*Personnel Selection and
Productivity*

WILEY SERIES IN
PSYCHOLOGY AND PRODUCTIVITY AT WORK

Series Editor
David J. Oborne

The Physical Environment at Work
Edited by D. J. Oborne and M. M. Gruneberg

Hours of Work–Temporal factors in work scheduling
Edited by Simon Folkard and Timothy H. Monk

Computers at Work–A behavioural approach
David J. Oborne

Psychology of Work and Unemployment
Gordon E. O'Brien

The Human Side of Advanced Manufacturing Technology
Edited by T. D. Wall, C. W. Clegg and N. J. Kemp

Women and Information Technology
Edited by Marilyn J. Davidson and Cary L. Cooper

Personnel Selection and Productivity
Mark Cook

Further titles in preparation

Personnel Selection and Productivity

Mark Cook
Centre for Occupational Research Ltd, London
and
*Department of Psychology, University College
of Swansea*

JOHN WILEY & SONS
Chichester · New York · Brisbane · Toronto · Singapore

Library of Congress Cataloging-in-Publication Data:

Cook, Mark.
  Personnel selection and productivity.

  (Wiley series in psychology and productivity at
work)
  Bibliography: p.
  Includes index.
  1. Employee selection. I. Title II. Series.
HF5549.5.S38C66 1988   658.3'112 87-21070

ISBN 0 471 91148 8

British Library Cataloguing in Publication Data:

Cook, Mark
  Personnel selection and productivity. —
  (Wiley series in psychology and productivity
  at work).
  1. Recruiting of employees 2. Employee
  selection
  I. Title
  658.3'11   HF5549.5.R44

ISBN 0 471 91148 8
ISBN 0 471 92967 0 (pbk)

Typeset by Witwell Ltd, Liverpool
Printed and Bound in Great Britain by
Courier International Limited, East Kilbride

Contents

Series Preface

With continuing pressures placed on organizations both to maintain and even to increase their output and efficiency, this series has been produced to present to the interested reader the many facets that contribute to productivity at work. The format of the series, which contains edited, single- and multi-authored volumes, helps greatly in this endeavour. Indeed, even the most cursory glance at the series contents illustrates the multi-faceted approach that needs to be taken, and the range of interests and disciplines involved.

Personnel selection must lie at the heart of any consideration of how psychology can relate to working productivity. Choosing the most appropriate employees, in terms of features like working efficiency and trainability, is likely to represent a central consideration for any organization looking to increase its output and effectiveness.

In this book, Mark Cook has approached the question from a number of interesting and useful viewpoints. He considers the importance of selection and illustrates the means not only of making appropriate selections, but of ensuring that the methods employed are both reliable and valid. Throughout the book, the theme constantly re-appears that many of the selection techniques used by organizations both in the past, and even during present times, leave much to be desired.

This book, then, has clear relevance to anyone with an interest in understanding how the various aspects of psychology can provide significant inputs to our everyday economic and working lives.

D. J. Oborne

Preface

When I first proposed writing this book I thought it self-evident that personnel selection and productivity are closely linked. Surely an organization that employs poor staff will produce less, or achieve less, than one that finds, keeps and promotes good staff. So it was surprising when several people, including one anonymous reviewer of the book proposal, challenged this assumption, and argued there was no demonstrated link between selection and productivity.

Critics are right, up to a point; there has never been an experimental demonstration of the link. The experiment could be made—but might prove very expensive. First create three identical companies. Second, allow company A to select staff using the best techniques available; require company B to fill its vacancies at random (so long as staff have the minimum necessary qualifications); require company C to employ the people company A's selection programme had identified as the least suitable. Then wait a year, and see which company is doing best, or—if the results are very clear-cut—which companies are still in business. No such experiment has been performed to my knowledge, although 'fair' employment laws in the USA have caused some organizations to adopt personnel policies not far removed from strategy B.

Perhaps critics meant only to say that the outline overlooked other, more important, factors affecting productivity: training, management, labour relations, lighting and ventilation. Or factors the organization can't control: the state of the economy, technical development, foreign competition, political interference. Of course all these affect productivity, but that doesn't prove that—other things being equal—an organization that selects, keeps and promotes good employees won't produce more, or produce better, than one that doesn't.

Within-organization factors affecting productivity are dealt with by the other titles in this series; ones outside the organization, like the state of world trade, fall outside the scope of psychology.

I would like to thank the many people who have helped me prepare this book, in particular those who have commented on earlier drafts, especially Paul Humphries, John MacArthur, Chris Potter, Graham Edwards and Ken Bennett.

Centre for Occupational Research Ltd
14 Devonshire Place, London W1N 1PB

CHAPTER 1

The Value of Good Employees

The best is twice as good as the worst

In an ideal world, two people doing the same job under the same conditions produce exactly the same amount. In the real world, some employees produce more than others. This poses two questions:

How much do workers vary in productivity?
How much are these differences worth?

The short answer to both questions is 'a lot'. The answer to the first question is good workers do twice as much work as poor workers. The answer to the second question says the difference in value between a good worker and a poor one is roughly equal to the salary they're paid.

HOW MUCH DOES WORKERS' PRODUCTIVITY VARY?

Clark Hull is better known, to psychologists at least, as an animal learning theorist, but very early in his career he wrote a book on aptitude testing (Hull, 1928), and described ratios of output of best to worst performers in a variety of occupations. The best spoon polishers polished five times as many as the worst. Ratios were less extreme for other occupations—between 1.5 to 1 and 2 to 1 for weaving and shoe making jobs. (Unfortunately Hull doesn't answer several fascinating questions—how many spoon polishers were studied? and did they polish spoons full time?) Hull was the first psychologist to ask how much workers differ in productivity, and he discovered the principle that should be written in letters of fire on every personnel manager's office wall: 'The best is twice as good as the worst'.

Comparing best to worst worker is an index of *range* (see Note 1), so it isn't very informative. Tiffin (1943) drew graphs of the *distribution* (see Note 1) of output for electrical fixture assemblers, for workers who solder the ends of insulated cables, and for 'hosiery loopers' (who gather together the loops of thread at the bottom of a stocking to close the opening left in the toe) (Figure 1.1).

1

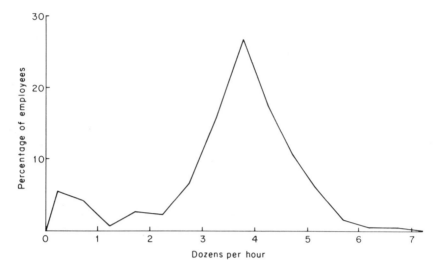

Figure 1.1. Distribution of productivity for 199 hosiery loopers (Tiffin, 1943). (Reproduced by permission)

Tiffin confirmed Hull's finding; the best fixture assembler's output is over twice that of the worst. He also showed that most workers fall between the extremes to form a roughly *normal* (see Note 1) distribution of output. Tiffin checked the effect of practice, and the consistency of differences between workers. Hosiery loopers' output increases after a year's experience, and the range of individual differences narrows, but the best looper still loops twice as many as the worst. The loopers' individual outputs were measured twice in successive weeks, and proved very consistent.

Later work by Rothe (1946) measured differences in output for workers wrapping blocks of butter, for workers hand-dipping chocolates, for coil-winders, and for several samples of machine operators. Differences in output were normally distributed, except in one group of machine operators where 'output norms'—tacit agreements among the workers to limit output—distorted the distribution. Sometimes the structure of work imposes uniformity on output; the best worker on a car assembly line does under 10 per cent more work than the poorest, because both work at the pace of the assembly line itself.

Hull, Tiffin and Rothe all analyse output in repetitive production work, where it is (relatively) easy to measure. Dorcus and Jones (1950) list a few more occupations where output is fairly easy to measure—typing, accounting machine operation, book-keeping. Selling too is usually easy to quantify. Schmidt and Hunter (1983) review all available evidence on range of worker ouput, with Hull's ratio of best to worst worker; the ratio is very consistent across a wide range of occupations: welders, typists, cashiers, card punch operators, lathe operators, lamp shade manufacturers, sewing machinists and 'wool pullers'. Schmidt and Hunter define 'best' as the 95th *percentile* (see Note 2) and 'worst' as the 5th percentile; the best 5 per cent of workers usually do twice as much as the worst 5 per cent. If the workers are paid piecerate, the ratio is slightly 'compressed'—to 1.69/1. Does output increase at the expense of quality? So that workers who do more are no more valuable? Not necessarily—faster keypunch operators and proof machine operators make fewer mistakes.

Not all occupational psychologists try to quantify output; many ask the wider question—Is the employee satisfied? The early work of the (British) National Institute for Industrial Psychology (NIIP) emphasized the worker's 'attainment of [his/her] self-chosen goal', rather than output as such. The current generation of occupational psychologists are more 'hard-nosed', and hark back to the 1920s, when Bingham defined the 'successful employee' as the one who 'does more work, does it better, with less supervision, with less interruption through absence from the job' (Bingham and Freyd, 1926). If the worker is happy, that's nice—for the worker.

Defining productivity in more complex or intangible work poses great problems. Is a good dentist one who fills more teeth per day? Or one who fills fewer because he/she prevents cavities forming? Is a good researcher one who publishes more articles? Or one who makes important discoveries? Who decides a discovery is important? Many occupations have no identifiable output. What defines productivity of a lifeboat crew, or ministers or religion, or TV announcers? It's impossible to decide if a selection method works without a criterion. Yet it's often very difficult to find a good criterion (Chapter 11).

HOW MUCH IS A PRODUCTIVE WORKER WORTH?

If some workers produce more than others, an employer that succeeds in selecting them will make more money—but how much more? A lot of ingenious effort has gone into putting a cash value on the productive worker. Accountants tried first, and weren't very successful, which left the field to psychologists.

Accountants can, at least in theory, calculate the value of each individual worker: so many units produced, selling at so much each, less the worker's wage costs, and a proportion of the company's overheads. In practice such calculations prove very difficult. Roche (1965) tried to quantify the value of individual radial drill operators (and the increase in profits the company might make by selecting new workers using a mechanical comprehension test). He arrived at an estimate of $0.203 worth per hour increase in output—a 3.7 per cent increase in the company's profits. Even Roche's detailed calculations were criticized (Cronbach and Gleser, 1965) as oversimplified. The drill operators machined a great variety of different components, but the company's figures didn't record output per operator, *per type of component*; pooled estimates had to be used. But if accountants can't put a precise value on an individual production worker's output, how can they hope to do so for a manager, supervisor or personnel director?

For many years accepted wisdom held that the financial benefit of employing good staff couldn't be directly calculated. Hence the psychologist couldn't tell employers 'my selection method can save you so many thousand pounds or dollars per year'. (Most psychologists are reluctant to make extravagant claims for their methods, so find it difficult to compete with people who lack their scruples.) The same wisdom made governments and pressure groups think 'selection procedures [could] be safely manipulated to achieve other objectives, such as a racially representative workforce' (Schmidt and Hunter, 1981)— because no one could prove that not employing the best people cost the organization money.

Rational estimates

Recently psychologists have devised a technique for putting a cash value on the people doing any job, no matter how varied and complex its demands, or how indefinable or intangible its end products. 'Rational Estimate' technique was invented by two psychologists, Schmidt and Hunter; they argue that people supervising a particular grade of employee 'have the best opportunities to observe actual performance and output differences between employees on a day-to-day basis' (Schmidt *et al.*, 1979b). So the best way to put a value on a good employee is simply to ask supervisors to judge the employee's worth.

Rational Estimate technique has two stages: data collection and data analysis. Rational estimates are collected using these instructions:

> Based on your experience with [widget press supervisors] we would like you to estimate the yearly value to your company of the products and services provided by the average supervisor. Consider the quality and quantity of output typical of the average supervisor and the value of this output.

To make the task easier, the instructions say:

> in placing a cash value on this output, it may help to consider what the cost would be of having an outside firm provide these products and services.

Similar estimates are made for a good supervisor, and for a poor one. 'Good' is defined as a supervisor at the 85th percentile, one whose performance is better than 85 per cent of his/her fellows. 'Poor' is defined as a supervisor at the 15th percentile, better than only a few other supervisors, and worse than most.

Why 15 per cent and 85 per cent? Because these values correspond roughly to one *standard deviation* (Note 3) either side of the mean. Therefore assuming the value of supervisors is normally distributed, the three estimates—15th percentile, mean and 85th percentile—can be used to calculate the standard deviation of employee productivity, cryptically referred to as 'SD_y'. SD_y summarizes the distribution in value to the employer of differences in output between employees (Figure 1.2). SD_y is a numerical index of differences in productivity within a workforce; it tells the employer how much the workers' work varies in value.

SD_y is a vital term in the equation for estimating the return on a selection programme. The smaller SD_y is, the less point there is putting a lot of effort and expense into selecting staff, because there's less difference in value between good and poor staff. The bigger SD_y is, the greater the difference between good and bad, and the more money can be saved by selecting more productive workers.

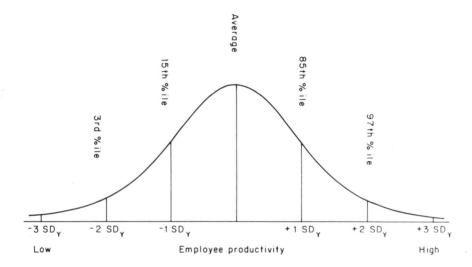

Figure 1.2. The distribution of employee productivity, showing the percentile points used in Rational Estimate technique to measure it.

After a large number of supervisors and managers have made Rational Estimates, averages are calculated (stage two). In their first study Schmidt and Hunter obtained estimates by 62 supervisors of the value of average and good budget analysts. The mean difference between average and good was $11,327 a year, meaning a good budget analyst is rated as worth $11,000 a year more than an average one. Any selection procedure that increases the proportion of good budget analysts recruited stands to save many thousands of dollars a year.

The study of budget analysts only made estimates for the average and the 85th percentile, which doesn't prove value to the organization is normally distributed. The distribution might be skewed. The difference between *average* and *poor* budget analysts might be far *less* than $11,000, if most analysts were much the same with only a few producing oustanding work, or it might be far *more* than

$11,000, if bad budget analysts were disastrously bad. If employee productivity is normally distributed, the difference between average and poor should be about the same as the difference between average and good. Schmidt and Hunter's second study made Rational Estimates for good, average and *poor* computer programmers (Schmidt *et al.*, 1980a). The differences betwen average and good, and average and poor, programmers were $10,513 and $9955 respectively; the two estimates don't differ significantly, so they can be averaged to obtain a single estimate for SD_y of just over $10,000.

Good programmers are worth over $10,000 more to their employers, *each year*, so it's clearly worth spending a fraction of that sum to make sure of finding some. (Many employers will cheerfully pay thousands of pounds to advertise for staff, but won't pay a few hundred to assess them.)

A worker at the 97th percentile of productivity is *two* standard deviations above the mean (Figure 1.2). If a worker at the 85th percentile is worth £12,000 more than an average worker, a worker at the 97th percentile should be worth 2 × £12,000 = £24,000 more. Rational Estimates for workers who produce more than 97 per cent of their peers should differ from Estimates for the 85th percentile by the same amount as Estimates for the 85th percentile differ from Estimates for the average; two studies find that they don't. In both (Bobko *et al.*, 1983; Burke and Frederick, 1984) the estimate for the 97th percentile was lower than predicted. Perhaps there really is an upper limit to what the most productive employee can achieve, imposed by peer pressure, or what the organization itself can cope with. Bobko *et al.* disagree, because the distribution of *actual* sales wasn't 'compressed' at the upper end.

Variations on the Rational Estimate theme

US Army tank commanders were unwilling to make Rational Estimates, saying soldiers' lives and performance in battle weren't describable in dollar terms. Eaton *et al.* (1985) devised the 'Superior Equivalents' technique, in which commanders estimate how many tanks with *superior* (85th percentile) crews would be the match of a standard company of 17 tanks, with *average* crews. Estimates converged on a figure of nine. An elite tank company need number only nine to be the match of an average company, neatly confirming Schmidt and Hunter's estimate that the best is twice as good as the worst. Given the price of modern tanks, the US Army could clearly save a fortune if it could be sure of recruiting only superior tank crews. Superior Equivalents technique is particularly suitable for workers who, while modestly paid themselves, need very expensive equipment.

Cascio (1982) describes a more complex way of calculating differences in productivity: CREPID (Cascio Ramos Estimate of Peformance In Dollars). The job is divided into different components—e.g. teaching, research and administration; the relative importance of each is rated—e.g. equally important;

the value of the worker's contribution to each area estimated, multiplied by its weighting, then summed. CREPID is obviously better suited for jobs with a range of activities that mightn't be done equally efficiently. Weekley *et al.* (1985) find CREPID gives much lower estimates of SD_y than Rational Estimates.

The 40–70 per cent rule

SD_y for budget analysts worked out at 66 per cent of salary; SD_y for computer programmers worked out at 55 per cent. These values prompted Schmidt and Hunter to propose a rule of thumb:

SD_y is between 40 and 70 per cent of salary.

'Best and worst' workers are each one SD_y from the average, so the difference between 'best' and 'worst' is *two* SD_ys. So if SD_y is 40–70 per cent of salary, the difference between 'best' and 'worst' is between 80 and 140 per cent of salary, allowing us to state another rule of thumb:

Value of a good employee minus value of a poor employee is roughly equal to the salary paid for the job.

So if the salary for the job in question is £15,000, the difference in value between 'best' and 'worst' worker is roughly £15,000 too. This makes the £300–600 it typically costs to assess someone before employing them look very modest. (And remember the 'best' and the 'worst', at the 85th percentile and 15th percentile, are far from being the extremes.)

The 'worse than useless' worker?

It's self-evident the average value of each worker's output must exceed average salary; otherwise the organization will lose money, and go out of business, or require a subsidy. Schmidt *et al.* (1982) review the evidence, and propose another rule of thumb:

Yearly dollar value of output of the average worker is about twice his/her salary.

Certain combinations of values of the two ratios—productivity/salary and SD_y/salary—have alarming implications for employers. Suppose salary is £10,000. The first rule of thumb implies SD_y is about £7000 (70 per cent of salary). The second rule of thumb implies average productivity is about £20,000 (twice salary). Consider a worker whose productivity is *three* SD_y below the mean. That worker is worth £20,000 less £7000 × 3, i.e. *minus* £1000 (Figure 1.3). The 'goods and services' he provides wouldn't cost anything to buy in from outside, because they aren't worth anything. In fact that employee actually loses the employer £1000, *on top of the cost of his salary of £10,000.* Two informants in one study (Burke and Frederick, 1984) did value an inferior sales manager at zero dollars, or at *minus* $100,000.

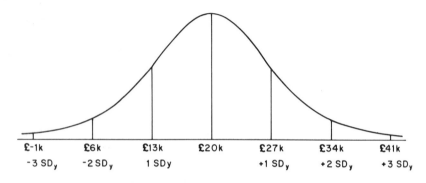

£-1k	£6k	£13k	£20k	£27k	£34k	£41k
-3 SD_y	-2 SD_y	1 SDy		+1 SD_y	+2 SD_y	+3 SD_y

Figure 1.3. The distribution of employee productivity, where average value is £20,000, and SD_y is £7000.

Only one or two in a thousand employees falls three SDs below the mean so, for this employer, 'worse than useless' employees are fortunately scarce. But suppose the productivity/salary ratio were nearer unity. Schmidt *et al.* (1984) report a ratio of 1.29 for park rangers (average Rational Estimate $13,530, average salary $10,507). If SD_y were 70 per cent of salary for park rangers, 7 per cent would be 'worth' negative sums to their employer. Could an organization survive a handicap like that? Fortunately later research, including that on park rangers, finds SD_y typically nearer 40 per cent of salary level than 70 per cent, which implies relatively few employees are 'worse than useless'. However estimates still derive from a fairly narrow range of employers; many commentators feel they would nominate organizations where 'worse than useless' workers proliferate.

Are Rational Estimates valid?

Some critics think Rational Estimates are dangerously subjective. Schmidt *et al.* disagree; the instructions specify estimating the cost of employing an outside firm to do the work, which provides a 'relatively concrete standard'. Furthermore 'the idiosyncratic tendencies, biases, and random errors of individual judges can be controlled by averaging across a large number of judges'. In any case, they argue, cost accounting calculations are often fairly subjective too, involving 'many estimates and arbitrary allocations' (Roche, 1965).

Some research has proved Rational Estimates are valid. Bobko and Karren (1982) compared Rational Estimates for 92 'telephone counsellors' (a euphemism for insurance salespersons) with counsellors' sales figures. The standard deviation of counsellors' actual sales was $52,308; SD_y, calculated by Rational Estimate, was $56,950. The second study (Ledvinka and Simonet, 1983) used data on insurance claims processed by individual claims supervisors. The average worker processed 5345 claims per year, and the standard deviation of 15 workers' outputs was 1679 claims a year. Differences in productivity were very consistent; one month's figures were nearly identical with another's. Dividing total wage cost by number of claims processed gives an average cost per claim of $3.30. The number of claims each individual worker processed was then multiplied by $3.30, to give a dollar estimate of the value of his/her output. The standard deviation of these 15 dollar estimates is SD_y—measured 'objectively', not by Rational Estimate. 'Objective' SD_y was $5542, which equalled 43 per cent of salary, and confirmed the lower estimate of the '40–70 per cent rule'.

IMPLICATIONS OF RATIONAL ESTIMATE RESEARCH

Rational Estimates calculate the savings made by using effective selection methods, and the cost of not using them. Research on Rational Estimates reaches some startling conclusions:

1. A 'small' employer, such as the Philadelphia police force (5000 employees), could save $18 million a year by using psychological tests (Schmidt and Hunter, 1981).
2. Dunnette devised a selection programme for workers in the US electricity generating industry, and claimed 'it does not seem too great a stretch of the imagination to expect a potential annual gain in the neighbourhood of $800 million when these selection procedures are adopted by the [70] companies participating in this research project' (Dunnette *et al.*, 1962).
3. A 'large' employer—the US Federal Government (4 million employees)—could save $16 billion a year by using psychological tests to select employees. Or, to reverse our perspective, the US Federal Government is losing £16 billion a year by *not* using tests (Schmidt and Hunter, 1981).
4. Critics see a major flaw in Schmidt and Hunter's calculations. Every company in the country can't employ the 15 per cent best computer programmers or budget analysts; someone has to employ 'the rest'. Good selection can't increase national productivity, only the productivity of employers that use psychological assessment to grab more than their fair share of talent. At present, employers are free to do precisely that. The rest of this book explains *how*.

NOTES

1. *Range and the normal distribution.* The Astronomer Royal of Belgium in the nineteenth century, Adolphe Quetelet, plotted a graph of the height of 100,000 French soldiers (Figure 1.4); the soldiers' heights formed a bell-shaped distribution, called the *normal distribution.*

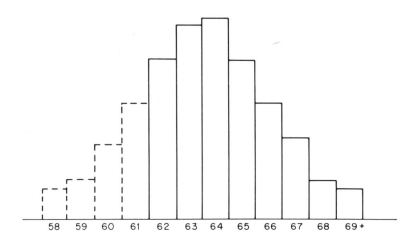

Figure 1.4. Distribution of height, in inches, for nineteenth-century French soldiers. NB: the distribution has been estimated for men less than 5′ 2″ who weren't accepted as soldiers.

Other naturally occurring measurements, when plotted, also produce a normal distribution: chest diameter, 'vital capacity' (how much air the person can drawn into his/her lungs—still a selection requirement for the fire brigade), time it takes to react to a sound, and activity of the autonomic nervous system. (Quetelet's distribution has been estimated for men under 5′ 2″, who weren't in the army because they were too short.)

Range. Quetelet's soldiers varied in height from under 5′ 2″ to over 5′ 9″. A statistic summarizing variability is needed. While everyone understands averages, measures of variability are harder to grasp. *Range* is the difference between the tallest and shortest. Range describes extremes which can be fairly uninformative; the modern *Guinness Book of Records* gives the tallest authentic male height ever recorded as 8′ 11″, and the shortest as 2′ 2″.

2. *Percentiles.* Range isn't a very useful statistic, especially to personnel managers who rarely want employees who will feature in the *Guinness Book of Records.* Ways of describing variability in the mass of people between the extremes are more useful. One is the *percentile.* Average male height is now

5′ 8.5″, which is another way of saying 50 per cent of men are as tall as 5′ 8.5″ and 50 per cent are taller. How many men are taller than 6′ 2″—about 2 per cent. How many men are shorter than 5′ 6″—some 16 per cent. Percentiles can describe a man's height to someone who doesn't understand feet and inches, by saying 'He is taller than 98 per cent of men', or 'He is at the 98th *percentile* for height'.

3. *Standard deviation.* The standard deviation does two things: it describes how one person compares with other, *and* it summarizes the variability of the whole distribution. 'Standard deviation' is usually abbreviated to 'SD'.

A distribution is completely summarized by its mean and SD, so long as it is 'normal', i.e. bell-shaped and symmetrical. (Distributions of some 'natural' scores, such as height, are normal; distributions of constructed scores, such as IQs, are made normal.)

The SD can be used, like the percentile, to describe someone's height, without reference to any particular system of measurement. A man 6′ 2″ high is 2 SDs above the mean. Anyone who understands statistics will know how tall that is, be the local units of height metres, feet and inches, or cubits.

CHAPTER 2

The Classic Trio and its Rivals

We've always done it this way

Figure 2.1 summarizes the successive stages of selecting a lecturer (assistant professor) for a British or North American university., The *advertisement* attracts *applicants*, who complete and return an *application form*. Some applicants'*references* are taken up; the rest are excluded from further consideration. Candidates with satisfactory references are *short-listed*, and invited for *interview*, after which the post is filled. The details vary from university to university; the basic principle remains: attract as many applicants as possible, then pass them through a series of 'filters', until the number of candidates equals the number of vacancies.

Advertisement

Most jobs are advertised, locally or nationally. People who answer the advertisement are sent 'further information' about the job, the pay and the organization. Many organizations still use recruiting methods dating from times of full employment and labour shortage; they paint a rosy picture of what's really a boring and unpleasant job, because they fear no-one will apply otherwise. In the USA 'realistic job previews'—films, brochures, visits—are increasingly used to tell applicants what being e.g. a telephone operator is *really* like—fast-paced, closely supervised, routine to the point of being boring, and solitary except for the occasional unfriendly or 'nasty' customer (Wanous, 1978). The more carefully worded the advertisement and the job description, the fewer unsuitable applicants will apply. (Except for the inevitable handful who don't read the advertisement, or think employers don't really mean it when they say successful candidates must have an engineering degree, or belong to the I(nstitute of) P(ersonnel) M(anagement) or A(merican) S(ociety) of P(ersonnel) A(dministration).

Applicants are sometimes recruited by word of mouth, usually through existing employees, which is cheaper. (A small— 7 × 7 cm—advertisement in a British national daily—*Telegraph* or *Guardian*—costs over £800.) Besides being cheaper, the 'grapevine' finds employees who stay longer (low 'voluntary turnover'), and who are less likely to be dismissed (low 'involuntary turnover') (Breaugh and Mann, 1984). People recruited by word of mouth stay longer because they have a clearer idea what the job really involves. But beware: the

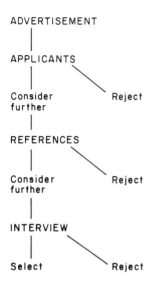

Figure 2.1. Main stages of selecting academic staff in a British university.

(UK) Commission for Racial Equality may claim employing an all-white workforce's friends is just a subtle way of maintaining an all-white workforce. To date a high proportion of the Commission's enquiries have deal with 'unfair' recruitment.

Sometimes people seek jobs, or employers seek staff, through employment agencies—public or private. Some grades of staff are 'head-hunted' by 'recruitment consultants'. The 'head-hunter' advertises without naming the prospective employer, or approaches likely candidates and invites them to apply. 'Head-hunters' assess candidates, usually by interview, before deciding whose names to pass on to the employer, which adds yet another stage to assessment. Staff are 'head-hunted' when good candidates are in short supply, for example in advanced manufacturing technology. Occasionally, in tightly unionized jobs, vacancies are filled by the union, not the employer. This practice has little to commend it. Seniority, the criterion unions usually use, doesn't predict productivity (Chapter 6).

Table 2.1 shows (some of) the results of a recent survey of US recruitment methods. Most employers use a combination of methods, and most are willing to consider employee referrals and 'walk-ins'—the person who comes in off the street and asks if they need any widget press operators that day. Employers are less likely to turn to public employment agencies for sales, professional/ technical, or management vacancies, preferring private agencies, or 'head-hunters' (Bureau of National Affairs, 1979).

Table 2.1. Methods used by US employers to find five types of staff. Figures are percentages (Bureau of National Affairs, 1979). Reprinted by permission from *Personnel Management*, copyright 1979 by the Bureau of National Affairs, Inc., 1231 25th Street, NW Washington, DC 20037.)

	O/C	P/S	S	P/T	M
Employee referral	92	94	74	68	65
Walk-ins	87	92	46	46	40
Newspaper advert	68	88	75	89	82
Radio/TV advert	5	8	2	7	4
Specialist publication advert	12	6	43	75	57
US Employment Service	63	72	34	41	27
Private employment agency	44	11	63	71	75
(employer pays fee)	(31)	(5)	(49)	(48)	(65)
College/university	17	9	48	74	50
Professional societies	5	19	17	52	36
Head-hunters	1	2	2	31	54
Union	1	12	0	3	0

O/C – office/clerical; P/S – production/ skilled;
S – sales; P/T – professional/technical; M – management.

THE 'CLASSIC TRIO'

Most organizations select their staff by the tried and tested trio: application form, letter of reference and interview.

Application form

The (UK) Industrial Society surveyed 50 British application forms; name, address, date of birth, previous employers and reasons for leaving last job are the only 'universals'. Only half ask for age, and only 4 per cent ask the bureaucrat's classic—mother's maiden name. (The British Civil Service also asks where and when she was born, to check if the applicant is 'British born of British parents'.) Surprisingly few forms ask about hobbies and leisure interests. Forty per cent want to avoid nepotism, and ask if the applicant has any relatives working for the company. Two-thirds ask for an educational history, and 26 per cent about details of membership of professional bodies.

Application forms can converted into 'Weighted Application Blanks' (WABs), by analysing past and present employees for predictors of success, or low turnover, or honesty (Chapter 6). One study found American female bank clerks who left prematurely tended to be under 25, single, to live at home, with a mother who herself works, to have had several jobs, etc. (Robinson, 1972); so American banks that want to recruit employees who will stay longer should avoid employing women with these characteristics. The WAB is economical, effective and difficult to fake. All the items on Robinson's WAB are routine application form questions.

Drawing up the shortlist

In the 1960s, when unemployment in Britain was 'nearing half a million', drawing up a shortlist was often difficult because personnel managers would be lucky to have as many as five passably good applicants (three of whom wouldn't show up for the interview anyway). In the 1980s personnel managers typically face a 'mountain of applications' to sift through, which gives researchers a new problem to study: which applications make the short list, and why. Wingrove *et al.* (1984) analyse how personnel managers use information on application forms. In a transport company, 80 per cent of decisions—reject or consider further—can be predicted from six facts: maths grade (at A level), degree in maths or computer science, work experience in a transport organization, belong to societies related to transport, work experience in computer programming, been on 'Insight into Management' course. People who wrote a lot were considered further, as were people who wrote neatly, and people who used 'certain keywords'—unspecified. People from certain parts of Britain—also unspecified—were more likely to be rejected.

American research on application sifting (Arvey, 1979a) finds women widely discriminated against at short list stage. Women are also 'stereotyped' as more suitable for some jobs, or for working with other women. Both male and female interviewers are equally biased against women. However the *size* of the effect was often very small; in one study (Dipboye *et al.*, 1977), preference for male applicants, while statistically significant, was so slight as to be entirely trivial. Arvey found no evidence of discrimination against non-whites in shortlisting.

Herriot and Wingrove (1984) recorded personnel managers 'thinking aloud' while sifting applications, and heard comments like 'Two As and a B at A level, pretty good' (has good exam grades), 'Hasn't bothered to read the brochure', or 'Oh dear—supermarket work every vacation'. One in five comments mention 'presentation': 'He hasn't written much on this form, and what there is I can't read'.

References

Two-thirds of major British employers always take up references; only a handful never do (Robertson and Makin, 1986). In the British public sector—higher education, Health Service, Civil Service—references are taken up before interview. The commercial sector often doesn't take up references until someone has been offered the job, so the reference is little more than a safety check, that the succesful candidate really did work for his/her last employer, and that he/she wasn't dismissed for stealing. British 'references' are usually letters saying whatever the referee feels like saying about the candidate, in whatever form he/she feels like saying it. Very few British employers ask for ratings, or for any structured or quantified opinion of the candidate. US employers are more likely to use structured reference forms.

Some employers don't limit themselves to asking people nominated by the applicant what they think of him/her; police and parts of the civil service check the applicant's background, associates and even attitudes very thoroughly. Other employers usually haven't the resources or authority to do this, although many gain unofficial access to criminal records by employing former police officers.

Interview

In both sectors the final hurdle is the interview. A 1957 survey in the USA reported that 99 per cent of employers interview job applicants (Ulrich and Trumbo, 1965). Robertson and Makin's survey of top UK employers, taken from the *Times 1000*, found only one who never interviewed.

BUILDING ON THE CLASSIC TRIO

Psychologists have long known the classic trio isn't very effective. Scott published the first research on the interview in 1915, showing six personnel managers didn't agree about a common set of applicants. Dozens more research studies since have confirmed Scott's conclusions (Chapter 3). Early research on what one person said about another's personality soon found such opinions highly unreliable.

The classic trio's failings prompted both personnel managers and psychologists to look for something better. The various offerings over the years divide into:

(a) psychological tests,
(b) group exercises,
(c) work sample tests,
(d) 'weird and wonderful' measures,
(e) miscellaneous,

or any combination of these, and the classic trio; long complicated assessments of a group of applicants are often dignified by the title 'assessment centre'.

(a) Psychological tests

Alfred Binet wrote the first intelligence test in 1904; it crossed the Atlantic, to become the Stanford–Binet. It wasn't the world's first test of mental ability, but it was the first general *intelligence* test, and the first to be (rather roughly) standardized.

The Binet tests children individually; personnel selectors test adults in groups. A committee of American psychologists wrote the world's first adult group intelligence test, to classify recruits to the US Army when America entered the

First World War in 1917; 1.7 million recruits were tested. (The British Army didn't use intelligence tests in the First World War, preferring, as Raymond Cattell (1936) said rather bitterly, '[to use] some of the best brains from civilian life to stop bullets in front-line trenches'.) The Army Alpha was released for civilian use as the National Intelligence Test, and sold 400,000 copies within six months. The Army Beta was a 'non-verbal' test for recruits who didn't speak English, or couldn't read; the instructions were given by gesture and example.

General intelligence tests usually contain a mixture of items—verbal, numerical, and abstract questions. *Aptitude* tests limit themselves to one type of item, and measure a specific ability: mechanical comprehension, spatial relations, clerical speed and accuracy, or ability to program computers. Aptitude tests often correlate (see Note 1) highly with general intelligence tests, so the distinction between the two isn't always clear.

The *personality questionnaire* also owes its origin to the Great War. By 1917 armies had discovered that many men couldn't stand the stress of continuous battle. The US Army acted on this knowledge, and devised a screening test for men who would crack up so quickly they weren't worth sending to the front line. The 'Woodworth Personal Data Sheet' had 116 items, and was surprisingly sophisticated for its day. Questions were excluded if more than 25 per cent of the healthy controls gave the keyed answer, or if the neurotic group didn't give the keyed answer at least twice as often as the controls. The PDS wasn't finished in time to be used in the war, but was released for civilian use, as the Woodworth Psychoneurotic Inventory, and was the ancestor of a long line of tests. Many items from PDS still give good service in modern questionnaires:

Do you usually sleep well?
Do you worry too much about little things?
Does some particular useless thought keep coming into your mind to bother you?

Other psychological assessments can claim even longer histories. The Utopian reformer Robert Owen used the first known *rating scale* in 1825; children in the New Harmony colony in Indiana were rated on ten 100-point scales of 'courage', 'imagination' or 'excitability'. But it wasn't a paper-and-pencil measure; Owen's scale was cast in brass, and can still be seen in the New Harmony museum.

Behavioural tests have been used for at least 3000 years. The Book of Judges (Chapter 7, Verses 4–7) tells how Gideon raised an army to 'smite' the Midianites, and found he had too many volunteers. He used a simple test of fieldcraft to exclude the inexperienced from his army; he told them to go and take a drink from the nearby river, and selected only those who kept on their guard even while slaking their thirst.

Psychological tests gained acceptance in the USA in the 1920s, and proliferated during the 1930s. Progress was slower in Britain. The National

Institute for Industrial Psychology (NIIP) was founded in 1920, and used aptitude tests during the 1920s and 1930s.

Studies of selection by psychological tests between 1910 and 1948, reported by Dorcus and Jones (1950), are plotted in Figure 2.2. Test use increased steadily throughout the period of the USA, whereas it started later, grew slower and peaked earlier in Europe and the UK. There was, of course, a lot of wartime military research in Britain that wasn't published until later, if at all—but so there was too in the USA, which didn't halt the growth of civilian testing during the war years. The wartime testing programme in the USA inspired more civilian test use post-war, whereas UK wartime developments, notably the War Office Selection Board (WOSB), inspired few civilian imitations (except the Civil Service Selection Board—CSSB).

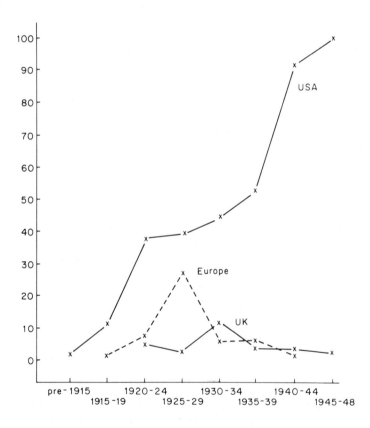

Figure 2.2. Number of studies using psychological tests for personnel selection published in the USA, Europe and the UK, between 1914 and 1948.

(b) Group exercises

Until 1942 the British Army selected officers by Commanding Officer's recommendation and a panel interview. By 1942 this system was proving ineffective, because the panel didn't like, or couldn't understand, candidates with grammar school education or 'communist' opinions. The WOSB replaced the panels, and a key element of the WOSB was the group exercise—leaderless group discussions, as well as more practical tasks, including the one still featured in British Army officer recruitment ads—building a bridge across a wide gap with short lengths of timber.

Some group tasks were part of a 'cover plan' (Vernon and Parry, 1949) to introduce the measures the psychologists wanted, while persuading the military to accept the new system; Vernon is (?deliberately) vague about which group exercises were 'unstandardised and unscoreable, and their diagnostic worth extremely dubious'. WOSB was partly inspired by German military selection methods, which had also used group discussions. The WOSB was the model for the (UK) CSSB (Vernon, 1950; Anstey, 1977).

In the USA a similar intensive assessment programme, using group discussions alongside many other measures, was used by the Office of Strategic Services (OSS), forerunner of the CIA, to select spies. The OSS programme, and WOSB, eventually inspired the 'assessment centre' for evaluating managers, first used by American Telegraph and Telephone in 1956; assessment centres are now commonly used in America and Britain, and include a wide range of group exericses. Assessment centres are discussed in greater detail in Chapter 9.

(c) Work sample tests

Most applicants for typing jobs are given a 'work sample' test—they are asked to type something. (Usually a bad work sample test—unstandardized, subjectively scored, and fairly uninformative.) In 1913 Boston (Mass.) tramways asked Hugo Munsterberg to find a way of reducing the number of accidents, without slowing down the services too much. Munsterberg found some tram drivers were 'accident-prone'; (some of) this accident prone minority were poor at judging speed and closing distance. Munsterberg devised a work sample test, of judgement of closing distances and relative speeds.

Many more work sample tests were devised in the 1920s and 1930s in Britain and Europe as well as America. Work samples were used very extensively in military selection and classification programmes in the Second World War. Work sample tests have two limitations. Because they're samples of work they're necessarily job-specific, so a tramway company needs different work samples for drivers, conductors, inspectors, mechanics, electricians, track maintenance workers, etc. Work samples are also more difficult to plan, where the work is diverse or abstract or involves other people. It's much easier to plan work samples for routine production workers than for supervisors and managers. The 'In-Basket' or 'In-Tray' is a management work sample test—a dozen letters, memos, and policy documents to read and deal with.

(d) Weird and wonderful methods

It's very difficult to select good staff, and quite impossible to make the right choice every time, so most personnel managers are conscious of frequent failures, and always on the look-out for better methods. Some are led astray by extravagant claims for semi-magical methods.

Graphology

'. . . a hail-fellow-well-met who liked to eat and drink; who might attract women of the class he preyed on by an overwhelming animal charm. I would say in fact he was a latent homosexual . . . and passed as a man's man . . . capable of conceiving any atrocity and carrying it out in an organised way'—a graphologist's assessment of 'Jack the Ripper', based on what might be one of the killer's letters (Figure 2.3). No-one knows who 'Jack' really was, so no-one can contradict the graphologist's assessment.

Graphology is widely used in personal selection in Europe, by 85 per cent of all companies, according to Klimoski and Rafaeli (1983). Fewer companies in Britain and the USA use it. Robertson and Makin (1986) found 7–8 per cent of major UK employers sometimes used graphology. But Klimoski and Rafaeli conclude that all the hard evidence indicates 'graphology is not a viable assessment method'; two graphologists analysing the same handwriting sample independently agree very poorly about the writer's personality. Graphologists' ratings of realtors (estate agents) are completely unrelated to supervisors' ratings and to actual sales figures (Klimoski and Rafaeli, 1983). Graphologists' ratings of insurance salesmen similarly failed to predict their success (Zdep and Weaver, 1967). Graphologists often ask subjects to write pen pictures of themselves, so the assessment isn't solely based on handwriting. (The *content* of the letter in Figure 2.3 reveals quite a lot about the writer's mentality.)

Handwriting can be a 'sign' or a 'sample'. A personnel manager who complains that he/she can't read an applicant's writing judges it *as a sample*; legible handwriting may be needed for the job. The graphologist who infers repressed homosexuality from handwriting interprets it *as a sign* of something far removed from putting pen to paper.

Astrology

It's not absurd to suppose people reveal their personality in their handwriting— just wrong. It does seem absurd to many people to suppose the sky at the instant

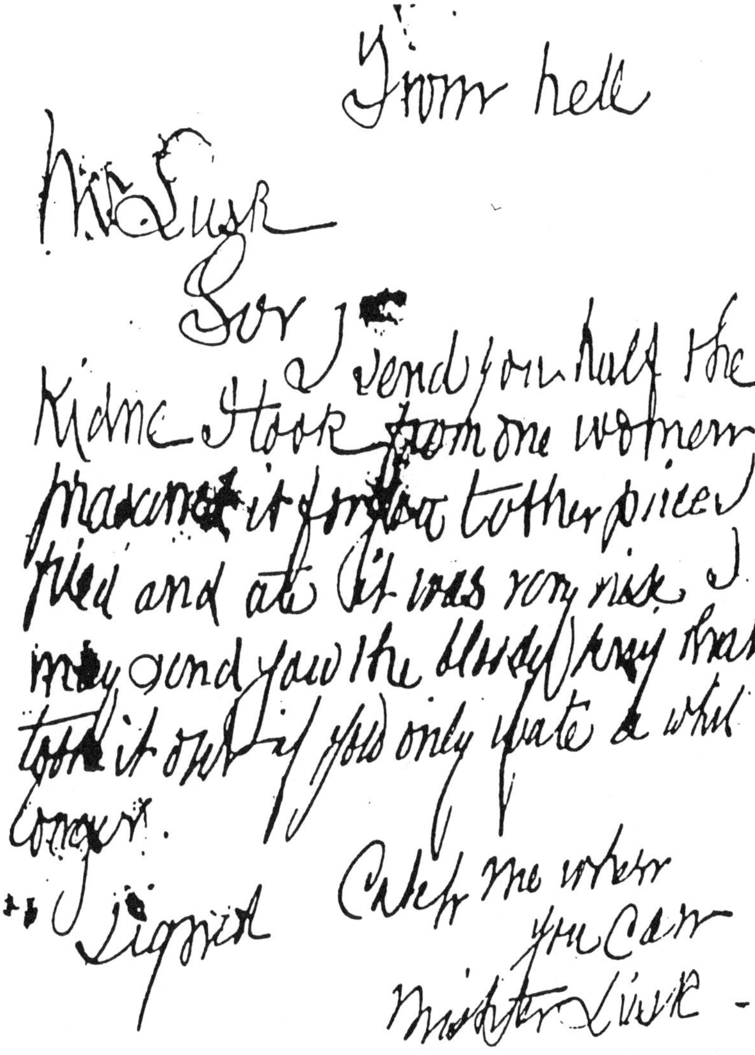

From hell

Mr Lusk
Sor
I send you half the
Kidne I took from one women
prasarved it for you tother piece
I fried and ate it was very nise I
may send you the bloody knif that
took it out if you only wate a whil
longer.
signed Catch me when
you Can
Mishter Lusk

Figure 2.3. A letter attributed to 'Jack the Ripper'.

of someone's birth could shape their personality. Nevertheless astrology is taken seriously by some psychologists, and there is evidence of personality differences in people born under different star signs. The difference is fairly basic—more introverts are born in 'even'-numbered months—and not very relevant to personnel selection.

Palmistry

Bayne (1982) notes that palmistry would be a very good selection device—convenient, cheap, unfakeable—if it worked. Unfortunately it doesn't.

Pseudo-tests

There are a number of these about, or a number of versions of the same one about. It's difficult to be more precise, because the most characteristic feature of the pseudo-test is that it's very wary of psychologists. Pseudo-tests are generally very short, typically a couple of dozen items; they're often checklists of adjectives, or use forced choice—'most like me'/'least like me'; they're often printed in several bright colours; they're complicated to score, and often use 'derived' scores (in which further scores are produced by adding, subtracting, multiplying or dividing the basic scores). Pseudo-tests are usually very expensive, especially as one almost always has to pay handsomely to be trained to use them.

Pseudo-tests rarely come with any information about reliability or validity, and are rarely, if ever, mentioned in occupational psychology journals. They tempt personnel managers because they're short, and they're available. Pseudo-tests are generally too short to measure anything, let alone the impressive lists of traits they claim to measure.

Polygraph

Polygraph, also known as the lie detector, is widely used in the USA for 'honesty tests' on staff who have the opportunity to steal—shop assistants, warehouse staff, bank employees. In 1983 the British government proposed using the polygraph to 'vet' staff with access to secret information, but eventually abandoned the idea in the face of union opposition. The principle of the polygraph is sound—anxiety causes changes in respiration, pulse and skin conductance—but its practice has drawbacks, principally a high rate of 'false-positives' in people nervous about the test, not because they're lying. The polygraph is likely to miss genuine criminals, because they don't see lies as lies, or because they don't respond physically to threat, and the test would probably miss a spy trained to mask physical reactions. The polygraph is forbidden by law as a selection test in nineteen states of the USA; it's legal in Britain but the British Psychological Society disapproves of its use for selection or 'honesty testing'.

'Trial by sherry'

Mixing 'informally', over drinks, coffee or even dinner, with existing staff features in some selection programmes. It's an important element in many assessment centres, where candidates are told they're being observed and assessed at all times. In one sense 'trial by sherry' is beyond criticism; if the candidate's 'face doesn't fit' he/she is clearly unsuitable. On the other hand, perhaps the organization needs new faces to shake it up. Or the 'jurors' might just be biased, perhaps even prejudiced.

CLASSIFICATION/PLACEMENT

In a classification programme everyone who 'applies' is found work; the question is *how and where*, not *whether*, to employ. Conscript armies need to classify recruits; personnel managers in a deep economic recession don't. People must find their own answers to the question 'what work am I suited for?'. Schools offer their pupils advice, of varying quality; adults have to pay for career guidance, also of varying quality. Classification uses interviews, tests and biographies, like selection, but can't follow the selector's often wasteful rule 'Always employ the best'. The best wireless operator might also be a good navigator and a passable pilot. He might be overqualified for wireless work, and better employed as a navigator. He might even need to be trained as a pilot, if pilots are in short supply.

CURRENT SELECTION PRACTICE

In 1975 a survey by the American Society of Personnel Administration found 60 per cent of large US employers used psychological tests, whereas only 39 per cent of small employers did. Many employers tested only for clerical jobs. Testing was in decline; three-quarters of employers had cut back their testing programmes since 1970, and 14 per cent intended to drop all testing.

Schmitt *et al.* (1984) review research on selection in North America between 1964 and 1982, and give an interesting analysis of the types of assessment used for six broad classes of job (Table 2.2). The Weighted Application Blank was the most commonly reported method. Personality and intelligence tests were widely used, followed by aptitude tests, peer evaluations, assessment centres, physical tests and job samples. Personality and intelligence tests are used fairly generally, with some exceptions. Clerical staff are rarely given personality tests, and sales staff are rarely given intelligence tests (which is odd—Ghiselli (1966) says intelligence tests have good predictive validity for sales). Assessment centres are used only for management; physical tests are used only for skilled and unskilled labour. Schmitt *et al.'s* data aren't a true survey of recent/current North American practice, since they draw their information solely from articles published in *Personnel Psychology* and *Journal of Applied Psychology*, which describe innovations rather than routine assessment methods.

At least 5000 North American employers use honesty tests, for employees who have access to cash or merchandise. Sackett and Harris (1984) describe these tests—questionnaires of varying lengths from 37 to 158 items—as 'largely outside

Table 2.2. Predictors and Criteria Used With Various Occupational Groups (Schmitt *et al.*, 1984). (Reproduced by permission)

	Professional No. of validities	Managerial No. of validities	Clerical No. of validities	Sales No. of validities	Skilled labor No. of validities	Unskilled labor No. of validities
Predictor						
Special aptitude	9	4	8	1	7	2
Personality	21	17	1	6	11	6
Gen. ment. abil.	8	18	12	3	5	7
Biodata	23	4	9	31	13	19
Job Sample	8	3	3	0	4	0
Assess. center	3	15	0	3	0	0
Supervisory/ peer evaluations	4	24	0	3	0	0
Physical ability	0	1	0	0	6	15
Criterion						
Performance rating	43	31	12	15	17	22
Turnover	5	0	9	11	12	11
Achievement/grades	8	11	3	4	14	3
Productivity	7	0	0	20	0	3
Status change	4	33	0	0	0	9
Wages	13	17	0	0	0	3
Work samples	0	1	12	0	2	9

the mainstream of psychological testing'; they are not published by major test publishers, no research on them appears in scientific psychology journals; it's often difficult to get any technical information about them. The validity of 'honesty tests' is reviewed in Chapter 8.

Surveys of use of psychological tests in Britain have appeared quite regularly (British Psychological Society, 1985); information about other methods is more sketchy (proving that psychologists like measuring things, even themselves).

Income Data Services (1985) describe some current UK selection programmes. The seventeen organizations surveyed include nine in the private sector (including J. Sainsbury, Blue Circle and Rank Xerox), three in the national public sector (Civil Service, Civil Aviation Authority and the Post Office), one in the local government sector (London Borough of Hammersmith and Fulham), and three of indeterminate or transitional status—British Telecom, British Airways and Trustee Saving Bank.

Blue Circle Industries select graduates from campus interviews—the 'milk round'—then use a group exercise, three aptitude tests, a personality inventory—described as experimental—and three interviews.

J. Sainsbury also select their graduate intake from the 'milk round', then use an assessment centre, consisting of: 60-minute interview, 'In-tray' test, scheduling test (a problem in stock control), making a speech ('oral presentation'), group exercise and two aptitude tests. Candidates for the buying department also complete a personality questionnaire, but this part of the battery is still 'on trial'.

The Civil Aviation Authority recruits about 50 air traffic control officers a year, for an expensive 3-year training programme. Applicants are preselected at application form stage, on the basis of age, educational qualifications and nationality; only 400–500 are 'weeded' at this stage, leaving 800–900 for interview and a battery of six aptitude tests. An unspecified number go on to the Final Selection Board, consisting of panel interview and two personality questionnaires. The Authority is currently investigating the predictive validity of its selection procedures.

British Airways have devised their own 'trainability' tests (a form of work sample test) for reservation agents, covering computer use, dealing with customers and telephone use. Cabin crew are selected by Weighted Application Blank, and a one-day assessment centre consisting of tests, group exercises, presentations and a final interview.

The national public sector uses its own elaborate and well-validated methods. The Civil Service has been using assessment centres—the Civil Service Selection Board (CSSB)—for 40 years. Both Civil Service and Post Office are large enough to employ their own psychologists and develop their own tests. Applicants for Executive Officer in the Civil Service are screened for age and A levels, then face the Executive Officer Qualifying Test, a 3-hour battery of five intelligence and aptitude tests, and finally a panel interview. British Telecom's Occupational Psychology Unit has developed aptitude tests for clerical assistants and apprentices, trainability tests for telephone installation engineers and verbal and numerical reasoning tests for graduate management trainees.

Local government has been slower to adopt modern methods, and rumours of arbitrary or ineffective procedures abound, alongside occasional allegations of nepotism. The IDS survey reports one local authority, Borough of Hammersmith, that uses a battery of aptitude tests and a group discussion exercise, as well as a panel interview, to select graduate trainees. Higher education in Britain remains firmly wedded to the 'classic trio', usually in its most antiquated and useless forms, despite employing the psychologists who prove its futility, and maintaining the libraries that house the results of their work.

Recently the National Health Service has launched a pilot scheme for psychological assessment of managers, to supplement the traditional system of references, one-to-one interviews, panel interviews and 'trial by sherry'. Candidates for District General Manager and Unit General Manager in ten Health Districts are tested with intelligence tests and a personality inventory.

Of the seventeen organizations described in the IDS survey, eleven use assessment centres for graduate intakes, with group exercises, intelligence or aptitude tests, and one or more interviews. Five include an 'in-tray' test, and seven a personality questionnaire. Two graduate assessment programmes include 'trial by sherry'; one includes peer assessments, in which candidates rank each other as 'preferred boss' and 'preferred candidate'. The IDS survey finds personality questionnaires aren't widely used except for graduate intakes; two organizations use them for senior managers, a third uses them for air traffic controllers. Assessment of apprentices and clerical workers is limited to interviews and aptitude tests. Two organizations use Weighted Application Blanks.

Surveys of British test use confirm that management trainees and apprentices are the most frequently tested groups. Engineering and electrical apprentices are particularly likely to face aptitude tests. Personality tests are not often used; they are never used for selecting clerical staff, apprentices or shopfloor workers. Graduate trainees are probably Britain's most extensively, and intensively, assessed class of employee—because they're vital to the organization's future? or because they're least likely to complain? Surveys of test use find employers much less likely to test *existing* employees than *prospective* employees, perhaps because present employees have 'rights', and probably a trade union, whereas applicants haven't. Robertson and Makin (1986) report 4 per cent of major UK employers always use personality tests, while 64 per cent never do, and the rest use them sometimes.

CONCLUSIONS

Most British organizations still use the 'classic trio'. Most probably still have no doubts about the value of application form, reference and interview.

Organizations that haven't heard that the classic trio has its faults probably haven't heard either that application forms, references and interviews can be improved. This implies a lot of organizations are using old-fashioned, inefficient methods.

Bad personnel selection is often little better than no selection at all, so many organizations in Britain are probably choosing their staff more or less randomly. Schmidt and Hunter (1981) estimate that poor or non-existent selection by the US Federal Government—4 million employees—costs $16 billion a year. Suppose 90 per cent of people employed in Britain are selected more or less randomly, how much does this cost Britain each year? Do they manage things more efficiently in Britain's competitors?

Some organizations in Britain have supplemented the classic trio, although hardly any have abandoned it altogether. Work sample tests have been used since the 1920s, and trainability tests are being adopted. Aptitude tests are quite widely used for apprentices, while intelligence tests are used for managers and management trainees. Assessment centres have been used by Civil Service and armed services since the 1940s, and have re-crossed the Atlantic back into the commercial sector. Personality testing remains fairly rare. WABs are even rarer.

What the USA does today, Britain does tomorrow (apart from WOSB/ assessment centre). 'Today' and 'tomorrow' are decades apart—but how many? Suppose Britain is 20–30 years 'behind' the USA. The future in Britain will see intelligence tests being used very widely in all organizations at all levels. The future will see personality tests used quite widely at supervisory level and above, WABs used quite widely below. The future will see the demise of the unstructured interview, and the free-form reference, and a proliferation of rating systems.

But the future could turn out quite differently. In one important respect Britain is only 10 years 'behind' the USA—equal employment legislation. British personnel managers might now be belatedly adopting methods the law will shortly force them to abandon. By 1997 intelligence tests could be virtually outlawed, personality tests suspect and WABs unthinkable. Selectors would be forced back onto the classic trio, or forced out of business altogether. Only time—and the efforts of professional bodies such as the Institute of Personnel Management and the British Psychological Society—will tell.

NOTE

1. *Correlation.* Height is normally distributed. So is weight. The two also 'correlate'; tall people usually weigh more than short people, and heavy people are usually taller than light people. Height and weight are not perfectly correlated; there are plenty of short fat and tall thin exceptions to the rule (Figure 2.4).

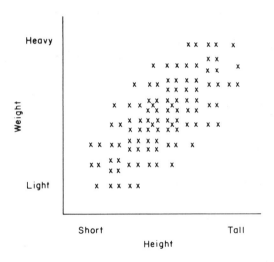

Figure 2.4. Height plotted against weight,
showing a positive correlation of 0.75.

The correlation coefficient summarizes how closely two measures such as height and weight go together. A perfect 'one-to-one' correlation gives a value of +1.00. If two measures are completely unrelated the correlation is zero—0.00. Height and weight correlate about 0.75. Sometimes two measures are inversely, or negatively, correlated: the older people are, the less fleet of foot they (generally) are.

CHAPTER 3

Job Description and Job Analysis

If you don't know where you're going, you'll end up somewhere else

Selectors should always start by deciding what, or who, they are looking for. In Britain this is often done very inefficiently (but not necessarily very quickly; I once sat through a 3-hour discussion of what or who we wanted in a new head of department (chairman), which succeeded only in concluding that we didn't really want a psycho-analyst, but would otherwise like the 'best' candidate. I didn't feel my time had been usefully spent.) American practice, partly under the pressure of 'fair' employment laws, has become very much more systematic.

Current British practice recommends selectors to write a *job description* and a *person specification*. Job descriptions start with the job's official title—'Head of Contracts Compliance Unit'—then say how the job fits into the organization— 'organizing and leading a team of seven implementing [a London borough] Council's contracts compliance policy'—before listing the job's main duties:

1. devise and implement management control systems and procedures;
2. introduce new technology to the Unit;
3. develop strategies for fighting discrimination, poverty, apartheid and privatization.

Job descriptions commonly fall into one of two traps. They list every duty— large or small, important or unimportant, frequent or infrequent, routinely easy or very difficult and demanding—without indicating which is which. Secondly, they lapse into value 'managementspeak' about 'liaising', 'co-ordinating', 'expediting', 'motivating', 'monitoring', etc., instead of explaining precisely what the successful applicant will find him/herself doing.

'Person specifications' also often suffer from vagueness and management-speak. Having dealt with specifics—must be over 30 and under 45, must have personnel experience and IPM (ASPA) membership, must speak Mandarin Chinese—many British 'person specifications' waste time saying the applicant must be keen, well-motivated, energetic, etc., as if any employer were likely to want idle, apathetic, unmotivated employees. American job descriptions emphasize *KSAs*—knowledge, skills, aptitudes. Ideally the person specification finishes by saying what selection tests to use, and what—*precisely*—to look for.

Advertisements include a condensed job description—'survey and inspect proposed work, prepare specifications and works schedules, arrange submission of quotations and tenders, supervise work under progress, and take measurements for valuation'—and person specification—'preferably hold an HNC in building or equivalent and have suitable experience in the building industry'; more detailed job description and person specifications are sent to people who reply to the ad.

The (US) Department of Labor has *task analysis inventories* for collecting job information. The inventory lists fourteen general headings:

1. what the worker does
2. education and training requirements
3. licensure, certificates, rating, etc.
4. communication responsibilities
5. area of responsibility
6. work aids used
7. machines and equipment
8. techniques used
9. specializations
10. products
11. services
12. registry and association requirements
13. union affiliation
14. environmental setting.

The Department of Labor also uses *general education development* ratings, which assess the level of reasoning, mathematics and language development needed. The lowest point on the language scale reads: 'recognise meaning of 2500 (two- or three-syllable) words ... print simple sentences ... speak simple sentences'; the highest point reads: 'read literature ... scientific and technical journals ... write novels, plays, editorials ... converse using the theory, principles and methods of effective and persuasive speaking.'

JOB ANALYSIS

Job descriptions and person specifications can be drawn up by a committee in half a day. Job *analysis* is much more ambitious, much more detailed, and has many more uses. Some methods require complex statistical analysis.

An example

Krzystofiak *et al.* (1979) wrote a 754-item *Job Analysis Questionnaire* for use in a power utility (power station) employing nearly 1900 individuals in 814 different jobs. Employees rate how often they perform nearly 600 tasks, on a five-point scale (never–frequently). Krzystofiak *et al.* first factor-analysed (see Note 1) their data, and extracted 60 factors, representing 60 themes in the work of the 1900 employees. One particular employee's work had six themes (in order of importance):

personnel administration
legal, commissions, agencies, and hearings
staff management
training
managerial supervision and decision-making
non-line management

The sample profile belongs to the company's Administrator of Equal Employment Opportunity. Similar profiles were drawn up for every employee. So what? The profiles have a number of uses:

1. Armed with the knowledge that a particular job has six main tasks, one has a clearer idea of how to recruit and select for it.
2. If one could find a good test of each of the 60 factors—a tall order admittedly—one would have a perfect all-purpose test battery for every one of the 800+ jobs in the plant.
3. Arguments with staff about whose job is more demanding, or deserves more money, can be settled more easily.

Krzystofiak *et al.* then cluster-analysed their data (Note 2), to sort employees into groups whose jobs were fairly similar. One of their clusters comprised:

Rate Analyst III
Statistical Assistant
Research Assistant
Affirmative Action Staff Assistant
Co-ordinator, Distribution Service
Environmental Co-ordinator
Statistician
Power Production Statistician

These eight jobs have quite a lot in common, but they all come from different departments, so their similarity might easily have been overlooked. Analysis of a matrix of 1700 × 60 ratings was required to uncover this group; human judges are notoriously very bad at interpreting large masses of data. The groupings revealed by the cluster analysis have a multitude of uses:

simplifying and standardizing selection procedures
centralizing training
planning promotions
substituting for absent workers
finding avenues to promote women and non-whites

Collecting information for job analysis

The job analyst tries to understand behaviour at work, so there are as many approaches to job analysis as there are to studying human behaviour itself. Here are nine methods of collecting information about work, arranged in a rough order from the most mechanistic and behaviourist to the most subjective or phenomenological.

1. Film is essential for detailed analysis of motor skills and physical tasks.
2. Written records, of sales, accidents, etc. can be useful.
3. Observation is useful for purely motor jobs, although it may overlook quality of work. Workers react to outsiders with stopwatchs and clipboards by working faster (or by going on strike). Observation alone rarely makes sense of higher-level jobs.
4. Structured questionnaires, which are usually completed by the worker, but sometimes by supervisors. Commercially prepared questionnaires are available.
5. Diaries, which are used for jobs with very little structure, such as university lecturer (college professor). Diaries are easy to 'fake', consciously or unconsciously.
6. Open-ended questionnaires are more suitable for higher-level jobs with diverse tasks.
7. Interviews take account of things observation can't: plans, intentions, meaning and satisfaction. The man who sees his work as 'laying bricks' differs from the man who sees it as 'building a cathedral'. Interviews take time and cost money; it's essential to interview more than one worker. Workers have a vested interest in describing the job as complex and difficult, and themselves as highly skilled and hard-working.
8. Group interviews with workers are more economical, and iron out idiosyncrasies, but just as likely to suffer from the 'vested interest' problem, which may go so far as a conspiracy to misinform.
9. Participation. Some psychologists think the only way to understand a job is

to do it, or spend as much time as possible alongside someone doing it. Some psychologists researching USAAF flight crew selection in the Second World War went to the lengths of learning to fly themselves.

Using two methods provides a cross-check—but also creates a familiar dilemma. If both methods give the same account, one is redundant. If they give different accounts, one doesn't know which to accept.

Ways of analysing information

Having collected information about the work being done, the researcher faces the task of making sense of it; this can be done subjectively, by a committee, or by formal statistical analysis.

(a) Subjective

After spending a month, or a week, or an afternoon, watching people doing the job or talking to them, the 'analyst' writes down his/her impressions. This is often good enough as the basis for writing a job description, but doesn't really merit the title 'analysis'.

(b) Rational

Official analyses of jobs group them by rational methods. The (US) *Dictionary of Occupational Titles* (*DOT*) provides detailed descriptions of thousands of jobs, e.g.:

> Collects, interprets, and applies scientific data to human and animal behavior and mental processes, formulates hypotheses and experimental designs, analyses results using statistics; writes papers describing research; provides therapy and counseling for groups or individuals. Investigates processes of learning and growth, and human interrelationships. Applies psychological techniques to personnel administration and management. May teach college courses.

DOT's account of a psychologist's work is actually a composite of several types of psychologist: academic, clinical and occupational; few psychologists do everything listed in *DOT*'s description.

(c) Factor analysis

This correlates scores for different jobs, to find factors of job performance (Note 1). Factor analysis can be misleading; if secretaries make tea, as well as type, typing and tea-making may appear on the same factor, although *rationally* they have little in common.

(d) Cluster analysis

This groups jobs according to similarity of ratings (Note 2). Salesmen for 3M ranked sales activities—e.g. 'arranging product displays for customers', 'entertaining customers'—in order of importance for their particular job (Dunnette and Kirchner, 1959). Sales jobs at 3M divided into five clusters:

Cluster 1: Direct retail contact
    arranging product displays for customers
    canvassing store to store
    calling directly on retail dealers
Cluster 2: Jobber and wholesaler contact
Cluster 3: Retail follow-up and service
Cluster 4: Industrial selling
Cluster 5: General selling and service

Cluster analysis groups *people*, whereas factor analysis groups *tasks*. Each is useful to the selector, in different ways.

USE OF JOB ANALYSIS

Job analysis has a variety of uses, in selection in particular, and in personnel work in general—so many uses in fact that one wonders how personnel departments ever managed without it. Job analysis is useful at every stage of the selection process.

1. Write selection tests (I)

Content validation. Job analysis allows selectors to write a selection test whose content so closely matches the content of the job that it is *content valid* (Chapter 11), which means it can be used, legally in the USA, without further demonstration of its validity.

2. Write selection tests (II)

Synthetic validation. Krzystofiak *et al* (1979) found 60 factors in power station jobs; if the employer could find an adequate test of each factor they could *synthesize* a different set of tests for every job, according to the factors involved in each (Chapter 11).

3. Write accurate, comprehensive job descriptions

These help recruit the right applicants, and help recruitment agencies send the right applicants.

4. Choose selection tests

A good job analysis identifies the knowledge, skills and abilities needed, allowing the selector to choose the right tests, and set minimum scores.

5. Aid interviewer

If the interviewer knows exactly what the job involves, he/she can concentrate on assessing knowledge, skills and abilities. Otherwise the interview can only assess the candidate *as a person*, which (a) may give poor results and (b) may be illegal in the USA (Chapter 12).

6. Classification

Assigning new employees to the tasks they are best suited for, assuming they haven't been appointed to a specific job.

7. Vocational guidance

Job analysis identifies jobs which are similar in the work done and the attributes needed, so someone interested in job X where there are presently no vacancies can be recommended to try jobs Y and Z instead.

8. Transfer selection tests

Jobs can be grouped into 'families', for which the same selection procedure can be used. If jobs are similar, then (1) selection tests for job A can be used for job B, without separate validation; and (2) selection procedures in plant or organization C can be used in plant or organization D, again without separate validation. However US 'fair' employment legislation doesn't allow selection procedures to be transferred, without proof there are no significant differences between jobs. Job analysis provides the necessary proof.

9. Criterion development

The success of selection can't be judged without a *criterion*—a way of of deciding which employees have proved *productive or unproductive*. Detailed analysis of the job makes it easier to distinguish good from bad employees.

10. Defend selection tests

In the case of *Arnold* v *Ballard* a good job analysis allowed an employer to require high school education—although general educational requirements are rarely accepted as 'fair' in the USA (Chapters 10 and 12). Job analysis is legally required by the Equal Employment Opportunities Commission in the USA, if the employer wishes to use selection methods that happen to exclude women, non-whites, anyone over 40, or the handicapped. The EEOC's Guidelines say: 'any method of job analysis may be used if it provides the information required for the specific validation strategy used'. The Guidelines don't say how detailed the job analysis has to be.

SELECTED JOB ANALYSIS TECHNIQUES—an OVERVIEW

Over the past 20 years job analysis schemes and inventories have multipled almost as prolifically as personality inventories. This chapter has space to describe only four or five of the most widely used, or most important. In general terms, job analysis techniques divide into: *job-oriented, worker-oriented* and *attribute-oriented.*

(a) *Job-oriented* techniques concentrate on what work is accomplished—'install cable pressurization systems', 'locating the source of an automobile engine knock'; they are usually checklists completed by the workers themselves.
(b) *Content-oriented* techniques are more concerned with what the worker does to accomplish the job—'attention to detail', 'use of written materials'; McCormick's Position Analysis Questionnaire (PAQ) exemplifies this approach.
(c) *Attribute-based* techniques describe jobs in terms of traits or aptitudes needed to perform them: 'good eyesight', 'verbal fluency', 'manual dexterity'. Fleishman classifies physical abilities (Chapter 10); psychologists have extensively analysed intellectual abilities (Chapter 7) and biographical factors (Chapter 6).

1. Critical incident technique (CIT)

This is the oldest job analysis technique, devised by Flanagan (1954) to analyse failure in flying training during the Second World War. Flanagan found the reasons given for failure too vague to be at all helpful: 'lack of inherent flying ability', 'poor judgement'. Opinions about qualities needed for success were equally vague: 'Too often statements regarding job requirements are merely lists of all the desirable traits of human beings.'

Flanagan identified flying's *critical* requirements by asking why, precisely, men failed flight training. He collected accounts of 'critical incidents' which caused men to be rejected: what led up to the incident, what the man did, what the consequences were, and whether the man was responsible for them.

In modern CIT hundreds, or even thousands, of accounts are collated to draw a composite picture of the job's requirements, from which checklists, ratings, etc., can be written. Observers are asked for accounts of strikingly good, as well as bad, performance. CIT is the basis of Behaviourally Anchored Rating Scaling (Chapter 5).

2. Position Analysis Questionnaire (PAQ)

PAQ is *content-oriented*, and covers nearly 200 elements, divided into six main areas (McCormick *et al.*, 1972). Table 3.1 lists the areas, and illustrative elements.

Table 3.1. Position Analysis Questionnaire

PAQ division	Illustrative job elements
1. Information input	Use of written materials Near-visual differentiation (good visual acuity, at short range)
2. Mental process	Level of reasoning in problem-solving coding/decoding
3. Work output	Use of keyboard devices assembling/disassembling
4. Relationships with other people	Instructing Contacts with public or customers
5. Job context	High temperature Interpersonal conflict
6. Other	Specified work space Amount of job structure

Each element is rated on six scales, e.g. Extent of Use, Important to the Job, etc. The ratings have been factor-analysed to discover 32 dimensions, e.g.:

Watching things from a distance
Being aware of bodily movement and balance
Making decisions
Dealing with the public.

McCormick *et al.* (1972) also obtained ratings of the *attributes*—aptitudes, interests or temperament—needed to carry out the job elements. PAQ can be completed by job analysts, supervisors or by workers, but its 'reading difficulty' level is very high, so less literate staff may find it hard to use.

3. Occupational Analysis Inventory (OAI)

This was developed originally for vocational education and guidance. OAI is a very long inventory, listing 602 elements, because it's *job-oriented*, whereas PAQ is *content-oriented* and much shorter. OAI also uses factor analysis, yielding 28 factors. Typical factors are:

(a) *Electrical/electronic repair maintenance, and operation:* radio mechanic, aircraft electrician, communications electrician.
(b) *Food preparation:* short-order cook, chef, school lunch supervisor.
(c) *Activities requiring co-ordination, balance and quickness:* fishing vessel first mate, aeroplane pilot, brick sorter.

The researchers used the factors to develop a pilot vocational interest inventory, whereas other vocational interest inventories—Chapter 8—use rational classifications of jobs, or factor analysis of questionnaire answers. However the factor analysis of over 1000 jobs left a lot of variance unaccounted for, implying a lot of tasks are too specific to be grouped in any meaningful way (Cunningham *et al.*, 1983).

4. J coefficients

The J coefficient, developed by Primoff (1959), uses a 'lens' model (Figure 3.1).

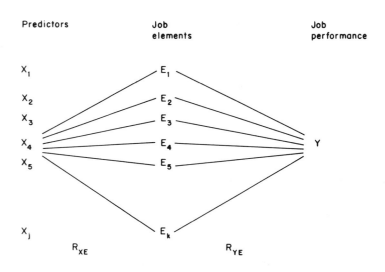

Figure 3.1. The J coefficient, showing predictors on the left, performance on the right, with job elements in the middle.

Job elements are the intermediate steps between *predictors* and *performance*. The J coefficient is calculated from the links between *predictors* and *job elements* (Rxe), and the links between *job elements* and *performance* (Rye), using a complex formula.

Predictor × *job element* links (Rxe) are estimated by expert judgements of the relevance of test items for each *element*. *Element* × *performance* links (Rye) can also be estimated by expert judgement, or by 'policy capturing', in which experts make overall judgements based on profiles of estimates, and their decision rules are inferred statistically.

The job elements themselves are: Knowledges, Skills, Abilities and Other personal characteristics (KSAOs). Supervisors first list the KSAOs, then rate how important they are.

5. Job Components Inventory

This was developed in Britain (Banks *et al.*, 1983) for jobs requiring limited skill, and has five principal sections: Tools and Equipment, Perceptual and Physical Requirements, Maths, Communication, Decision-Making and Responsibility.

6. Physical Abilities Analysis

This is a set of nine factors (listed in Table 10.2, page 180), each rated on a seven-point Behaviourally Anchored Rating Scale (BARS). Detailed *physical* job analysis is particularly important when women and the handicapped apply for jobs traditionally done by men, and which have physique requirements (Fleishman, 1979).

Relative merits of different systems

Levine *et al.* (1983) surveyed experienced job analysts, who found PAQ, J coefficients, Fleishman's Physical Abilities Analysis, and four other job analysis methods equally useful for selection work, with only Flanagan's Critical Incident Technique getting a poor rating. PAQ was rated the most practical of the seven schemes, being ready to use 'off-the-shelf'. Subjects disliked PAQ's 'non-job-specific language' and 'esoteric terminology'. On the other hand PAQ was cheaper to use.

Reliability

Job analysis techniques obviously need acceptable inter-observer reliability, and intra-observer reliability. McCormick *et al.* (1972) report acceptable inter-rater reliabilities for PAQ; Banks *et al.* (1983) found Job Components Inventory ratings by workers and supervisors correlated reasonably for most scales and most jobs.

Validity

Research on validity of job analysis faces a familiar dilemma. If results agree with 'common sense' they are dismissed as redundant—'telling us what we already know'; if results don't agree with common sense they are simply dismissed. *Construct* validation (Chapter 11)—proving the analysis makes sense—is the most promising approach.

Job analysis should differentiate jobs that differ, but give the same picture of the same job, in different plants or organizations. Banks *et al.* found Job Component Inventory (JCI) ratings distinguished four clerical jobs from four engineering jobs, proving JCI could find a difference where a difference ought to be. Banks *et al.* also showed JCI ratings were the same for mailroom clerks in different companies, providing JCI didn't find a difference where there shouldn't be one.

Arvey and Begalla (1975) used PAQ to reach some surprising conclusions. They obtained PAQ ratings for 48 home-makers (housewives), and compared their composite 'home-maker' profile with 1000 other jobs in the PAQ Manual.

Table 3.2. Factors in senior (UK) Civil Service jobs (Dulewicz and Keenay, 1979) (Reproduced by permission)

1. *Personnel.* Organizing the work of one's staff, supervising and appraising them. Training and lecturing to staff. Selecting, and giving careers guidance, to staff. Consulting and negotiating with Staff Associations. Knowledge of a wide range of personnel management techniques.
2. *Resource utilization.* Knowing how to manage projects/programmes and how to plan/evaluate the utilization of resources. Planning computer operations and knowledge of computers/ADP.
3. *Finance.* Knowledge of financial parliamentary procedures and of financial disciplines and techniques—accountancy, economics, investment appraisal and cost-benefit analysis.
4. *Figure-work.* Carrying out numerical calculations. Assimilating and making inferences from statistical information. Knowledge of descriptive and analytical statistical techniques.
5. *Foreign.* Consulting and negotiating with representatives from foreign governments, etc. Speaking foreign languages.
6. *Local government.* Consulting or negotiating with representatives of local authorities. Knowledge of local government constitution, procedures and finance, and of social studies.
7. *Contracts.* Consulting or negotiating with representatives of local authorities and industry, and specialists. Knowledge of legislative parliamentary procedures and law.
8. *Parliamentary.* Advising ministers. Writing explanatory briefs on policy, speeches and answers to Parliamentary Questions. Knowledge of legislative parliamentary procedures and law.
9. *Generalist.* Consulting and negotiating with other senior civil servants. Acting as a committee member or chairman. Assimilating critically and commenting on written material. Writing persuasive expositions to colleagues. Writing instructions and other authoritative communications.

The most similar job was police officer, followed by home economist, airport maintenance chief, kitchen helper, and fire fighter—all 'trouble-shooting, emergency-handling' jobs. Arvey and Begalla calculate the average salary paid for the 10 jobs most like housewife; that average was $740 a month, at 1968 prices. Most people hadn't seen the housewife's role in this light, nor had they reckoned its true worth.

Analysis of the work of senior (UK) Civil Servants found nine factors (Table 3.2), and thirteen clusters, which were aggregated into four main groups (Table 3.3). Dulewicz and Keenay (1979) sent details of the clusters to the Civil Servants who contributed the data, and asked if they agreed with the classification, and whether they had been correctly classified. Only 7 per cent thought the classification unsatisfactory, and only 11 per cent disagreed with their personal classification.

Table 3.3. Clusters in senior (UK) Civil Service jobs (Dulewicz and Keenay, 1979) (Reproduced by permission.)

1. *General administration*
   A—parliamentary
   B—international
   C—local government and other outside bodies
   D—general work

2. *Financial and economic administration*
   A—general finance
   B—resource allocation and control, general
   C—resource allocation and control, regional and local government

3. *Resource management*
   A—central and advisory
   B—regional
   C—physical resource management (computers and equipment)

4. *Personnel management*
   A—general personnel work
   B—staff management

PAQ ratings by experts, supervisors, people doing the job and students inter-correlate almost perfectly (Smith and Hakel, 1979), which poses a disturbing question. If workers or students can analyse jobs, why pay for experts? The students were given only the name of the job, so how could they describe it accurately? Unless PAQ is only measuring stereotyped impressions of jobs, and not really *analysing* them? However Cornelius *et al.* (1984) were able to show that the more the students knew about the job, the better their PAQ ratings agreed with the experts', which confirms PAQ's validity. Furthermore very high levels of student–expert agreement are partly an artefact, based on PAQ's 'Does Not Apply' ratings; everyone knows that college professors (university lecturers) don't use powered hand tools as part of their job. When 'Does Not Apply' ratings were excluded from the analysis, agreement between students and experts was further reduced. These results imply PAQ genuinely analyses jobs, and isn't just a very complicated way of measuring stereotypes.

USING JOB ANALYSIS to SELECT WORKERS

An obvious idea, first suggested by Viteles in 1923, is to classify jobs by the tests used to select staff. Ghiselli (1966) collated all the data he could find on test validity, and then classified jobs *twice*: first into broad rational categories— managerial, supervisory etc.; second by test validity. The two classifications were completely different: 'by and large the clusters and subclusters [based on test validity] are made up of jobs with little apparent similarity'. However Ghiselli didn't correct validities for sampling error, unreliability, etc.; perhaps groups of *corrected* validities would be more meaningful (Chapter 7).

Less ambitiously, several attempts have been made to link aptitude batteries to job analyses. For example Mecham (see McCormick *et al.*, 1979) analysed 163 jobs for which both General Aptitude Test Battery (GATB) and PAQ data were available. PAQ scores predicted the average GATB profile of a job; people who have 'gravitated' to a job, and 'survived' in it have a particular profile of abilities. Correlations between GATB and PAQ, across jobs, were generally quite high. This research implies each job needs a particular set of attributes, that can be identified by PAQ, and then assessed by GATB. Similar research by Cunningham (cited in Pearlman, *et al.* 1980) using the Differential Aptitude Test (DAT) and Occupational Analysis Inventory (OAI), was less successful, possibly because the samples were too small.

Analysis by PAQ of the job of plastics injection-moulding setter in a UK plant identified seven attributes: long-term memory, intelligence, short-term memory, good near visual acuity, perceptual speed, convergent thinking and mechanical ability. Sparrow *et al.* (1982) recommended the employer to use: Wechsler Memory Scale, Raven's Standard Progressive Matrices, Thurstone's Perceptual Speed Test, Birkbeck Test of Mechanical Comprehension, and a standard eye chart read at 30 cm. Sparrow's work illustrates the use of job analysis to make sense of a job, then decide how to select the right people to do it.

However the work of Schmidt, Hunter and Pearlman, reviewed in greater detail in Chapter 7, suggests analysis of jobs doesn't need to be very detailed. US Army jobs needed only to be grouped into very broad categories—clerical, general technical, electronics, etc.—to achieve good predictive validity. Pearlman *et al.* (1980) concluded that deciding a job is 'clerical' was all the job analysis needed to choose tests that predicted productivity.

CONCLUSIONS

Does job analysis contribute to selection of more productive workers? Research using GATB and PAQ has been moderately successful; PAQ ratings predict fairly accurately what profiles of abilities will be found in people doing different jobs. Attempts to analyse the job, then select the right tests—known as 'synthetic validation' (Chapter 11)—are criticized by Mossholder and Arvey (1984) as amounting so far only to a promising plan, not a proven, workable system.

Job analysis inventories are moderately successful at choosing the right tests to select workers for a job, but are they necessary? They are time-consuming to complete, and quite expensive to use. Sparrow *et al.*'s analysis of plastics injection moulding work with PAQ came up with a very unsurprising list of tests to use, and could be accused of not really telling us anything we didn't already know, or couldn't have discoverd much more quickly and cheaply. Pearlman *et al.* tend to agree, and conclude 'analysis' of a job, when selecting tests, need be no more elaborate than deciding it's 'clerical'.

However, job analysis shouldn't be dismissed out of hand. It is worth using in personnel selection in the USA, if only because it's risky not to. Deciding a job is 'clerical', and using a 'clerical' test for selection, may satisfy common sense, and may be good enough for Pearlman *et al.*, but it won't satisfy the Equal Employment Opportunities Commission, if there's a fuss about the composition of the resulting workforce. The full detail and complexity of PAQ may be needed to prove a clerical job really is clerical.

Similarly an American employer who has proved that GATB selects woolpullers in Plant A, and want to use GATB to select woolpullers in Plant B, may have to analyse both wool-pulling jobs to prove they really are the same. In fact, American employers, ever conscious of 'fair employment' agencies, usually find they can't have too much information about their employees, so enormously detailed, complexly analysed inventories such as PAQ are often a godsend.

Nor should one forget that selection is just one of several personnel functions job analysis serves. Some of these other functions, or all of them combined, may justify the time and cost of job analysis.

NOTES

1. *Factor analysis.* Table 3.4 shows correlation between performance on eight typical school subjects, in a large sample. (A table of correlations between every pair of a set of measures is called a correlation *matrix.*) The correlations between English language, English literature, French and German are all fairly high; people who are good at one tend to be good at the others. Similarly the correlations between maths, physics, chemistry and biology tend to be fairly high. However correlations between subjects in the two sets of four—e.g. English literature × physics—are much lower. All of

Table 3.4. (Fictitious) correlations between school subject marks

	Maths	Physics	Chemistry	Biology	English	French	German
Maths							
Physics	67						
Chemistry	76	55					
Biology	60	61	70				
English	33	23	25	21			
French	23	31	30	15	77		
German	11	21	22	14	80	67	
English Literature	33	23	24	55	45	56	69

this suggests that people who are good at one language tend to be good at another, while people who are good at one science are good at another. There are *eight* school subjects, but only *two* underlying abilities.

Clear groupings in small sets of measures can be seen by inspection. Larger sets of less clear correlations can be only be interpreted by *factor analysis*, which calculates how many *factors* are needed to account for the observed correlations. Two factors account for performance in the eight school subjects. Fleishman's analysis of dozens of measures of physical strength and activity shows nine factors are needed.

2. *Cluster analysis.* In Krzystofiak *et al.*'s study, each one of 1710 workers who completed the JAQ has a profile on 60 factors, giving a 1710 × 60 (= 102,600)

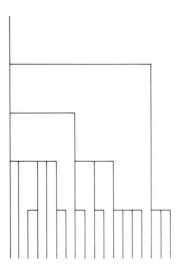

Figure 3.2. A dendrogram, produced by cluster analysis, showing the structure of similarity of different jobs within an organization.

matrix. One could check through this by hand/eye, to pick out people with similar profiles, but this would be very tedious, and very inaccurate. Cluster analysis calculates 'intersubject distance' D^2 for every possible pair of profiles, where D^2 is the sum of the squared differences between the 60 pairs of scores. The pair whose D^2 is lowest have the most similar profiles of 60 scores. Cluster analysis then seeks the person with most similar profile to the composite of the first two subjects, and adds that in, and so on.

Cluster analysis generates a 'dendrogram', a diagram showing which subjects resemble each other and which do not, and adding clusters together according to levels of similarity. At the left of a typical dendrogram (Figure 3.2), are individual workers; at the right is a single cluster comprising all workers. In between is the information the researcher wants—the structure of similarity of jobs.

CHAPTER 4

The Interview

'I know one when I see one'

I described the interview that got me my job at UC Swansea as 'assembly of a dozen or so people, with no experience or training in selection and no idea what they're looking for, ask[ing] whatever questions come into their heads' (Cook, 1979). Only one of the dozen was a psychologist, and he an expert on colour vision rather than selection or the fields I was being employed to teach.

I describe interview practices at UCS not, or not solely, to mock them, but to make an important point. Research on the interview describes a very small tip of a very large iceberg. The small tip is what employers who are willing to be researched do when the researcher is watching. The rest of the iceberg is the other 200 million interviews conducted each year in the USA and UK. Some of these interviews may as good as the best the researcher sees; rumour, anecdote and one's own experience suggest many aren't. One hears of personnel managers who judge applicants by the look of the back of their neck while they're standing at attention, or by the manager's dog's reaction, or by the ratio of hat size to shoe size, but these employers aren't likely to invite psychologists to study their activities.

Interviews vary widely. They can be as short as 3 minutes, or as long as 2 hours. The public sector in Britain favours the 'panel' interview, in which the candidate faces five, ten or even twenty interviewers. In campus recruitment, the 'milk round', candidates usually face a series of interviews. Robertson and Makin's (1986) survey shows interviews by two or three interviewers (together) slightly more popular than one-to-one interviews; British industry, as sampled from the *Times 1000*, doesn't favour large panel interviews.

Some interviewers are psychologists or psychiatrists; some are personnel managers; some are line managers; a lot are nobody in particular. Robertson and Makin's survey shows line managers and personnel people usually interview in British industry.

Sometimes the interviewer is friendly and tries to establish rapport; sometimes the interviewer makes the applicant try to sell him/her something; sometimes the interviewer tries stress methods; quite often he/she has no particular strategy. The armed services favour psychiatric screening, which Ulrich and Trumbo (1965) think could prove useful in industry, 'in the light of evidence that a majority of dismissals are for reasons of interpersonal inadequacies and maladjustments'.

Bad interviews are legion, and they are clearly a waste of time. They also cost a lot of money—over a billion dollars a year in the USA according to Hakel (1982). The question is whether a good interviewer, asking sensible questions, listening to the answers, attaching the right weight to each of them, can out-perform other selection methods, or can add anything to them, or can even do better than sticking a pin in the list of applicants.

Doubts about the value of interviewing date from an early study by Hollingworth, in 1922, of twelve sales managers who interviewed 57 would-be salesmen, and generated some spectacular disagreements. Research on the interview has been reviewed increasingly frequently since (Wagner, 1949; Mayfield, 1964; Ulrich and Trumbo, 1965; Wright, 1969; Schmitt, 1976; Arvey, 1979a; Hakel, 1982; Reilly and Chao, 1982).

ARE INTERVIEWS USEFUL?

What defines a *useful* selection method? A good selection method is *reliable*; it gives a consistent account of the person being assessed. A good selection method is *valid*; it selects good applicants and rejects bad ones. A good selection method is *cost-effective*; it saves the employer more in increased output than it costs to use. (Psychologists call cost-effectiveness *utility*; see Chapter 13.)

Reliability

Interviews are moderately reliable. Interviewers usually agree with each other; inter interviewer reliability (Note 1) coefficients range from 0.62 to 0.90, 'with a few exceptions ... lower than usually accepted for devices used for individual prediction' (Ulrich and Trumbo). Interviewers also agree with themselves if they re-rate candidates (Mayfield, 1964), (although most studies can't prove inter-viewers don't remember what they said the first time).

Interviewers share a stereotype of 'the good applicant' which ensures they agree, but not that they're accurate. Canadian Army interviewers agreed very well on the 'ideal officer', using 120 items derived from previous interviews (Sydiaha, 1961). But while interviewers collectively agree what they're looking for, each individual interviewer's own stereotype has idiosyncratic elements. Some interviewers see 'is presently active in eight outside organizations' as a very good sign, while others see it as a very bad sign (Mayfield and Carlson, 1966).

Validity

Interviews aren't a very good way of choosing productive workers, and rejecting unproductive ones. Ulrich and Trumbo concluded validity coefficients of less than 0.50 were the rule, and validities of less than 0.30 very common (Note 2).

Research since 1965 hasn't changed this pessimistic conclusion. Grant and Bray (1969) describe the role of the interview in the Bell/American Telegraph and Telephone management assessment centre (Chapter 9). Interviews lasted up to 2 hours; interviewers recorded their impressions immediately afterwards. Interview *reports* (not interviews) were rated on eighteen dimensions; ratings predicted salary progress—an idex of productivity—8–10 years later, with at best moderate success. A 1-hour interview by a psychologist showed a 'an essential lack of predictive validity' in selecting Peace Corps volunteers, while a 'board rating'—the consensus of between seven and 24 experts—generated 'predictions with a high degree of consistency, even if not always with a high degree of accuracy' (Harris, 1972). Interview ratings of officer cadets in 'a national defense organisation' didn't correlate at all with training grades after 6 and 12 weeks (Zedeck *et al.*, 1983).

Dunnette (1972) summarizes 30 interview validity coefficients for the American petroleum industry, and finds a very low median validity ($r = 0.13$); only 25 per cent of validity coefficients exceeded $r = 0.21$. Reilly and Chao (1982) review twelve validity studies, eight of them unpublished, and calculated a similar low average validity coefficient ($r = 0.19$) against supervisor ratings. Hunter and Hunter (1984) pool ten studies, about which they say very little except that none were included in Reilly and Chao's analysis. 'Validity generalization' analysis (see Chapter 7) reaches even gloomier conclusions than previous reviewers; the interview has a very low ($r = 0.11$) average correlation with supervisor ratings. Validity generalization analysis sees the occasional fairly high validity coefficient that reviews, including this one, seize on with relief as just a 'fluke', the upper tail of a distribution of validity coefficients that vary widely about a low true mean. (Validity coefficients vary widely because they contain seven sources of error, see Chapter 7).

Ulrich and Trumbo make an important point: 'studies purporting to validate the interview have, instead, tested the validity of the interviewer's predictions, to which the contribution of the interview, *per se*, was unknown'—because the interviewer almost always has application form or CV, references, sometimes even test data. Perhaps these other sources contribute most of the interview's limited predictive power, in which case the face-to-face encounter is an expensive waste of everyone's time.

Criterion reliability

Validity coefficients are low because the interview is trying to predict the unpredictable. The interviewer's judgement is compared with a 'criterion' that defines a good employee. This criterion is never perfect, and is often another person's judgement, which may be just as fallible as the interviewer's judgement. Supervisors' ratings, one commonly used criterion, have fairly good reliability (around $r = 0.60$); one supervisor agrees fairly well, but far from perfectly, with

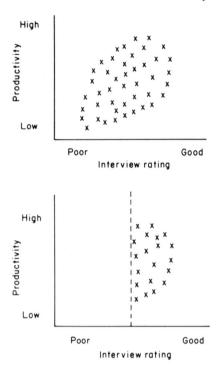

Figure 4.1. Restriction of range. In the lower distribution, everyone with a low interview rating has been excluded from the analysis (necessarily, because they weren't employed, so their productivity can't be known). A very low correlation results. The upper distribution shows the results that would have been obtained, if everyone were employed, regardless of interview rating.

another supervisor. Training grades, another common criterion, usually have higher reliabilites (around $r = 0.80$). A selection procedure can't have a validity coefficient higher than the reliability of the criterion, so a study using supervisor ratings can't achieve a validity higher than 0.60. Validity coefficients can be corrected for criterion unreliability. Such correction raised Hunter and Hunter's pooled estimate for the interview's validity from $r = 0.11$ to 0.14.

Range restriction

Validity coefficients are low because 'range' is 'restricted'. Validity ought to be calculated from a sample of *applicants*, but usually has to be estimated from a sample of *successful* applicants. Few organizations can afford to employ everyone who applies, or to employ people judged unsuitable, simply to allow psychologists to calculate better estimates of validity. Nearly all research settles for the less radical method of correlating interview ratings with success, *within the minority of selected applicants*. Figure 4.1 shows the effect on the validity coefficient. If only the top 20 per cent are employed, a (potentially) large correlation is greatly reduced, because none of the unsuccessful applicants are employed. This 'restricts range', because only applicants with good interview ratings are included in the calculation.

Validity coefficients can be corrected for 'restricted range' (Note 3), as well as criterion unreliability. Hunter and Hunter (1984) corrected for range restriction, and increased their estimate of the mean true validity of the interview from $r = 0.14$ to 0.22. Reilly and Chao report a very similar value ($r = 0.23$). Even making every possible allowance the interview does poorly; it has limited validity. Chapter 13 compares the interview with other methods, and answers the question 'Is it worth using a selection method that does so poorly?'

Occasionally everyone who is assessed *is* accepted; for a trial period, candidates for Royal Navy commissions were interviewed, but the ratings weren't used (Jones and Harrison, 1982). The interviews were brief; the interviewers themselves naval officers; their ratings of 'overall suitability' correlated moderately well with success at Admiralty Boards.

Qualities that can be accurately estimated by interview

Intelligence can be judged fairly accurately in the interview. It used to be said—correctly—that tests should be used to measure intelligence, because tests are more consistent, more accurate and therefore fairer. Intelligence tests are also quicker—because applicants can all be tested at once—and cheaper. But intelligence tests have fallen foul of 'fair' employment laws in the USA, and might one day face similar problems in Britain. Hence an employer who wants to assess intelligence, but doesn't want to use tests, could make a reasonable approximation by interview. Snedden (1930) devised an interview that purposely used 'high-level vocabulary', such as 'stamina' or 'pertinacity'; interview assessments achieved a very high correlation with test intelligence. (However interviews are legally 'tests' in the USA, so a vocabulary test thinly disguised as an interview might be challenged.)

Rundquist (1947) asked what can the interview assess that other methods can't, and answered 'social interaction'—ability to get on well with others and create a good impression. A panel interview, designed to be stressful, achieved very high reliability, and correlated moderately well with ratings of overall efficiency by brother officers, in a very large sample of US Naval officers.

Ulrich and Trumbo identify the other question the interview can answer as 'What is the applicant's motivation to work?'; analysis of selection of US Naval officer cadets found the interview best at assessing career motivation. American Telephone and Telegraph's management follow-up study later confirmed that interviews were best at assessing 'career passivity'—no strong need to advance, willingness to wait and desire for job security (Grant and Bray, 1969).

Gifford et al. (1985), however, found motivation couldn't be assessed in the interview, whereas social skill could be, up to a point. Gifford et al. used the 'lens' model (Figure 4.2) to explain why interviewers could assess social skill, but not motivation. Social skill is visible in the interview. Interviewees who rated themselves socially skilled smiled more, gestured more and said more; the more the candidate smiled, gestured and spoke, the higher the interviewer's rating of social skill. Motivation too is 'visible' in the interview; highly motivated candidates dressed more formally, and leaned back more during the interview.

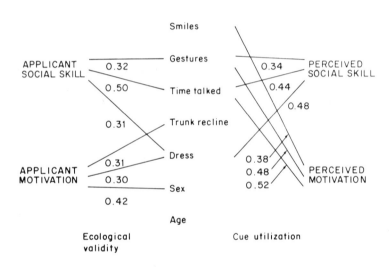

Figure 4.2. The 'lens' model, showing the link between interviewee's personality (motivation and social skill) and interview behaviour, and the link between interview behaviour and interviewer rating (Gifford et al., 1985). (Reproduced by permission.)

But interviewers didn't base assessments of motivation on dress and posture; they rated as highly motivated candidates who smiled, gestured and said more—behaviour which didn't relate to motivation. Gifford's interviewers could have judged motivation if they'd used the right cues; but suppose they'd been asked to judge something that wasn't reflected in the candidates' behaviour? Clearly their task would be impossible.

Interview plus other data

'Credentials' alone predict success in graduate psychology training with only moderate validity; an interview increased validity, but a battery of tests—without an interview—did rather better. Anderson (1960) found a 30-minute interview greatly improved decisions about graduate psychologists based on college grades and tests. However neither of two long interviews added anything to 'credentials' and test data when selecting clinical psychologists (Kelly and Fiske, 1951). Success in clinical psychology proved very hard to predict accurately by any means.

REAL and IDEAL INTERVIEWS

Models

Books on how to interview, and schemes for improving interviewing, abound—generally unsupported by proof that they work. Critics (England and Paterson, 1960) have suggested no more should be written.

The (UK) Engineering Industry Training Board recommends a 'six-point plan' for interviewing apprentices: general personal questions, educational questions, engineering questions, motivational questions, supply information, questions from candidates.

Forty years' research on officer selection in Britain identifies five areas to cover in interviews (Vernon and Parry, 1949):

1. *Outward impression*—manner, ability to communicate, self-presentation.
2. *Educational achievements.*
3. *Achievement in other areas*—sports, spare-time activities, positions of responsibility, employment record.
4. *Physical orientation*—liking for sports, physical stamina, keeping physically fit.
5. *Realistic career motivation*—knowledge of training and career, fit of service career to ambitions and interests.

Anstey (1977) gives detailed advice on panel interviews. The best number is three, including chairman; large boards are uneconomic and cumbersome, while even-numbered boards may be deadlocked in a vote. An interview for a specialist might follow the sequence:

Chairman—8 minutes on present job, education and career to date, and reasons for wanting the job.
Internal specialist—10 minutes on qualifications and experience for the specific post.

Outside specialist—10 minutes on qualifications and experience in general.
Chairman—5 minutes on interests and leisure pursuits.
Final review, with opportunity for candidate to add information and ask
questions.

Knatz and Inwald (1983) discuss highly specialized interviews for 'screening'
police officers who might 'break' under stress; the interviewer should set a fast
pace, asking leading questions, 'when did you stop beating your wife' questions,
and surprise questions ('when was the last time you were in a fist fight?'). The
interviewer looks for excessive fearfulness, phobias, uncontrolled impulsivity,
inability to handle hostility, as well as overt psychoses, alcoholism, etc.

A lot of interviews remain very haphazard; Keenan and Wedderburn (1980)
found some 'milk round' interviewers 'failed to use an interview guide or any
form of structured format'.

The interview in practice

How long do selection interviews last? What do interviews ask about? How
much information does the candidate supply? What do interviewees think about
interviews and interviewers?

While the literature on interview reliability and validity is vast, information
about what actually goes on in interviews remains sketchy. Some research has
'debriefed' students after 'milk round' (campus recruitment) interviews, and
interviewed the interviewers about their aims and methods. American graduate
recruiters ask about extracurricular activities, whereas British interviewers are
more interested in academic work, and knowledge of job and company (Taylor
and Sniezek, 1984; Keenan and Wedderburn, 1980). Interviewers often ask a lot
of factual, biographical questions, which are usually redundant because the
answer's on the application form. Interviewers often 'lead' the candidate, which
is usually a mistake.

Interviewers don't agree among themselves which are the most important
topics, nor is there a high 'level of agreement between recruiters' importance
ratings and applicants's reports of interview content' (Taylor and Sniezek, 1984).
Interviewers discuss different topics with succesive candidates (Keenan and
Wedderburn, 1980). Applicants expect interviewers to tell them more about the
job, while interviewers expect applicants to say more about themselves, about
their reasons for applying for the job, and about the company (Herriot and
Rothwell, 1983). Interviewees describe interviews as generally superficial and
easy to deal with.

'Hard' information about what happens in interviews is scarcer. Several
studies find interviewers talk more than candidates (Mayfield, 1964), which is
obviously undesirable since they're supposed to be getting information, not
giving it.

Content analysis of interviews shows the interviewer decides how long the interview should last, while the interviewee determines how many questions are asked (by the length of his/her answers). Daniels concluded that interviewers are fairly efficient, although the more talkative do tend to irrelevance at times. 'Non-directive' open-ended questions get more information out of the interviewee. Applicants who talk more are more likely to be selected (Anderson, 1960). Is this because applicants who talk more improve their chances? Or because interviewers encourage applicants they like to say more?

Arvey (1979a) thinks interviewers in the USA will have to choose their questions carefully in future. The Washington (State) Human Rights Commission objects to eight classes of question, unless they're 'job-related': marital status, home ownership, criminal record, military discharge, pregnancy, citizenship, spouse and family and 'overgeneral enquiries'.

The (UK) Equal Opportunities Commission's Code of Practice says 'questions posed during interviews [should] relate *only* to the requirements of the job. Where it is necessary to discuss personal circumstances and their effect upon ability to do the job, this should be done in a neutral manner, equally applicable to all applicants'. A woman who didn't get a job as a golf professional complained about being asked: 'Are there many women golf professionals in clubs?' and 'Do you think men respond as well to a woman golf professional as to a man?' The court didn't, however, consider the questions discriminatory, and refused to accept the plaintiff's argument that it was unlawful to ask a woman questions that wouldn't be asked of a man (or vice-versa).

Several studies have shown that successful candidates look the interviewer in the eye more, smile more, gesture more, move their head more (shaking and nodding), and generally both look and sound more friendly and enthusiastic (Imada and Hakel, 1977). It doesn't follow, of course, that smiling, looking, etc., *causes* the candidate's success; he/she may look, smile, etc., more because he/she thinks—rightly—the interview is going well.

IMPROVING the INTERVIEW

One could recommend abolishing the interview altogether, on the grounds that it wastes the candidate's time, and tells employers nothing about candidates they couldn't discover from the application form, except what candidates look and sound like (which matters, sometimes). But people expect to be interviewed, and feel cheated if they aren't. Hakel (1982) says 'most people have faith in the process. The interview is the place to "put your best foot forward". . . . 'If you can just get in to see the interviewer you can tell your whole story.' Interviews *look* fair, especially when they are large and elaborate; many organizations' rules require them to interview five candidates even when they already know who they want.

Given the interview is here to stay, what can be done to improve it?

(a) Select the selectors

Vernon and Parry (1949) found one naval recruiting assistant who made much better decisions than the Royal Navy's test battery, which was generally far better than interviewers. Other research finds different interviewers' decisions differ widely in accuracy. But selecting the selectors creates problems. Research on the 'good judge of others' (Cook, 1979) has generally failed to find such a person. Judging people accurately isn't a generalized ability. People who are good at rating traits aren't necessarily good at rating someone's vocabulary. This implies Vernon and Parry's recruiting assistant may have been a 'fluke', who wouldn't be so accurate if her task changed, or even with her next batch of recruits. If there's no generalized trait of being good at summing up other people, there's no simple way of finding good judges. Social intelligence tests and 'empathy' scales haven't proved very useful. A 'track record' of good judgements is presently the only sure way of finding a good interviewer, so an organization that thinks it has one should hang on to him/her.

(b) Train interviewers

Training schemes abound, but have yet to be proved effective. Nevertheless, telling the interviewer what to look for, how to look for it, and how likely he/she is to miss it, can't be a bad idea. Interviewers can be warned of common sources of bias and inaccuracy, and taught how to use rating scales efficiently. Training makes ratings more reliable (Wright *et al.*, 1967), so one trained interviewer can replace a panel of untrained judges. Interviewers can be successfully trained to change their style of questioning (Mayfield, 1964). Interviewers trained in traditional interview techniques still achieved near zero validity predicting supervisor ratings and sales, whereas interviewers trained in structured interview methods achieved impressive results predicting supervisor ratings, and sales (Orpen, 1985).

The interview has largely escaped the legal problems that beset psychological tests in the USA, even though it's the easiest way of all to discriminate, consciously or unconsciously. But the interview hasn't gone entirely uncriticized; the case of *US* v. *Hazelwood School District* noted that 'No evidence was presented which would indicate that any two principals apply the same criteria— objective or subjective—to evaluate applicants.' One school principal (headteacher) said, rather unwisely, choosing a teacher was 'like dating a girl, some of them impress you, some of them don't'.

(c) Provide a good job description

Interviewers working from a good job description agree with each other better, pay less attention to irrelevant information and are less likely to make up their minds too quickly. Interviewing without a job description is risky under current US law (Arvey, 1979).

(d) Tell the interviewer what to look for

Interviewers can assess the applicant's social skill and motivation, but can't predict if he/she can fly an aircraft. More specifically research can supply the interviewer with a list of points to cover. Vernon and Parry (1949) list proven 'contraindications' for military responsibility: poor work record, inability to give an intelligible account of present job, hypochondria, preference at school for handiwork/athletics/geography over maths/science, underachievement at school.

(e) Listen to the candidate

The average interviewer isn't very good at answering questions about what happened, immediately after the interview (Carlson, 1967); more experienced interviewers are more accurate, as are ones who use a structured interview guide. Anstey (1977) thinks 'effective listening' the hallmark of good interview. 'Effective listening' goes beyond merely staying awake: 'One should note not so much what the candidate has said . . . as what one has learnt from it', not whether he/she is in favour of the EEC but whether his/here arguments are sound and well presented. People who remember what someone looked like, said and did are better at predicting what that person will do in the future (Cline, 1964).

(f) Use the information efficiently

No-one knows how many facts the typical interviewer collects in the typical interview, but it presumably runs into double figures. (Janz (1982) recorded an average of seventeen answers answers in a 30-minute interview.) Some facts will point one way, some the other. People are generally very bad at interpreting inconsistent information; they ignore or distort information that doesn't fit their overall impression. Tullar *et al.* (1979) found that interviewers who rejected a candidate said he/she didn't look them in the eye, while interviewers who accepted the same candidate thought he/she *did*. Interviewers should list all the facts about the candidate, preferably as they emerge, decide which way each points and calculate a score. More important facts can be given greater weight. Better still the interviewer's judgement, or questions, or both, can be *structured*.

(g) Structure the interviewer's judgement

Most interview 'models' give the interviewer a set of categories to work from, or supply rating scales. It's tempting to elaborate lists of ratings, but interviewers rarely have the time or inclination to use something too long or complicated. Nor can interviewers use more than a handful of scales; a proliferation of scales simply results in the interviewer making the same judgement again, under another name.

(h) Structure the interview

Hovland and Wonderlic first proposed a standardized interview in 1939, taking the Terman–Binet intelligence test as their model. Their form covers work history, family history, social history and personal history. Some questions are answered by the applicant, others by the interviewer: 'Does the applicant indicate a sincere interest and attitude towards his work?' The form proved quite successful and predicted quite well which employees were later dismissed.

Another early structured system was McMurray's 'patterned interview'. McMurray (1947) reported very high validity coefficients (as high as $r = 0.68$) for three samples of factory workers, perhaps because the interview ratings weren't used in the selection, so there was no 'restriction of range'. McMurray's interview lists not only questions for the interviewer to ask—'What plans do you have for your children?'—but questions for the interviewer to *answer*, about the candidate's reply—'Do dependents provide adequate motivation?' McMurray's Patterned Interview was designed to measure personality traits, which makes its high predictive validity all the more surprising.

All reviews agree structured interview methods give more reliable and accurate results. (Structured interviews almost always use ratings or checklists, so it isn't clear whether structuring the interview or the interviewer's judgement, or both, increases reliability.)

'Situational' interviews (Latham *et al.*, 1980) use 'Critical Incidents' (Chapter 3) of particularly effective or ineffective behaviour:

> The employee was devoted to his family. He had only been married for 18 months. He used whatever excuse he could to stay at home. One day the fellow's baby got a cold. His wife had a hangnail or something on her toe. He didn't come to work. He didn't even phone in.

The incidents are rewritten as questions:

> Your spouse and two teenage children are sick in bed with a cold. There are no friends or relatives available to look in on them. Your shift starts in 3 hours. What would you do in this situation?

The company supervisors who describe the incidents also agree 'benchmark' answers for good, average and poor workers:

I'd stay home—my spouse and family come first (poor).
I'd phone my supervisor and explain my situation (average).
Since they only have colds, I'd come to work (good).

At the 'interview' the questions are read out, the candidate replies, and is rated against the 'benchmarks'. The 'situational' interview is very reliable, and predicts supervisor ratings of overall effectiveness very well. Latham argues the method is 'fair' because it deals with very specific behaviour, of proven direct relevance; it avoids mention of legal risky abstractions such as abilities or dispositions. An American police force's structured interview was ruled 'fair'—even though it rejected three times as many women as men—because it used critical incidents (and because it predicted performance at police academy) (Arvey, 1979a).

Like most very structured interviews, Latham's technique blurs the distinction between interview and paper-and-pencil test. Why not read the questions to a group of interviewees, or even print them as a questionnaire?—unless the raters attend to the interviewee's manner when rating his answers (Latham doesn't say).

Janz (1982) proposes the 'patterned behaviour description interview', which also starts by analysing the job using critical incident technique, and ends by rating the applicant's responses, but places more emphasis on what happens in between—questioning and recording. The interviewer has a more active role than in the 'situational' interview, being 'trained to redirect [applicants] when their responses strayed from or evaded the question'. Janz trains his interviewers to record what the applicant says, and *not* to interpret it—the exact opposite of Anstey's 'effective listening'. Janz compared interviewers trained his way with ones trained in conventional interview technique, and found his method achieved good validity, where a conventional interview did not.

Mayfield (1964) cautions that a structured interview devised for insurance companies didn't work when applied to office machine reps, and vice-versa, and suggests structured interviews may not be 'transportable'. In the light of evidence that ability tests prove very 'transportable' when large enough samples are tested (Chapter 7), one study doesn't prove structured interviews are necessarily 'local'.

HOW the INTERVIEWER REACHES a DECISION

(a) Interviewers make up their minds quickly

They may be ready to pass a verdict on the candidate after 4 minutes of a 15-minute interview (Springbett, 1958). Tucker and Rowe (1977) found interviewers accepted or rejected after an average of 9 minutes. Surprisingly, interviews who *hadn't* seen the interviewee's application form took exactly as long as ones who did know his/her background, which implies factual information didn't play a very big role in the interviewer's decisions. What happens in these 4–9 minutes?

(b) The interviewer forms a first impression

Rating of application blank and candidate's appearance predicted final ratings for 85 or 88 per cent of candidates (Springbett, 1958). Advice to 'be on time and dress smartly' is obviously sound. Candidates who look and sound enthusiastic, and who look the interviewer in the eye, create a better impression (Imada and Hakel, 1977). Male interviewers react against scent or after-shave, regardless of sex of applicant; female interviewers favour it, also regardless of sex of applicant (Baron, 1983). Female applicants for management positions create the best impression by being conventionally but not severely dressed (Forsythe *et al.*, 1985). But beware—order effects are notoriously 'fickle'. Interviewers 'normally' rely on first impressions, but if they're asked to make a series of ratings they rely more on 'last impressions' (Farr, 1973)—so a 'structured' interview system might not over-weight first impressions.

Moreover research doesn't always find 'first impressions' count (McDonald and Hakel; 1985); interviewers saw good and bad resumés, which created a first impression, then chose which ten of a list of 30 questions to ask. Contrary to expectations interviewers didn't choose 'negative' questions—'What course did you have most problems with at school'—when interviewing 'poor' candidates. Nor did interviewers ignore candidates' answers, even though they contradicted the 'first impression'; if a 'bad' resumé candidate gave 'good' answers, he/she got a *good* final rating.

(c) The interviewer looks for reasons to reject

Springbett (1958) found just one bad rating was sufficient to reject 90 per cent of candidates. Bad news shifts interviewers' ratings more readily than good news. Hollman (1972) argues interviewers pay *too little* attention to the candidate's *good* points, not *too much* to his/her *bad* points. Interviewers are more sensitive to bad news, because they get more criticism for hiring poor workers—who remain visible—than for rejecting good ones, who necessarily remain an unknown quantity. Looking for reasons to reject is a perfectly rational and efficient strategy *if* the organization has plenty of good applicants.

(d) The interviewer uses an 'implicit personality theory'

Andrews (1922) describes an interviewer who hired a salesman, who proved a disaster, and for ever after wouldn't employ anyone who'd ever sold adding machines. Why not? Because the disastrous salesman has previously sold adding machines. The interviewer reasoned:

People who sell adding machines are terrible salesmen.
This candidate formerly sold adding machines,
Therefore he will be a terrible salesman.

Andrews's interviewer's reasoning is obviously at fault; someone must be good at selling adding machines.

COMPLEX JUDGEMENT in the INTERVIEW

Defenders of the interview argue a good interviewer can see patterns in the information, that pre-set, mechanistic methods, like checklists and Weighted Application Blanks, miss. Thorndike argued many years ago that the value of technical skill *interacts* with general intelligence multiplicatively. Skill—say with a paint brush—is invaluable in a genius, but useless in a stupid person. A mechanistic assessment that gives points to each separately ignores the relation between them. In selecting sonar operators in the Second World War, selectors initially gave marks for general intelligence, mechanical comprehension and tone discrimination, added them up, and selected applicants whose total exceeded the pass mark. This allowed an applicant whose ear was poor to 'make up' on the other tests; unfortunately intelligence or mechanical comprehension can't help a sonar operator who is tone deaf. A good interviewer's 'judgement' helps him/her avoid such silly mistakes.

However, research casts considerable doubt on the interviewer's claim to be doing something so mysterious and complex that no other method can replace him/her. Research shows:

1. human 'experts' never do better than a system, and
2. human experts don't use information as complexly as they claim.

1. Expert v. system

Over 30 years ago Meehl (1954) reviewed 20 studies comparing systems with experts, and concluded system always predicted as well as expert; often better. Expert never did better than system. Three of the 20 studies were of personnel selection, for the US Navy or Coast Guards. Research since 1954 hasn't disproved Meehl's conclusion (Cook, 1979).

Reilly and Chao (1982) review six studies in which experts, usually psychologists, used test data to rate applicants, and in which the ratings (not the test scores) were used to predict potential, sales, tenure, income or survival. Experts did fairly poorly overall, achieving a mean validity well below that achieved by the test themselves. Of particular interest is a study by Roose and Dougherty (1976) which compared directly experts' opinion based on tests, biography, and interview, with multiple regressions (Note 4) calculated from the same data. Regressions predicted productivity far better than experts.

2. Does the expert use information complexly?

Experts like to think 'combining [of information] is done intuitively ... hypotheses and constructs are generated during the course of the analysis ... and the process is mediated by an individual's judgment and reflection' (Gough, 1962). Some experts make a positive virtue of not being able to explain how they reach their judgements—citing 'nose', 'ear' 'eye', 'gut' or 'hunch'.

Research on how experts make decisions mostly uses the ANOVA (analysis of variance) paradigm. The researcher:

(a) constructs sets of cases in which information is systematically varied,
(b) asks the expert to assess each case,
(c) deduces how experts make their decisions.

If the expert 'passes' one set of cases and 'fails' another, and the only feature distinguishing the two sets is exam results, it follows that the expert's decisions are based on exam grades, and exam grades alone. Experts claim they don't think as simplistically as this; they say they use 'configurations', e.g. exam grades are important in young candidates but not for people over 30—an *interaction* of age and grades. Experts like the layman to credit them with very complex decisions: pass candidates with good exam grades (1), unless they're 'mature students' (2), but then not if they have low IQ (3), or if they had the opportunity to study (4) but didn't use it (5), unless of course they're housewives (6)—a six-way interaction.

ANOVA studies find experts rarely use configurations, even simple ones like 'exam grades count but not for older candidates'. Most of their decisions fit a *linear additive* model: superior exam grades—plus point, good vocabulary—plus point, young—plus point, keen—plus point, equals four plus points. Hiring decisions based on academic standing, experience and interests, showed 'little or no' evidence of complexity (Hakel *et al.*, 1970). Choice of secretary based on five cues also yielded no evidence of complex decisions (Valenzi and Andrews, 1971). Personnel managers join an illustrious company: doctors, nurses, psychologists, radiologists, prison governors and social workers. All claim to make very sophisticated judgements; all show little evidence of actually doing so. Only one class of expert really does make complex configural decisions – the stockbroker.

ANOVA studies construct a 'model' of the expert's thought processes, which model can then be used to make a fresh batch of decisions. The results are unexpected:

3. A 'model' of the expert is better than the expert

The model never has 'off-days'; it always performs as well as the expert's best performance. An organization could 'preserve' the wisdom of its best personnel manager, by constructing a model of his/her decisions, and continue as 'use' him/her after he/she had left. Computerized 'expert systems' already exist that know everything the medical profession knows about reactions to different antibiotics. But constructing a model could prove humiliating for the expert, if his/her decisions turn out to be so inconsistent or so simplistic that they're not worth modelling. Miner (1970) found interviewers influenced by only three of nineteen aspects of the candidate: height, weight and having been an officer in the armed services. Dawes (1971) found the decisions of medical school admissions committees could be 'forecast' fairly accurately from candidates' admission test scores and college grades. It's unlikely this information—already 15 years old—will prevent the highly paid staff of medical schools wasting their time discussing candidates. Cook's Law states: 'the more important the selection decision, the more man hours must be spent arriving at it'.

ANOVA studies use 'cut-and-dried' information, like exam grades, which are easily analysed statistically. Thirty years go Meehl (1954) pointed out it's a waste of time using an expert interviewer to do things a clerk or a Weighted Application Blank can do. Experienced interviewers should be used to assess qualities they can measure, and other methods can't—social skill, motivation, perhaps intelligence.

Very often the interviewer can't be replaced by a system, because the interview is needed to define the problem. The psychiatrist seeing a new patient starts with an open mind about symptoms and diagnosis; similarly the personnel manager, wearing a welfare or IR hat, may need to interview to formulate the problem. But selection interviews should always have a clear goal, and shouldn't be allowed to turn into 'fishing expeditions'.

ERROR and BIAS in the INTERVIEW

(a) Are interviewers biased against minorities?

Hakel says the interview is 'far more susceptible to bias, error ... than is testing or the statistical use of biographical information'; in fact 'if one's intent is to discriminate against the members of one group ... the simplest way to do so is through the employment interview'. Research on application sifting (Arvey, 1979) finds consistent bias against women, but no research on 'real' interviews has demonstrated discrimination against women or racial minorities.

However there is evidence interviewers have stereotypes that may bias them. Cecil *et al.* (1973) listed the characteristics seen as desirable in male and female applicants for a white-collar job. The ideal male candidate can change his mind readily, is persuasive, can take a lot of pressure, is highly motivated and aggressive; the ideal female candidate has a pleasant voice, excellent clerical skills, excellent computational skills, expresses herself well, is immaculate in dress and person and is a high school graduate.

(b) Attractiveness

Dipboye *et al.* (1977) found assessors strongly biased by physical attractiveness. Being good-looking was worth two rank positions, in twelve, regardless of sex of applicant or sex of assessor. Some people say attractiveness is a legitimate requirement for some jobs; others see 'face-ism' as akin to racism.

(c) Behind the quota

Interviewers are more likely to offer a job, when 'behind their quota'—short of suitable candidates to appoint—(Carlson, 1967), which obviously increases their chances of appointing less suitable applicants.

(d) Clones and mirror-images

Do interviewers look for 'clones' or 'mirror-images'? People generally do prefer others who share their outlook and background, but research on interviewer-candidate similarity has mixed results (Schmitt, 1976). Some interviewers are biased in favour of candidates like themselves, others aren't. Similar applicants *are* rated more competent, but *aren't* more likely to be offered a post, but *are* offered a higher salary if employed.

(e) Are interviewers biased by the previous candidate?

The two preceding candidates can exert a massive biasing effect on interviewers—but only if they hadn't been warned (Wexley *et al.*, 1972). Warning them reduces 'contrast effect' considerably, while a week's training virtually eliminates it. Other studies, however, have either found no contrast effects, or ones so tiny as to be quite unimportant (Schmitt, 1976).

CONCLUSIONS

Good interviews are structured; the interviewer knows what to look for, how to find it and how to rate it. Structured interviews are also 'safer' legally. Bad interviews are a waste of time, and a lot of interviews are bad.

Interviews can assess social skill and career motivation better than other traits. Interviews can assess intelligence, but shouldn't be used instead of tests, unless the selectors are afraid to use tests.

Good interviewers should be treasured, but employers shouldn't expect their skill to transfer very well. Interviewers aren't good at synthesizing information; they should collect data, not analyse it.

The selection interview serves other purposes—to answer the applicant's questions, to 'sell' the organization, to clarify gaps in the applicant's CV or to negotiate terms of employment.

The interview isn't a very good way of selecting staff—but no method is perfect. Only charlatans claim to have infallible methods.

NOTES

1. *Reliability.* A 'reliable' measure gives consistent results. Physical measurements are usually so 'reliable' their consistency is taken for granted. Subjective measures such as interview assessments aren't so consistent. At their worst they may be so inconsistent they convey no information at all.

    Reliability is usually measured by the correlation between two sets of measures. If two interviewers each rate 50 applicants, the correlation between their ratings is 'inter-rater reliability', aka 'inter-observer reliability', or 'inter-judge reliability'. If two interviewers don't agree in their ratings, one of them must be wrong, but which?

    If the same interviewer rates 50 applicants twice, the correlation between the two sets of ratings is 'intra-rater reliability'. If this is very low, it means that person's judgements are inconsistent, and so not much use.

2. *Validity.* A 'valid' test measures what it claims to measure. In personnel selection this means it selects productive employees. Productivity is defined by a criterion, such as supervisor ratings. The correlation between criterion ratings and interviewer ratings is the 'validity coefficient'. Different types of validity are discussed in Chapter 11; so are different types of criterion.

3. *Criterion reliability.* Criteria of productivity are not perfect—not reliable *in the technical sense*; one supervisor's ratings don't agree perfectly with another's; the same supervisor's rating may vary from one occasion to another. Other criteria are similarly not perfectly consistent.

    Criterion (un)reliability imposes limits on validity. An interview can't predict supervisor ratings with perfect accuracy, because the ratings themselves aren't consistent. If one supervisor's ratings don't agree with a second supervisor's ratings, an interview can't be expected to predict either set perfectly accurately.

    Validity cannot be higher than criterion reliability. The reliability of supervisor ratings averages around $r = 0.60$, so no selection whose criterion is supervisor rating can achieve a validity exceeding 0.60.

4. *Multiple Regression.* A correlation (Note 1 in Chapter 2) describes the relationship between *two* variables, e.g. predictor and criterion. Often the selector has several predictors: a set of test scores, a number of interview ratings, etc. A *multiple regression*, denoted by R, takes account of inter-correlations between predictors. A multiple regression summarizes the information in a set of ratings, or a set of tests.

    The multiple regression also identifies redundancy in a set of ratings or tests. Suppose four interview ratings all predict productivity quite well: 0.40, 0.45, 0.42, 0.45. If each rating provides independent information the combination of the four would give a very much better prediction than any one of the four. If the four ratings are highly inter-correlated—as is much more likely—the prediction from all four combined will not be much better than the prediction from any individual rating.

Selection research shows that adding new tests to a selection battery soon brings diminishing returns; adding new tests after the third or fourth rarely increases R by a significant or worthwhile amount.

CHAPTER 5

References and Ratings

The eye of the beholder

Interviews allow the applicant to speak for him/herself, on the principle that 'the best way of finding out about someone is to ask them'. References and ratings work on a different principle: 'the best way of finding out about someone is to ask someone who knows him/her well' – former employers, school teachers, colleagues or fellow trainees. The standard US book on references argues: 'Reference givers who have closely and frequently observed an applicant peforming a job similar to the job being applied for can provide the most potentially useful information' (Levine and Rudolph, 1977). References are the traditional approach to finding out what others think of the applicant, part of the 'classic trio'. Ratings try to get more systematic and useful information from the same source.

'REFERENCES'

Known in the USA as: letter of recommendation, recommendation form, referee report, voucher, or 'perif'. In Britain, generally called 'references' or even 'a character'. References are usually written, although people in a hurry, or who don't want to commit themselves, may use the telephone. Virtually all American employers take up references on new employees (Muchinsky, 1979); three-quarters of the US companies felt selection would suffer if references couldn't be checked. However not one company had investigated the effectiveness of references.

References are used (a) to check accuracy of information given by applicants, and (b) to predict success on the job. Forty-eight per cent of American employers use references only to check accuracy; the rest hope to learn something new about the candidate. Of these, 20 per cent (of the total) use the reference to search for negative information. Most employers want information about personality—cooperativeness, honesty and social adjustment. This makes sense. Personality is 'typical behaviour'—how the person behaves routinely, when he/she isn't making a special effort. 'Typical behaviour' is inaccessible to selectors, because it's easy for applicants to make a special effort for the duration of most selection tests; whereas previous employers or teachers have seen the candidate all day every day, perhaps for years, and can report how he/she usually behaves, and what he/she is like on 'off days'.

References may be structured—questions, checklists, ratings—or unstructured—'Do you think [John Smith] would make a good university lecturer (college professor)?—or a mixture of both. In Britain the completely unstructured reference is still very widely used. Sixty years ago American occupational psychologists recommended it be replaced by a list of specific questions, and some simple five-point ratings:

1. [Mr Henry B Smith] states that he was in your employ from [Jan 1 1928] to [Mar 16 1932] as a [machinist]. Is this correct?
2. He states that he left your employ because [he was anxious to attend day school and could not do it in your employ]. Is this true. If not, why did he leave?
3. Did he have any habits to which you objected? If so what?
(a) Powers of application. Exceptionally industrious (☐), Industrious (☐), Performs work assigned (☐), Shiftless (☐), Lazy (☐).
(b) Popularity. Very popular (☐), Good mixer (☐), Average (☐), Exclusive (☐), Unpopular (☐).

American industry listened; 51 per cent of American employers use structured reference reports, in which the most useful questions were 'Would you re-employ?' 'How long did the person work for you?' and 'Why did he/she leave?' (Mosel and Goheen, 1958).

There isn't much published research on the reference, which is odd, given the vehemence with which most occupational psychologists condemn it. There are two studies of the unstructured reference, and half a dozen studies of rating format references (Muchinsky, 1979).

	Candidate X		Candidate Y
		A	
Referee A		g	
		r	
		e	
	Idiosyncratic	e	Way of describing people
		m	
		e	
Referee B		n	
		t	

Figure 5.1. Schematic representation of Baxter *et al.*'s (1981) study of letters of reference.

Baxter *et al.* (1981) searched medical school files to find 20 cases where the same two referees had written references for the same two applicants (Figure 5.1). If references are useful, what referee A says about applicant X ought to resemble what referee B says about applicant X. Analysis of the qualities listed in the letters—intelligent, reserved, unimaginative, etc.—revealed a different, and much less encouraging, pattern. What referee A said about applicant X didn't resemble what referee B said about applicant X, but did resemble what referee A said about applicant Y. Each referee has his/her own idiosyncratic way of describing people, which came through no matter who he/she was describing. The free-form reference tells you more about its author than about its subject.

Peres and Garcia (1962) analysed 625 reference letters for engineering applicants, and found most used generalized trait descriptions, and didn't describe specific behaviour. Factor analysis found five factors that distinguished good from poor candidates: mental agility, vigour, dependability/reliability, 'urbanity', and co-operation/consideration. Good engineer applicants got favourable ratings on mental agility, vigour and dependability; poor applicants were 'damned with faint praise' as 'urbane' (talkative, cultured, poised) or 'co-operative'.

Reliability

American research suggests references are unreliable. Most research compares one referee with another and finds they agree poorly or not at all, which creates problems for employers: which—if either—is right? Referees agreed very poorly about applicants for (US) Civil Service jobs, for 80 per cent of correlations were lower than $r = 0.40$; references given by supervisors bore no relation to references given by acquaintances, while references by supervisors and co-workers (who both see the applicant at work) agreed only very moderately (Mosel and Goheen, 1959). Reilly and Chao (1982) cite an unpublished study by Sharon showing references for would-be judges were very unreliable. Another unpublished study by Bartlett and Goldstein found raters agreed whether a reference was favourable or not, but that different referees didn't agree about the same applicant.

The (UK) Civil Service Selection Board (CSSB) uses five or six references, covering school, college, armed services and former employers, and 'take[s] them very seriously' (Wilson, 1948). Thirteen CSSB staff achieved very high inter-rater reliability in assessments of candidates based on references alone. CSSB finds references reliable, in sharp distinction to most American research; CSSB used five or six references, not two or three, which may increase reliability. Or perhaps CSSB panels understand the reference's private language, or perhaps they can pick out and discount 'rogue' references.

Validity

Mosel and Goheen report several investigations of the Employment Recommendation Questionnaire (ERQ), a structured reference request form written by the US Civil Service, and widely used by private industry in America. ERQ covers:

1. *Occupational ability*: skill, carefulness, industry, efficiency.
2. *Character and reputation.*
3. 'Is the applicant specially qualified in any particular branch of trade in which he seeks employment?'
4. 'Would you employ him in a position of the kind he seeks?'
5. 'Has the applicant ever been discharged from any employment to your knowledge? If yes, Why?

Mosel and Goheen (1958) analyse ERQ data for US Federal Civil Servants (i.e. *successful* applicants). The US Civil Service normally uses ERQ data 'clinically', i.e. unsystematically. Mosel and Goheen quantified ERQs, correlated them with supervisor ratings, and found they had little or no predictive validity (Table 5.1). ERQ ratings didn't correlate at all with 'training and experience' ratings or 'unassembled examinations' (Chapter 10), in which experienced examiners rate the applicant's skills as listed on his/her application. Mosel and Goheen also compared ERQs with 'qualification investigations', in which US Civil Service investigators interview between three and six people who know the applicant—a sort of oral reference. For three occupations—economist, budget examiner and training officer—the two sources of information agreed moderately well. The persons interviewed included some of the people who had written the ERQs.

Table 5.1. Correlation of Mean ERQ Scores with Supervisors' Performance Ratings (Data from 1,117 Employees in 12 Skilled Trades) (Mosel and Goheen, 1958) (Reproduced by permission)

Trade	N	r
Carpenter	51	.01
Equipment repairman	40	.23
Machinist	100	.24*
Machine operator	108	-.10
Ordnanceman-torpedo	125	-.01
Radio mechanic	107	.29**
Aviation metalsmith	94	.24*
Highlift fork operator	108	.21*
Auto mechanic	98	.09
Painter	70	.07
Ordnanceman	100	.10
Printer	116	.11

*significant .05 level.
**significant at .01 level.

Browning (1968) compared reference ratings of teachers with criterion ratings of teaching performance by head teachers. The correlations were generally very low, across eleven categories of referee (median $r = 0.13$). Attempts to improve the reference have had mixed results. Carroll and Nash (1972) used a forced choice reference rating form. Items in each pair of items are equated for social desirability, but only one statement predicted job success:

has many worthwhile ideas
completes all assignments

always works fast
requires little supervision.

Scores predicted performance rating 4 months after hire quite well in university clerical workers.

Reilly and Chao (1982) cite unpublished studies by Rhea, on structured reference forms for US Navy officer cadets. Rhea devised a novel technique, in which references are *empirically keyed* to performance ratings (and cross-validated). Rhea didn't take what referees said at face value, but correlated each item with performance ratings, intending to use only those items that actually predicted performance. Unfortunately these items didn't prove numerous enough for the method to be successful.

Reilly and Chao also cite an unpublished study by Bartlett and Goldstein, showing telephone reference checks had very limited ability to predict 'voluntary' and 'involuntary' termination in airport workers. Few workers left, and even fewer were sacked, making it inherently difficult to predict which. Summarizing all available US data, Reilly and Chao conclude reference checks give poor predictions of supervisor ratings ($r = 0.18$) and turnover ($r = 0.08$).

Hunter and Hunter's (1984) review calculated mean validity of reference checks for four criteria:

supervisor ratings	0.26	(10 coefficients)
training grades	0.23	(1 coefficient)
promotion	0.16	(3 coefficients)
tenure	0.27	(2 coefficients)

Hunter and Hunter give no details of the studies analysed, but inspection of their Table 8 shows some were also included in Reilly and Chao's analysis. Hunter and Hunter quote higher average validities for the reference than Reilly and Chao, because they correct for criterion unreliability. The reference check achieves fourth place in Hunter and Hunter's 'final league table'—behind cognitive ability tests, job tryouts, and biodata. This 'fourth place' is only provisional because Hunter and Hunter found relatively few studies of reference validity. Neither review includes British data on reference validity for CSSB and Admiralty Selection Board.

UK research

Candidates for Royal Naval officer college are rated by head teacher on seven scales. Reference ratings were correlated with ratings of leadership and general conduct, an examination mark and the two combined. All seven ratings combined predicted 'total mark' moderately well. Ratings of leadership were best predicted by head teacher's rating of *sporting and extracurricular activities*, while exam mark was best predicted by rating of *application to studies* (Jones and Harrison, 1982). Jones and Harrison think these results are quite promising; overall (corrected) predictive validity of head teacher's report equals that reported for psychological tests predicting training grades (Ghiselli, 1966). Jones and Harrison find the prediction of leadership and conduct 'particularly encouraging', given how difficult these are to measure by any other test. They don't expect such good results every time; head teachers are more likely (than, say, former employers) to write careful, *critical* references, because they know they will be writing references for Dartmouth Naval College for future pupils, and because their own credibility is at stake.

Anstey (1966) reports an interesting finding. The British Foreign Office recruited 150 entrants to the Diplomatic Service between 1948 and 1959, including eight who had poor references from school or college. On follow-up in 1963, six of these eight were found to have poor, or very poor, performance reports, suggesting that the Foreign Office was unwise to decide to ignore their references.

Apart from Carroll and Nash's forced-choice method, 'references' haven't proved very promising. At their very best—Naval officer cadets—they do as well as intelligence tests. But references do have one great advantage—they're very cheap, because someone else does all the work, and doesn't expect to be paid.

Pollyanna effect

A very early (1923) survey, described by Moore (1942), found most reference writers said:

(a) they always gave the employee the benefit of the doubt,
(b) they only said good things about him/her,
(c) they didn't point out his/her failings.

In certain circles it's considered bad form to write a bad reference; one should either refuse to act as referee, or hint as strongly as seems necessary that one doesn't feel able to write anything very flattering. If referees *are* reluctant to say anything unkind, references are clearly a poor source of information (and can never demonstrate predictive validity, because range will be very severely restricted). Research confirms this pessimistic conclusion. Mosel and Goheen found ERQ ratings highly skewed, with 'outstanding' or 'good' opinions greatly outnumbering 'satisfactory' or 'poor' opinions. Candidates were hardly every rated 'poor'. Nearly all (97.5 per cent) referees said 'Yes' to 'Would you employ him?', while 99.1 per cent said 'No' to 'Has the applicant ever been discharged?'. However Mosel and Goheen were studying *successful* applicants, so perhaps this isn't surprising. Jones and Harrison (1982) analysed ratings given to *all* applicants for Dartmouth Naval College; average mark was well above the midpoint of the scale, and marks below the midpoint were rarely given.

Carroll and Nash (1972), however, disagree. They wrote a forced-choice reference questionnaire which contained only positive statements, and found a high proportion of subjects complained they were deprived of the opportunity to say anything negative about the applicants; perhaps a case of only wanting something when you can't have it.

RATINGS

American personnel practice uses ratings a lot, far more than British personnel work. Ratings are most widely used to appraise performance, usually annually. In personnel selection, ratings can be used as the 'predictor', but are more often used as the 'criterion'. Ratings used as *predictor* in a selection 'test', are usually made by external referees (vs), or by the candidate's peers. *Criterion* ratings are usually made by supervisor or manager.

Ratings are used for regular performance appraisals in American industry, so they're big business. Performance appraisals often determine promotion, salary, even survival, so rating systems come under keen scrutiny. Ratings are prone to systematic errors:

(a) *Halo.* First described by Thorndike (1918), over 60 years ago. Ratings on different dimensions aren't independent. The employee rated punctual is also rated ambitious, smart, able and conscientious. However, one can't infer halo simply because ratings on different dimensions correlate; the attributes might 'really' go together ('true halo'). Cooper (1981) reviews attempts to control 'halo', and concludes they are only partly successful. It's usually a mistake to multiply rating scales, because factor analysis (Note 1 in Chapter 3) almost always shows a large number of ratings reduce to a fairly small number of factors.

(b) *Leniency.* Reluctance to give poor ratings, which pervasively affects referees' ratings.

(c) *Central tendency.* Using the middle points of the scale, and avoiding the extremes. Particularly irritating to the researcher because it reduces variance and restricts correlations.

Attempts to reduce halo, leniency and central tendency divide into: (1) varying format of ratings (2) training.

Rating formats

Rating formats have multiplied over the past 20–30 years. Landy and Farr (1980) suggest calling a moratorium on writing new formats, because they don't seem to be solving any problems, except how to fill the pages of *Journal of Applied Psychology* and *Personnel Psychology*.

Graphic rating scale

This is the conventional rating scale format:

efficient  inefficient

Different formats vary the number of scale points, supply adverbs—'very', 'fairly', 'slightly' etc.—for each point, etc.

The dimensions to be rated are often very vague: 'quality', 'demeanour', 'production', 'organization'. American psychologists call these 'motherhood' traits; they sound warm and comforting, but are almost impossible to define.

Behaviourally Anchored Rating Scales (BARS)

BARS tries to make each point of the scale more meaningful to the rater, to make ratings less arbitrary, and so to reduce halo, leniency and central tendency. BARS writing proceeds by four stages:

1. Choose the dimensions. The supervisors who make the ratings meet, for a day or half a day, to identify what to rate. They are encouraged to avoid 'motherhood' concepts like 'initiative', 'dependability' or 'maturity'. Israeli tank commanders listed five dimensions for tank crews: *efficiency* with which weaponry is operated, *effort, proficiency in maintenance, proficiency in manouevre* and *teamwork* (Shapira and Shirom, 1980).
2. List examples of good, average and poor work. The same supervisors, working individually, write descriptions of 'critical incidents' (Chapter 3) of good, bad and average performance. Up to 900 incidents may be described. The incidents are sifted, to exclude duplicates, ones that are too vague, and ones raters couldn't observe.
3. Sort the items. Supervisors work through the revised list of incidents, and

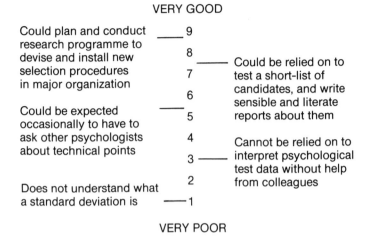

Figure 5.2. An (invented) example of a Behaviourally Anchored Rating Scale (BARS) for an occupational psychologist.

assign each to one of the dimensions listed in stage 1. Incidents that aren't assigned to the same dimension by 75 per cent of supervisors are discarded.
4. Scale the incidents. Supervisors scale incidents that survive stage 3, on a seven-point scale. If the *standard deviation* (Note 4 in Chapter 1) of supervisors' ratings exceeds 1.5 the incident is discarded, because supervisors don't agree well enough on its weighting.

The BARS is now ready to use, having taken 2–3 days to complete. Up to 30 supervisors contribute data, so BARS writing is expensive. Figure 5.2 illustrates a typical BARS. BARS are claimed to reduce halo and leniency, and to increase inter-rater agreement. Shapira and Shirom (1980) found correlations between different BARS fairly low, suggesting raters weren't just rating the same thing five times under different headings. Other authors are sceptical about the advantages of BARS over simpler rating formats (Borman, 1979). BARS are highly specific, so a new set has to be developed for each job, although Goodale and Burke (1975) wrote a set of ten generic BARS that could be used for every ancillary job in a hospital, except nursing.

Training schemes

Borman (1979) reviews a number, and describes his own. Training aims to reduce halo and leniency, without reducing accuracy. Borman's training consisted of group discussion of actual ratings, led by a trainer who pointed out inaccuracies and examples of halo and leniency errors. Another study (Pursell *et al.*, 1980) initially found five psychological tests failed to predict supervisor ratings of electricians; after the supervisors had been trained to reduce rating error, test validity increased dramatically. However Warmke and Billings (1979) found the effects of training short-lived; practice ratings made at the end of the training course were 'better', but 'real' ratings by senior nurses 2 months after training still showed halo.

PEER ASSESSMENTS

Research dating back to the 1920s finds that people are surprisingly good at predicting who among their peers will succeed, and surprisingly honest too. Even when they know their opinions will help determine who gets selected or promoted, people say (fairly) willingly what they think of each other, and are (relatively) uninfluenced by who they like and dislike.

Sometimes rating scales are used, sometimes forced-choice formats. In *peer nomination* each subject nominates the best or worst performers in the group, usually in order of effectiveness or ineffectiveness. In *peer ranking*, each subject rank orders the whole group from best to worst. Subjects don't usually judge themselves. Peer assessments don't work well unless the group numbers at least ten. Ratings and rankings describe everyone, whereas nominations ignore the middle of the distribution; between a quarter and half the candidates might receive no nominations at all. This doesn't matter if the selectors want the best 10 per cent, or want to screen out unacceptable candidates. Love (1981) found nominations and ranking were more reliable and had higher predictive validity than ratings.

Military research

The US and Israeli armed services have researched peer assessments extensively. Early research (Williams and Leavitt, 1947) found peer ratings of US Marine officers correlated well with combat ratings; peer ratings were 'a more valid predictor both of success in officer candidate school and of combat performance than several objective tests'. A series of studies by Hollander (1965) found peer evaluations of global potential in office candidates correlated fairly well with effectiveness ratings as regular officers, that peer nominations were very reliable and that they achieved good predictive validity within as little as 3 weeks. Recent Israeli research (Amir *et al.*, 1970; Tziner and Dolan, 1982) reports very high correlations betwen peer evaluations and admission to officer school, in large samples of males and females. Peer assessments had higher predictive validity than almost any other test, including intelligence tests, interview rating and rating by commanding officer.

Reviews (Lewin and Zwany, 1976) of US Army and Navy research finds correlations centring in the 0.20s and 0.30s, but varying very widely (up to $r =$

0.79). In military research, validity proves equally good whether ratings are collected for research purposes or for actual selection.

Civilian research

Peer nominations of insurance agents predicted appraisals of managerial effectiveness quite well (Mayfield, 1970). Peer ratings distinguish middle managers who get promoted from ones who don't (Roadman, 1964). Most data were collected for research purposes, but Mayfield's subjects were told the data would be used 'administratively'—to make decisions about pay, promotions, etc. Peer assessments have also been used to predict sales performance in salesmen (Waters and Waters, 1970); McBain's (1970) research implies peer assessments could predict accident rate in truck (HGV) drivers. Kraut (1975) found peer ratings of 'Impact' predicted future advancement, but not performance appraisal ratings. This suggests peer ratings, like the assessment centre (Chapter 9), may measure whose 'face fits' better than they predict productivity. Peer nominations retain their validity for long periods—up to 3 years (Hollander, 1965).

Reilly and Chao (1982) review peer evaluations for MBA graduates, managers, life insurance agents, sales staff, pharmaceutical scientists and secretaries, and calculate average validities for three criteria:

training	0.31
promotion	0.51
performance ratings	0.37

Reliability

Peer *nominations* achieve very high reliabilities—generally in the 0.80s—because only extremes are included (Kane and Lawler, 1978). Nominations achieve high reliability after a very short time, and regardless of whether they are used for research or 'administratively'. Army basic training squads are re-shuffled after 4 weeks, but once the groups had settled down, peer assessments retained their predictive validity, even though different peers were making them.

Friendship

Personnel managers usually dismiss peer assessments on the grounds they will prove little more than popularity contests. Researchers disagree. Hollander found subjects had on average three friends, but nominated only one as a leader. Love (1981) found friendship didn't bias the relationship between peer assessment and criterion rating. On the other hand Waters and Waters (1970) found nominations among friends had no predictive validity, whereas nominations among enemies or 'neutral' groups did, which implies friendship distorts judgements. However Waters and Waters's subjects were salesmen, where avoiding being disliked by others arguably genuinely increases productivity.

Positive/negative nominations

'Negative' nominations—who is 'selfish' or 'overbearing'—are more idiosyncratic, and more likely to be biased by dislike. Nominations of 'five most effective' had good predictive validity, whereas nominations of 'five least effective' had none (Kaufman and Johnson, 1974). 'Negative' nominations caused resentment; candidates described them graphically as being asked to 'cut their buddy's throat'.

Summary

Kane and Lawler (1978) analyse nineteen studies and conclude peer *nominations* achieve an average validity of $r = 0.43$; military studies achieve higher validities than civilian studies. However Kane and Lawler calculate these medians from the *best validity* achieved in each study, not from *all validities* reported. Peer nominations predict 'objective' criteria—graduation, promotion, 'survival'— better than supervisor ratings. Nominations for specific criteria—will make a good officer—are more accurate than nominations for vague criteria— 'extravert', 'emotional', Kane and Lawler conclude nominations are best used for predicting leadership. They also conclude peer *ratings* are less valid than nominations probably because everyone is rated, not just the highly visible extremes. Validity is equally good for civilian and military studies.

Hunter and Hunter (1984) calculate a new 'meta-analysis' (pooling the results of a large number of separate researches) for peer ratings, against three criteria:

supervisor ratings $r = 0.49$
training grades $r = 0.36$
promotion $r = 0.49$

In Hunter and Hunter's review of 'alternative' tests (alternative to ability tests), peer ratings are clearly superior to other 'alternatives': biodata, reference checks, college grades, interview, and Strong Vocational Interest Blank. Hunter and Hunter place peer ratings third (of six) measures in order of suitability for promotion decisions, but don't list it as a predictor for initial selection.

Schmitt *et al.*'s (1984) *validity generalization* analysis (see Chapter 7) of 31 validity coefficients for supervisor/peer assessments, mostly of managers, found a mean validity of $r = 0.43$, the highest of any of eight classes of predictor.

Why are peer assessments such good predictors? Mumford (1983) discusses several theories:

(a) *Friendship.* Popular people get good peer evaluations and promotion. Not necessarily mere bias, if making oneself liked is part of the job.
(b) *Consensus.* Traditional references rely on two or three opinions, where peer assessments use half a dozen or more. Multiple assessors cancel out each others' errors.
(c) *No place to hide.* In military research the group is together, 24 hours a day, faced with all sorts of challenges—physical, mental, emotional—so they really get to know each other, and can't keep anything hidden. Amir *et al.* (1970) argue peer assessments work, because soldiers know what's needed in an officer, and because they know their own survival may one day depend on being led by the right person.

Acceptability

Peer assessment has been most popular in the armed services—whose subjects are less likely (or less able) to complain. Peer ratings are unpopular if used 'administratively'. Love (1981) found peer assessments unpopular with policemen, who thought them unfair and inaccurate, and that they shouldn't be used for deciding who to promote.

Usefulness

Peer assessment is very cheap. The selectors get between 10 and 100 expert opinions about each subject, entirely free. Peer assessments generally have good validity; sometimes very good. Peer assessment has two big disadvantages: it's unpopular, and it presupposes applicants spend long enough together to get to know each other really well. Both of these factors effectively limit it to predicting promotability in police or armed services. Kane and Lawler question whether peer assessments often add any *new* information; Hollander found peer nominations correlated very highly with pre-flight training grade, so they didn't contribute any unique variance. (No other study seems to have considered this issue.)

In practice, peer assessments don't seem to be used very widely, if at all, to make routine selection or promotion decisions. Probably no-one really believes peer assessment would work if used, and *known to be used*, within an organization year in, year out. Hughes *et al.* (1956) describe how a Weighted Application Blank completely lost its initial high validity in 3 years' field use, because candidates, with the connivance of field managers, 'bent' their answers to fit. The same fate would surely befall peer assessments if used routinely.

'FAIRNESS' and the LAW

Defamation

Employers often assume references and ratings aren't covered by the usual law of libel. This isn't necessarily true, although surveys show few American employers have faced litigation over references. Nevertheless, many play safe, and restrict themselves to saying the person was employed by them from time A to time B, without offering opinions of any sort. Unstructured references allow a skilful writer to 'damn with faint praise', and an experienced recipient to 'read between the lines'—so long as they both speak the same private language.

Privacy

In the USA the 'Buckley Amendment' gives post-secondary students the right to 'elect to' see what referees have written about them. As a consequence, either selectors require students to sign statements relinquishing their rights under the Act, or referees write bland, unhelpful references (Shaffer *et al.*, 1976).

'Fairness'

The 'reference' is legally a 'test', which can differentially exclude minorities, and so be challenged. In the case of *EEOC* v. *National Academy of Sciences* a non-white female refused a job on the basis of a bad reference claimed the reference check had adverse impact on non-whites and wasn't job-related. Both claims were dismissed. In *Rutherford* v. *American Bank of Commerce*, a reference that mentioned the employee had filed a charge of sex discrimination was ruled unlawful.

Peer ratings don't seem to have been legally challenged as a selection test. Peer assessments demonstrated some racial bias in earlier research (Cox and Krumboltz, 1958), in which black and white alike rated their own race higher. A later study by Schmidt and Johnson (1973) found no racial bias in peer ratings— but then, as Kane and Lawler point out, Schmidt and Johnson's data were collected during a programme to improve race relations. Bias in peer assessment seems generally too small to have any practical significance, and can probably be removed by training (Mumford, 1983).

SUMMARY

References are traditionally dismissed by occupational psychologists, even though there hasn't been all that much research on them. Most research that has been reported finds references are unreliable, and have little or no validity.

However, some British research reaches different conclusions. References can be useful if the referee is careful, and concerned for his/her future credibility. A composite of six references, rather than the usual two, may be more reliable. References 'digested' by a panel may be more useful. (But the British research that supports these more optimistic conclusions is limited, rather sketchily reported, many years old and in urgent need of replication).

Peer ratings by contrast have consistently very high validity—in a very limited setting. Peer assessments are only feasible where the candidates already know each other well, and where the assessor has considerable power over them. Even then, peer assessments are rarely used 'for real'.

However, peer assessments prove the principle behind references is sound: people who know the candidate can describe him/her well. There is information to be gained, if selectors can go about it the right way.

CHAPTER 6

Weighted Application Blanks and Biodata

Were you born in Minnesota?

Over 60 years ago, Goldsmith (1922) devised an ingenious new solution to an old problem: selecting people who could endure selling life insurance. He took 50 good, 50 poor and 50 middling salesmen from a larger sample of 502, and analysed their application forms. Age, marital status, education, (current) occupation, previous experience (of selling insurance), belonging to clubs, whether candidate was applying for full- or part-time selling, whether the candidate himself had life insurance, and *whether* (not *what*) candidate replied to question 'What amount of insurance are you confident of placing each month?'—collectively distinguished good from average and average from bad.

Binary items—married/single—were scored +1/−1. Scoring age was more complicated:

−2 for 18–20
−1 for 21–22
0 for 23–24
+1 for 25–27
+2 for 28–29
+3 for 30–40
+1 for 41–50
0 for 51–60
−1 for over 60

Education was scored in the same asymmetric curvilinear way: 8 years scores +1, through 12 years scores +3, down to 16 years scores +2. Low scorers in Goldsmith's sample almost all failed as insurance salesmen; the small minority of high scorers formed half of a slightly larger minority who succeeded at selling life insurance (Figure 6.1).

Goldsmith had turned the conventional application form into a Weighted Application Blank (WAB). The WAB works on the principle that 'the best predictor of future behaviour is past behaviour', and the easiest way of measuring past behaviour is what the applicant writes on his/her application form. The principle is familiar to anyone with motor insurance. The insurance

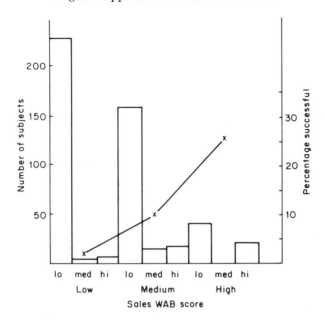

Figure 6.1. The first published Weighted Application Blank (Goldsmith, 1922). The proportion of successful life insurance salesmen is much higher in high-scoring applicants.

company knows from experience what sort of person has more accidents, and charges them higher premiums. People who drive sports cars, people who live in London, people who run bars—all are poorer risks. Insurers don't rely on common sense, which might well convince them that young drivers, with faster reflexes, will be safer; they rely on experience, which shows that young drivers, by and large, are a menace. If insurers can calculate premiums from occupation, age, address, perhaps selectors can find a better use for application forms than looking at them, telling the candidates where they live and where they last worked, then filing the form. Perhaps they can use application forms as a very cheap, very powerful way of selecting employees.

By the end of the 1930s the WAB technique was well developed; ready-made tables had been drawn up for WAB construction. Table 6.1 illustrates one of 88 WAB items from Mitchell and Klimoski's (1982) study of trainee realtors (estate agents). Columns 1 and 2 show successful realtors are more likely to own their own home, and less likely to rent a flat or live with relatives. Column 3 compares the percentages. Column 4 assigns a scoring weight, from 'Strong's Tables'; larger percentage differences get higher weights. The 'home' item weight is added to the weights from 87 other items, and a cut-off point chosen to maximize efficiency of selection. Finally the WAB is *cross-validated* on a second 'hold-out'

Table 6.1. A sample WAB item, from Mitchell and Klimoski (1982)

	Licensed	Unlicensed	Difference	Weight
Do you:				
Own your own home?	81	60	21	5
Rent home?	3	5	-2	-1
Rent apartment	9	25	-16	-4
Live with relatives?	5	10	-5	-2

sample. A WAB derived from sample A will usually 'shrink' when used on sample B, because some items 'predict' within sample A by chance, and don't work for sample B.

WAB construction is entirely empirical, *mindlessly* empirical in the eyes of its critics: 'The procedure is raw empiricism in the extreme, the "score" is the most heterogeneous value imaginable, representing a highly complex and usually unravelled network of information' (Guion, 1965a). It doesn't matter *why* an item differentiates successful estate agents from unsuccessful—only that it *does*. (Although one might argue an estate agent who hasn't succeeded in buying his/her own house can't be very good at his/her job.)

Department store staff

The classic WAB was often used to select department store staff. Mosel (1952) compared the best and worst saleswomen in a large department store, and found the ideal saleswoman was: between 35 and 54 years old, had 13–16 years formal education, had over 5 years selling experience, weighed over 160 pounds, had worked on her *next to last* job for *under* 5 years, lived in a boarding house, had worked on her *last* job for *over* 5 years, had her principal previous experience as a 'minor executive', was between 4' 11" and 5' 2" high, had between one and three dependants, was widowed, and had lost no time from work during the past 2 years (in order of predictive validity). It's particularly difficult to explain why the ideal saleswoman stayed a long time in her *last* job but left her *next to last* job more quickly.

Turnover

WABs have often been used to predict clerical turnover. Buel (1964) compared female clerks who left within 9 months with those who stayed longer, to find sixteen differentiating items. Buel cross-validated his blank on two 'hold-out' samples, and found a high correlation. Soon after, the company moved from city centre to suburb, which meant many more clerks were needed, and also that three of the sixteen items ceased to be relevant. The WAB still achieved a reasonable validity.

Pea-canners

WABs have been used for very humble jobs. The Green Giant Co. found its seasonal pea- and corn-canners often inexplicably left within a few days of starting work, causing the company great inconvenience and expense. Dunnette and Maetzold (1955) devised a WAB to reduce turnover:

> the typically stable Green Giant production worker lives [locally], has a telephone, is married and has no children, is not a veteran [not an ex-serviceman], is either young (under 25) or old (over 55), weighs more than 150 pounds but less than 175, has obtained more than ten years education, has worked for Green Giant, will be available for work until the end of summer, and prefers field work to inside work.

The WAB was only used for male applicants; female employees didn't present a turnover problem.

This profile retained its predictive validity over 3 successive years, and into three other Green Giant canning factories, but it didn't work for non-seasonal cannery workers. Scott and Johnson (1967) found *permanent* workers' turnover predicted by the regression equation:

Tenure = 0.30 (age) + 8.82 (sex) – 0.69 (miles from plant) + 5.29 (type of residence) + 2.66 (children) + 1.08 (years on last job) – 1.99

where female = 1; male = 0; live with parents, or in a room (bedsit) = 0; live in own home = 1.

Permanent cannery workers who stay the course have family and domestic responsibilities (and tend to be women), whereas the profile for seasonal workers identifies young college students, or semi-retired people, both wanting a short-term job.

Oil company executives

At the other extreme, Laurent (1962) used a biographical survey to predict managerial success in Standard Oil of New Jersey. The survey was double-checked, and any item that reflected age or experience, rather than effectiveness, was eliminated. Successful executives were good in college, pursue leadership opportunities and see themselves as forceful, dominant, assertive and strong.

Some WAB items are familiar to personnel managers: (absence of) 'job-hopping', being born locally, being referred by existing employee, owning a home, being married, belonging to clubs and organizations, playing sports or physical games. Others are less obvious—coming from rural or small-town home; some make sense when you know they work, but would need a very devious mind to predict—'doesn't want a relative contacted in case of emergency', as a predictor of employee theft; some are bizarre—no middle initial given (employee theft again). Physique is often mentioned; usually extremes of height or weight are bad signs.

Military WABs

The US Navy presently uses a very short WAB, combined with cognitive ability measures, to select recruits (Sands, 1978; Booth *et al.*, 1978). The Navy WAB covers only: years schooling completed, expulsions or suspensions from school, age at enlistment, and existence of 'primary dependents'. Using a huge sample (n = 68,616), the researchers calculated an 'Odds for Effectiveness' (OFE) table, which allows recruiting office staff to read off 'survival' probability of applicants with particular combinations of age, dependents, education and ability.

Large sample size helps US Navy researchers find an apparently genuine interaction between age at enlistment and education. Men with 12 or more years education were equally successful whether aged over or under 19, whereas less well educated men were more successful if aged 19 or over, which implies poorly educated 17 and 18-year-olds should be asked to come back when they're 19 (Hoiberg and Pugh, 1978).

BIODATA

The classic WAB is invisible, and unfakeable. It's invisible because the applicant expects to complete an application 'blank'. It's unfakeable because most of the items could be verified independently, if the employer could afford the time and expense. (Some can: it's called 'positive vetting'.) The classic WAB has tended to be supplanted since the 1960s, by 'Biodata', aka Biographical Inventories, aka Life History Data. Biodata uses questionnaire format with multiple-choice answers:

How old was your father when you were born?
1. about 20.
2. about 25.
3. about 30.
4. about 35.
5. I don't know.

Many studies use Glennon *et al.*'s (1963) *Catalogue of Life History Items*, which lists 484 'biographical' items. The questionnaire format of Biodata loses the 'invisibility' of the WAB.

Smith *et al.* (1961) used the *Catalog* to predict research creativity in scientists (using supervisor ratings and patentable ideas as criteria). On cross-validation the 22-item Biographical Inventory of Research and Scientific Talent achieved good validity for both criteria. Umeda and Frey (1974) use the *Catalog* to try to construct a Biodata predictor for ministers of religion. They were unusually *un*successful; only two items had predictive value: ministers who 'heard the call' later in life were more successful, and ministers who supported themselves as theology students were more successful. Miner (1971) reports successful management consultants show 'eliteness motivation' in their biography: small private school, small private college, prestige business school, Navy or Air Force rather than Army, commissioned rank, and better off or better educated than father.

Biodata have been used successfully to predict success as sales/research engineer, oil industry research scientist, pharmaceutical industry researcher, bus driver, 'custodial officer' and police officer (Reilly and Chao, 1982). Schmitt *et al.* (1984) found Biodata used for: professional, clerical, sales, skilled labour and unskilled labour. Biodata were used most frequently for selecting sales staff, least often for managerial occupations.

Rational or empirical construction?

Purely empirical WABs offend psychologists who like to feel they have a theory. They aren't happy knowing canary-breeders make dishonest employees; they want to know *why*. Ideally they would like to *predict* that canary-breeders will make dishonest employees. Critics of pure empiricism also argue a WAB with a foundation of theory is more likely to hold up over time, and across different employers.

The 'rational' school of WAB construction doesn't go in for very elaborate theories. Indeed, by the standards of personality research, their efforts too are mindless empiricism, for they generally rely on correlation and factor analysis to discover structure in biographical information. They 'attempt to quantify composites of items that measure an interpretable set of constructs', and to discover 'psychologically meaningful personal history variables' (Mitchell and Klimoski, 1982).

Matteson (1978) proposed item analysis of biographical data to find sets of closely related facts; his target was a group of four items homogeneous in item content and highly correlated. Analysis of 75 items in successful and unsuccessful applicants for oil refinery maintenance and construction work produced twelve keys. Each key contains at least six items, so scores will be more reliable, and less likely to capitalize on chance. Matteson predicts such keys will suffer less 'shrinkage' and be more 'transportable'.

Owens takes this idea a stage further, and uses Biodata to *classify* people. Scores on his Biographical Questionnaire are factor-analysed, yielding thirteen factors for men and fifteen for women. The factor scores are then cluster analysed (Note 2 in Chapter 3) to group people with common patterns of prior experience (Owens and Schoenfeldt, 1979). Different subgroups had different profiles on cognitive ability, personality and interest tests (which *hadn't* been used in the cluster analysis). For example the group of female *Active, conventional social leaders*, high on Biodata factors of *Social leadership* and *Athletic participation*, low on *Negative emotions*, scored high on tender-mindedness, social-religious conformity, interest in physical goals, extraversion and the social service and sales-managerial scales of SVIB, but low on the human and 'hard' science interests of SVIB.

Brush and Owens (1979) classified oil company employees into eighteen subgroups, and then compared unskilled employees in 'Bio-group' 5 (higher *Personal values* and very high *Trade skills interest and experience*) with those in 'Bio-group' 6 (low on *Family relationships* and very low on *Achievement motivation, Self-confidence,* and *Personal values*). Bio-group 5 members had lower termination rates, which implies the company could reduce turnover by selecting Bio-group 5 subjects, and rejecting Bio-group 6. Owens (1976) describes similar unpublished studies on salesmen and oil company executives. Taylor (cited Owens, 1986) found most salesmen came from only three (of nine) biodata groups (one time College Athletes, College Politicians, and Hard-workers). Pinto (cited Owens, 1986) found biodata group membership predicted survival as a salesman in two large samples, with astonishing power ($r = .66$). Owens (1976) suggests Biodata groups could be used for selection, classification and career counselling.

Mitchell and Klimoski (1982) compare predictive validity of *rationally* and *empirically* constructed Biodata inventories. The 'rational' inventory factor analysed rating format items 'Own your own home/Rent home/Rent apartment/Live with relative', to yield six factors, e.g.

> *Economic establishment:* financially established and secure, most likely married, tending to be older, active in community and civic affairs, socially ascendant, professional knowledge and contacts beyond what would be expected in a younger person.

The empirical inventory used classic WAB methodology, scoring the items by Strong's Tables, and summing the weights from all 87 items to give a single index. Mitchell and Klimoski predicted empirical Biodata would give better results with the original sample, but would cross-validate less well. Their predictions were correct, up to a point:

1. The empirical measure gives much better results on the original sample.
2. The rational measure doesn't 'shrink' at all.
3. But the empirical measure still gives better results on the cross-validation sample, even after 'shrinkage'.

Most modern researches use a mixture of classic WAB and Biodata. They're also generally much more reticent about item content, so it's often unclear how much of each they include. (Early studies published their WABs in full, presumably quite confident that pea-canners or shop assistants didn't read *Journal of Applied Psychology*, and couldn't discover the right answers to give.) The success of the classic WAB depends on the general public never suspecting application forms have any but the usual bureaucratic purpose.

The fine distinction between Biodata and personality inventory

Many 'biographical' items look remarkably like personality inventory items. What is the conceptual difference between personality inventory questions, like those listed in Chapter 8, and 'Biodata' questions?

(a) Biodata questions allow a *definite* answer, whereas personality questions often don't. Most Biodata questions could be answered by someone who knows the respondent well. Most Biodata questions could be argued about sensibly, which many personality questions can't be.

(b) Personality inventory questions are *carefully phrased*, to elicit a rapid, unthinking reply, whereas Biodata items often sound quite clumsy in their desire to specify precisely the information they want, e.g:

> With regard to personal appearance, as compared with the appearance of my friends, I think that:
> (a) Most of my friends make a better appearance.
> (b) I am equal to most of them in appearance.
> (c) I am better than most of them in appearance.
> (d) I don't feel strongly one way or the other.

In a personality inventory this would read more like: 'I am fairly happy about the way I look—TRUE–FALSE.'

(c) Personality inventories have *fixed keys*, whereas Biodata items are re-keyed for each selection task. (However, just to confuse the issue, the American insurance industry's *Aptitude Index Battery* has included questions from personality inventories, empirically keyed like WAB items. Personality questions lost their validity faster than biographical questions (Thayer, 1977).)

The distinction between personality inventory and Biodata inventory is often so fine that one wonders if the choice of title reflects the authors' outlook, or their perception of what's acceptable in their organization, rather than a real difference.

WABs and Biodata aren't used much in Britain. Robertson and Makin's (1986) survey found 5 per cent of major British employers using Biodata for selection. The (UK) Civil Service Commission are writing a Biodata inventory for income tax inspectors. British Airways use one for cabin crew. Source documents, like Glennon *et al*'s *Catalog* of Biodata items, are virtually unobtainable in Britain.

VALIDITY

It's vital to distinguish between the *original* sample, on which WAB or Biodata inventory is constructed, and *cross-validation* or *hold-out* samples. Validity can only be calculated from the *cross-validation* sample. A WAB or Biodata inventory that hasn't been cross-validated shouldn't be used for selection. Cureton (1950) calls un-cross-validated coefficients 'baloney coefficients'. WABs and Biodata are particularly likely to 'shrink' on cross-validation, because they are purely empirical, not to say arbitrary, and can easily capitalize on chance differences between the original samples. Several studies report validity 'shrinks' so fast the inventory ceases to have any predictive validity within a few years, and has to be re-written, with new scoring weights (Roach, 1971).

Several reviews of WAB and Biodata validity have reported impressively good results. Dunnette's (1972) meta-analysis of biographical inventories reported validity (r = 0.34), comparable with perceptual speed and psychomotor tests, but not quite as good as general intelligence tests, job knowledge tests or job tryouts. Owens (1976) summarized 72 studies and found Biodata had good predictive validity for success in selling (mostly insurance), high-level talent or creativity, and credit risk. Muchinsky and Tuttle (1979) review sixteen studies using WABs or Biodata to predict turnover, and found significant, cross-validated results in most cases, for a range of occupations: sales assistants, 'route' salesmen, professional workers, clerical workers and Dunnette's pea-pickers. Guion and Gottier (1965) found 'personal history data' had consistently better validity than personality inventories, and had usually been cross-validated (unlike personality inventories).

Reilly and Chao (1982) review published and unpublished American research, and found biographical inventories the best 'alternative' predictor, with an average validity of r = 0.38. Table 6.2 shows the effectiveness of Biodata in predicting five criteria, for six classes of occupation. Biodata are particularly effective in predicting clerical tenure. (The value of r = 0.62) for Sales × Productivity derives from only one study, with a small sample.)

Vineberg and Joyner's (1982) review of military research found WABs predicted global ratings of performance rather poorly, and predicted ratings of 'suitability' only a little better. Hunter and Hunter (1984) argue that 'suitability' may really mean the applicant's 'face fits', which might or might not indicate he/she is more effective.

Schmitt *et al.* (1984) review research published between 1964 and 1982, covering some of the same ground as Reilly and Chao. The weighted average of

Table 6.2. Summary of Validity for Biodata. (Reilly and Chao, 1982) (Reproduced by permission.)

Occupation	Criteria					
	Tenure	Training	Ratings	Productivity	Salary	Average for Occupation
Military	.30(3;4684)	.39(3;569)	.25(3;990)	NA	NA	.30(9;6243)
Clerical	.52(6;553)	NA	NA	NA	NA	.52(6;553)
Management	NA	NA	.40(4;2504)	NA	.23(3;320)	.38(7;2824)
Other non-management	.14(2;327)	NA	NA	NA	NA	.14(2;327)
Sales	NA	NA	.40(4;146)	.62(1;98)	NA	.50(5;244)
Scientific/engineering	.50(2;157)	NA	.32(4;360)	.43(5;563)	.43(4;360)	.41(15;1440)
Average for criteria	.32(13;5721)	.39(3;569)	.36(15;4000)	.46(6;661)	.34(7;680)	.35(44;11,631)

Note.—The number of coefficients and total sample size are shown in parenthesis.

99 validity coefficients was $r = 0.24$, definitely poorer than assessment centres, work samples and peer ratings, but definitely better than personality inventories. Biodata were used to predict:

performance ratings	$r = 0.32$
turnover	$r = 0.21$
achievement/grades	$r = 0.23$
status change	$r = 0.33$
wages	$r = 0.53$
productivity	$r = 0.20$

The high correlation with wages, based on seven samples and 1544 subjects, is unexplained.

Hunter and Hunter (1984) review Biodata research, using validity generalization analysis to arrive at a single estimate of Biodata validity, based on pooled samples of 4000–10,000, for four criteria:

supervisor ratings	$r = 0.37$
promotion	$r = 0.26$
training success	$r = 0.30$
tenure	$r = 0.26$

(Validity generalization analysis corrects for restriction of range, criterion reliability and sampling error, to give an estimate of the 'best' the measure can achieve. Chapter 7 gives fuller details.) Note that WABs predicted supervisor ratings better than training grades, a reversal of the usual pattern.

In Hunter and Hunter's 'final league' table of selection methods, Biodata came third, after ability tests and job try-outs. However Hunter and Hunter only included twelve validity coefficients in their analysis.

Validity generalization and transportability

Validity isn't the only criterion of a good selection test; *cost* and *practicality* matter too. A test that can be introduced 'ready-made' into any selection procedure is cheaper and more practical than one that has to be specially written, or re-written, for every new employer. Ability tests (Chapter 7) are 'transportable' or 'generalizable', as well as being good predictors of productivity. WABs and Biodata don't seem quite so versatile.

An unpublished study by Kirkpatrick (Owens, 1976) retested Chamber of Commerce managers after 5 years, using a different criterion, and found the WAB keys held up surprisingly well. Laurent (1970) found a Biodata inventory that predicted managerial effectiveness in New Jersey 'travelled' to Norway,

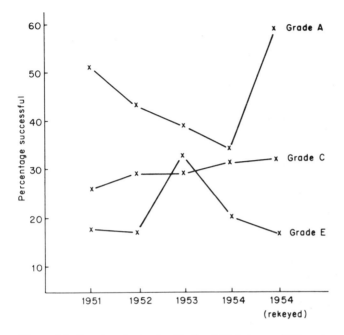

Figure 6.2. Results obtained with the AIB between 1951 and
1954. High and low grades converge, as the test's scoring is
'leaked'. Predictive validity is regained, and the grades diverge
again, when the AIB is re-keyed in 1954. Data from Hughes *et
al.* (1956).

Denmark and the Netherlands, survived translation, and still retained good
predictive validity. (Translating Biodata inventories is surprisingly difficult;
education systems differ from country to country, so 'How many O levels did
you pass?' means nothing outside Britain.).

Other research finds WABs and Biodata *don't* 'travel well'; they tend to be
specific to the organization they were developed in. They tend even to be specific
to the criterion they were developed against; a WAB that predicts supervisor
ratings doesn't predict tenure, and vice-versa (Tucker *et al.*, 1967).

The best data on 'transportability' come from the *Aptitude Index Battery*
(AIB), a Biodata inventory used by the North American insurance industry.
Brown (1981) analysed AIB data, for 12,453 insurance salesmen from twelve
large US life insurance companies. A *validity generalization* analysis (see
Chapter 7) showed the AIB's mean true validity coefficient was $r = 0.26$, and that
62 per cent of the variation between validity in the twelve companies could be
accounted for by sources of error—differences in range restriction, sample size
and criterion reliability. This means:

(a) the AIB was valid for all twelve insurance companies, but also
(b) that it is genuinely more valid for some than for others.

Brown divided the companies into group A, who recruited through press adverts and agencies, and group B who recruited by personal contacts. Group B had higher average production levels, and selected more people with higher AIB scores. Brown compared AIB validities in the two groups, and found it higher for group B companies.

WABs sometimes lose predictive power because they're misused. Hughes *et al.* (1956) wrote a new form of AIB which worked well while it was still experimental, but lost its validity as soon as it was used for actual hiring (Figure 6.2). Field managers scored the forms and were supposed to use them to reject unsuitable applicants; instead they 'guided' favoured applicants into giving the 'right' answers. In 1954 far more applicants reported they owned $7000 life insurance, $7000 'just happening' to be the border between one and two points. Since 1969, field managers have only been told if applicants pass or fail AIB, to prevent them 'stretching a point' for favoured borderline candidates. Clearly the scoring of any WAB must be kept secret. But if WABs lose predictive power as soon as their very existence gets known, they could never be used on a really large scale, for example to screen out unsuitable applicants for driving licences.

Validity of specific cues

Generalizable validity implies certain biographical pointers have fairly general predictive validity. Early WAB research occasionally gave some very contradictory results. Owning one's own home is generally a 'good' sign, but wasn't for Mosel's shop saleswomen, where the most efficient lived in boarding houses. Are there any biographical pointers that have fairly general predictive validity?

Experience has very moderate predictive validity supervisor ratings, but zero validity for training grades (Hunter and Hunter, 1984). Arvey *et al.* (1981) review half a dozen studies, and conclude there's little evidence that experience predicts productivity. *General* experience, in supervising people, or selling, has no predictive validity. Research on air traffic controllers finds experience was only used when it's *directly and specifically* relevant; having used a radio or flown an aircraft doesn't predict efficiency as an air traffic controller, but experience of instrument flying does.

Seniority—how long the person has been working there—is often used to decide who gets promoted: 'Buggins's Turn'. Unions, in Britain and America, often insist it should be the *sole* criterion. Seniority almost always plays a big part in deciding who is 'released' when the workforce has to be reduced: 'Last In, First Out'. There's no reason to expect seniority to be related to efficiency, and not much research on the link; Gordon and Fitzgibbons (1982) find seniority quite unrelated to efficiency in female sewing machine operators.

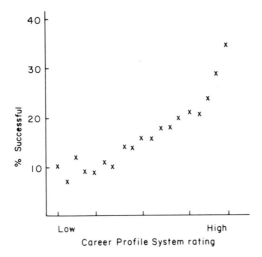

Figure 6.3 Predictive validity of the Career Profile System, the successor to AIB, showing that the higher the CPS score, the greater the proportion of applicants who 'survive'. Data from Thayer (1977).

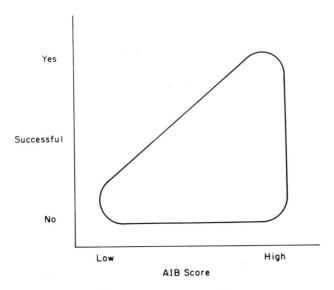

Figure 6.4. Schematic representation of the relation between AIB score and success in selling insurance. A low score means the applicant will fail, but a high score doesn't mean he/she will necessarily succeed.

Age. Hunter and Hunter reviewed over 500 validity coefficients, and found age alone has zero validity as a predictor, whether the criterion is supervisor rating or training grade. Age does predict turnover; younger employees are more likely to leave (Muchinsky and Tuttle, 1979). Age can distort WAB/Biodata scoring; older men tend to have more dependents, higher living expenses, and to belong to more organizations than younger men (Thayer, 1977), so a WAB using age-related items for subjects with diverse ages could give misleading results. Some tests, including *AIB,* have different norms for different ages.

Hunter and Hunter note that age does predict 'survival' in US Navy recruits. Vineberg and Joyner confirm that age predicts performance ratings and 'suitability' ratings, in the US armed services. These military data obviously cover a very narrow age range.

Consortium WABS. WABs and Biodata suffer 'decay of validity' over time, and need revising every few years. They also need very large samples—preferably 400–1000. They haven't in the past proved 'transportable' from one organization to another, or even from part of a single organization to another part. These problems are interlinked; any test devised on a small sample is less likely to work somewhere else. The answer for organizations that don't employ vast numbers is the *consortium WAB/Biodata inventory.*

Aptitude Index Battery (AIB) has been used by the (US) Life Insurance Marketing and Research Association since the 1930s, and dates in part back to 1919 (Thayer, 1977). AIB is a composite measure: biographical items, including dependents, employment history, educational level, financial status, membership of organizations, etc., as well as personality and interest items. AIB is now called *Career Profile System.* Figure 6.3 shows success closely related to AIB score (and also shows how few succeed in insurance, even from the highest score bands) Brown (1979). AIB predicts failure very well (Thayer, 1977); low scorers rarely succeed. AIB predicts success less well; many high scorers nevertheless fail to 'survive'. Figure 6.4 shows schematically the distribution of AIB scores against the composite 'survival' and sales criterion. AIB is essentially a screening test, that eliminates potential failures, but doesn't necessarily identify successes.

AIB has been re-written and re-scored a dozen times, but retains some continuity. Brown (1978) claims the 1933 keys still worked in 1969, showing AIB's validity doesn't decay over time; Hunter and Hunter (1984) disagree, and say validity of the 1933 key had shrunk badly by 1939, and had virtually vanished by 1969.

FAKEABILITY

A lot of psychologists tend to grow restless when fakeability of measures is discussed. Either because they object to the assumption that people don't tell the truth, or perhaps because they don't like to admit most selectors in the last analysis can't do very much about being lied to. Faking *does* matter. Computer programmers have a saying 'Garbage In–Garbage Out': if the information going in one end of a selection process is incorrect, the decision coming out the other end hasn't much chance of being accurate.

The traditional WAB can only be faked if the subject deliberately lies. Research gives conflicting accounts of how often people do this. Keating *et al.* (1950) report near-perfect correlations between what applicant and previous employer said. On the other hand Goldstein (1971) checked information given by applicants for a nursing aide post with what previous employers said. Half the sample overestimated how long they had worked for their previous employer. Overstating previous salary, and describing part-time work as full-time were also common. More seriously, a quarter gave reasons for leaving their last job the employer didn't agree with, and no less than 17 per cent gave as their last employer someone who had never heard of them. Moore (1942) noted that recruits to US Army during the First World War gave very unreliable accounts of their skills. Only 6 per cent who claimed a trade really knew it, while over 30 per cent were totally inexperienced 'trade bluffers'. Owens (1976) is right to say more research is needed on the accuracy of WAB and Biodata information.

Biodata inventories are more like personality inventories. They can be deliberately faked—sometimes called 'gross faking'. They can suffer from the natural desire of subjects to present themselves in a favourable light—'social desirability'. Klein & Owens (1965) studied fakeability of Biodata used to predict research creativity, and found students could double their chance of 'passing' one key, and increase their 'pass rate' on a second. Schrader and Osburn (1977) told half their subjects the inventory included a lie-detection scale (which in fact it didn't). Subjects improved their scores in both conditions, but faked less when warned there was a lie scale. An unpublished study by Larsen (Owens, 1976) found answers to questions about past behaviour less fakeable than 'self-evaluations'.

'FAIRNESS' AND THE LAW

Rosenbaum (1976) found one predictor of employee theft that he didn't have much hesitation in not using—being non-white. Other ways of discriminating against 'protected' groups are subtler; having a Detroit (city centre, as opposed to suburban) address distinguishes thieves from non-thieves (Pace and Schoenfeldt, 1977), but also tends to distinguish white from non-white, much as a Brixton or Handsworth address might in Britain. If WAB/Biodata items are linked to race, sex or age, they will exclude these protected minorities disproportionately, and give rise to claims of *adverse impact* (Chapter 12).

However, Biodata studies reviewed by Reilly and Chao didn't by and large create adverse impact for ethnic minorities. No adverse impact was found in studies of bus drivers, clerical staff, Army recruits, supervisors. Scores on a Biodata inventory of creativity were completely uncorrelated with race (Owens, 1976). Cascio (1976) found a WAB predicted turnover in white and non-white female clerical workers equally accurately.

However, while Biodata inventories seem more or less colour-blind, they do sometimes distinguish male and female. Biodata for US Navy recruits need different predictors for male and female (Sands, 1978). Nevo (1976) found different predictors were needed to predict male and female promotion in the Israeli Army. The American insurance industry's AIB can be used for male and female, but has to be scored differently. On the other hand Ritchie and Boehm (1977) developed a Biodata inventory for American Telegraph and Telephone managers, which achieved equally good cross validity for women and men; Ritchie and Boehm conclude: 'the same kinds of experiences and interests that characterise successful managers of one sex are also predictive of success for the other'.

If a selection procedure does create *adverse impact*, the employer must prove it's a valid predictor of effective performance. Pace and Schoenfeldt (1977) suggest WABs/Biodata are necessarily valid, 'since they are in fact derived in such a way as to assure it'. A cross-validated WAB necessarily has *predictive* validity. But WABs and Biodata often lack *face* validity; they look arbitrary, so a good lawyer would have a field day asking the employer to explain the connection between not using a middle initial and theft. Robertson and Smith (1987) found applicants greatly disliked Biodata inventories, and thought them both inaccurate and unfair, which suggests strongly Biodata measures are much more likely to be challenged than, for example, interviews.

WABs/Biodata inventories *as a whole* don't seem to create too much adverse impact—but many of their component items are likely to prove inherently objectionable to 'fair employment' agencies: age (if over 40), arrest record, convictions, height and weight, marital status, home ownership, etc. The Equal Opportunities Commission in Britain doesn't approve of any requirement that 'inhibits applicants from one sex or from married persons'. Mitchell and Klimoski (1982) say

> Items such as age, sex, and marital status may in fact be challenged by the courts if such items are included in inventories for the purpose of personnel selection. In that event, whatever gains in predictive power to be derived through the inclusion of these items must be weighed against the possible expense of legal defence.

But if no one notices them, or realizes their purpose . . .

Class. Social class pervades WAB and Biodata questions:

owns an automobile
owns own home
lives in suburbs
finished high school
persons/room ratio at home
father's occupation

mother's occupation
father's education, etc.

'Parental occupation', which appears in most WABs, is often used by researchers to *define* a person's social class. It's not against the law, even in the USA, to discriminate on grounds of social class. But it's potentially risky, for two reasons.

1. On both sides of the Atlantic being non-white tends to mean being poor, so indices of class are often also indices of race.
2. On both sides of the Atlantic an enterprising journalist or politician could make considerable capital attacking a selection process that looks both capriciously arbitrary, and blatantly biased in favour of middle-class applicants.

CONCLUSIONS

WABs and Biodata inventories have a number of disadvantages. They don't seem to 'travel' all that well, certainly not as well as ability tests. This makes them expensive, because each employer has to write and validate his/her own WAB/Biodata. WABs/Biodata haven't attracted a lot of criticism, but could prove hard to defend if claims of 'unfairness' were to be made.

On the other hand WABs/Biodata are cheaper than other 'custom' tests, e.g. work samples, because they're paper-and-pencil, and because employer's records can be used to provide 'instant' validation *and* cross-validation.

WABs/Biodata can be faked, but a true WAB is hard to fake, because the information can be checked—at a price. A true WAB is also proof against faking because the applicant doesn't realize the test is a test. The true WAB is *invisible*.

From another perspective, however, invisibility is a major weakness. The invisible WAB presupposes public ignorance of its every existence. What worked for pea-canners in rural America 30–40 years ago may not survive in an age of freedom of information and investigative journalism.

The biographical inventory has to be taken seriously, because it achieves consistently good results—but it's profoundly unsatisfactory in two, linked, respects. The distinction between Biodata inventories and personality inventories is hard to discern (except that Biodata inventories achieve better results). Most personality inventories reflect a *theory* of personality, whereas Biodata inventories are almost completely atheoretical. Owens has made a start trying to understand Biodata, but they mostly remain 'mindlessly' empirical: a set of answers that can predict an outcome. No-one knows why.

Tests of Cognitive Ability

'We know much less than we have proven' (Glass, 1976)

This book is easier to write in 1987 than in 1977; this chapter would have been very depressing to write 10 years ago, and would have become hopelessly out of date very quickly. Ten years ago, most people, even many occupational psychologists, were inclined to 'write off' tests of cognitive ability as having little or no value in predicting productivity. New research, and re-analysis of older research, has shown that most people, and many occupational psychologists, were wrong.

OVERVIEW OF COGNITIVE ABILITY TESTS

In the 80-odd years since the first tests appeared they have diversified into a number of forms, used for different purposes, and reflecting different approaches. Children and the mentally disturbed are tested *individually*; selectors usually test people in *groups*. US psychologists favour *multiple aptitude batteries*, sets of six to twelve tests that yield a profile of abilities; British psychologists traditionally prefer *general intelligence* tests, that yield a single score. Some tests of general intelligence use mostly *verbal* items, while some use mostly *non-verbal* items—numerical, diagrammatic or abstract.

Cognitive ability tests produce *raw scores*, which must be converted to *standard scores*; several systems are used:

(a) *Mental age* was used by the earliest ability tests; a person with a 'mental age' of 5 does as well on the test as the typical 5-year-old. The mental age system only works for children, because mental growth tapers off after age 16.

(b) *Intelligence quotient.* The IQ was orginally calculated by dividing mental age by actual (chronological) age, and multiplying by 100; this type of IQ is no longer used. IQ is now a standard score, in which mean is set at 100, and standard deviation at 15 (Figure 7.1).

(c) *Percentiles* (see Note 4, Chapter 1, page 10) are used by some tests, e.g.: Differential Aptitude Test, Watson Glaser Critical Thinking Appraisal and Graduate Managerial Assessment.

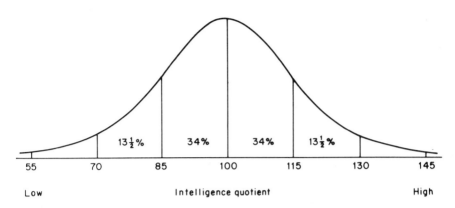

Figure 7.1. The distribution of intelligence, about a mean of 100, with a SD of 15.

(d) *Grades*. The AH series of tests, popular in Britain, use a very simple system: five grades, A to E.

Error of Measurement

IQs are increasingly avoided because they give a spurious impression of precision. No-one thinks the difference between IQs of 117 and 118 amounts to much; but what about the difference between 115 and 120? A simple formula based on re-test reliability and standard deviation of test scores allows *error of measurement* to be calculated. An IQ test with a re-test reliability of 0.90 has an error of measurement of five IQ points, meaning one in three re-tests will vary by five points *or more*.

Differential aptitude batteries

American preference for multiple aptitude batteries dates back to Thurstone's 'Primary Mental Abilities', an 'oligarchic' model which argued there are *seven* independent cognitive abilities: Verbal, Reasoning, Number, Spatial, Perceptual Speed, Memory, and Word Fluency.

Current US research often uses General Aptitude Test Battery (GATB) or US military aptitude batteries. GATB was written by the US Employment Service for career counselling, and measures nine abilities (Table 7.1). The other widely used aptitude battery is Differential Aptitude Test (DAT) which measures seven abilities: Verbal Reasoning, Numerical Ability, Abstract Reasoning, Clerical Speed and Accuracy, Mechanical Reasoning, Space Relations, Spelling and Language Usage.

Guilford (1967) proposes a complex 120-factor model of intelligence. Guilford's tests include a range of 'social intelligence' tests that look promising for personnel

Table 7.1. General Aptitude Test Battery, which measures nine abilities, using eight paper-and-pencil and four apparatus tests (Reproduced by permission)

G	General (composite of Vocabulary, Three-dimensional Space, and Arithmetic Reasoning).
V	Verbal (vocabulary)
N	Numerical (Computation, Arithmetic Reasoning)
S	Spatial (Three-dimensional Space)
P	Form Perception (Tool Matching, Form Matching)
Q	Clerical Perception (Name Comparison)
K	Motor Co-ordination (Mark Making)
F	Finger Dexterity (Assemble, Disassemble)
M	Manual Dexterity (Place, Turn)

work, perhaps even for selecting selectors, but which aren't very widely used. Guilford's 120 factors also include tests of 'divergent thinking', intended to measure creativity and originality.

American psychologists, from the 1930s on, hoped to analyse the demands of jobs and identify the right profile on a differential aptitude battery. GATB's manual gives Occupational Aptitude Patterns for different types of work. For example, Pattern 3—Applied Science (Professional)—specifies high General Aptitude (>125), together with fairly high Numerical and Spatial Aptitudes (>115). Not many Occupational Aptitude Patterns have been adequately validated.

General intelligence tests are sometimes scoreable for subtests; AH6 has keys and norms for 'Verbal' and 'Numerical + Diagrammatic' scores, as well as for Total score. However subscore differences must be interpreted with great caution, because they contain *two* sources of error. Suppose a test produces verbal and numerical subscores, each with a reliability of $r = 0.90$; differences up to six or seven IQ points will be found in two out of three retests, and differences up to 12 or 14 in one in three. Tests like DAT, which are intended to measure profiles of abilities, use specially designed profile sheets that allow the significance of differences to be checked easily.

Aptitude tests

Most are 'paper-and-pencil' but some require apparatus. Aptitude tests are widely used on both sides of the Atlantic; some of those currently available include: General Clerical Test, Bennett Mechanical Comprehension Test (MCT), Engineering Selection Test Battery (UK), Computer Programmer Aptitude Battery, and Crawford Small Parts Dexterity Tests (an apparatus test). Aptitude tests often correlate fairly highly with general intelligence tests; for example the Bennett MCT correlates around $r = 0.60$ with various general intelligence tests.

Achievement tests

Aptitude tests measure what a person *could* learn, achievement tests what a person *has* learnt. (In practice the distinction isn't always so clear.) British employers usually rely on professional qualifications, completed apprenticeships, diplomas, rather than achievement tests. In the USA, Short Occupational Knowledge Tests are available for a range of occupations: garage (auto) mechanic, electricians, machinists, plumbers, secretaries, etc. Achievement tests are also known as 'Shop-Knowledge' tests and 'Trade' tests. Hough *et al.* (1983) describe the 'Situational Judgement Inventory', in effect a trade test for lawyers.

Computerised testing

Everyone who completes AH6 has 35 minutes to answer the same 60 questions, whether they can't answer a single one, or whether they get them all right in 10 minutes (fairly unlikely—Heim tested 693 graduates, and not one got all 60 right). By contrast computerized testing can be 'tailored' to the individual's performance. If the subject does well, the questions get harder; if the subject does poorly, questions get easier, until the subject reaches his/her own limit. 'Individual' tests, like the Binet, have always had this flexibility; as the cost of computers falls below the cost of testing time, it becomes economic for group testing. The US Army has devised a Computerized Adaptive Screening Test which screens recruits in a third of the time, with a third of the items of the paper-and-pencil form (Sands and Gade, 1983).

THE VALIDITY OF COGNITIVE ABILITY TESTS

Early research

In 1918 Link published a validation study of 139 assorted munitions workers using a battery of nine tests, including an unidentified intelligence test. Some tests predicted hourly output well; the Woodworth Wells Number Checking Test correlated well for some employees, but not for 'shell gaugers' and 'paper shot shell inspectors' ($r = 0.02$ and -0.19). Card sorting and cancellation tests, as well as general intelligence, also had some predictive value. Link probably published the first validity coefficient.

Early validation research is summarized by Dorcus and Jones (1950), who give brief abstracts of 426 many and varied studies. Research during the 1950s is reviewed by Super and Crites (1962), who include the extensive wartime researches with Army General Classification Test. The Classification Test predicted success in training in 37 different military roles, and was also used to grade civilian occupations by average intelligence. Occupations with low average intelligence were: miner, farm worker, lumberjack, and 'teamster'; occupations

Personnel Selection and Productivity

with high average level were: accountant, personnel clerk, and students of medicine or mechanical and electrical engineering.

Herrnstein (1973) argues intelligence is *necessary but not sufficient* for productivity. Table 7.2 shows few accountants had IQs more than 15 below the accountant average, whereas quite a few lumberjacks had IQs well *over* their average of 85. Assuming the latter hadn't always wanted to be lumberjacks, the data imply they couldn't or didn't use their ability to find more prestigious work.

Table 7.2. Average scores of accountants and lumberjacks conscripted into US Army during the Second World War, and 10th and 90th percentiles.

	10th percentile	Median	90th percentile
Accountants	114	129	143
Lumberjacks	60	85	116

The period of disillusion

Disillusion with CA testing for personnel selection dates from the 1960s. It has two main sources: distrust of the very idea of individual differences in cognitive ability, and the apparent failure of tests to predict anything successfully.

Distrust

In 1969 Arthur Jensen published his *Harvard Education Review* article 'How much can we boost IQ and scholastic achievement', reprinted in Jensen (1969), which stated the evidence on heritability of intelligence rather more forcefully than people in the USA were used to, or cared for. The original researches were then read carefully, for the first time in years, and their defects noted. Burt's research on heritability proved not just badly done; substantial parts of it were fraudulent. Over-inclusive thinking then caused people to assert all research on heritability was suspect, or even that intelligence tests in general had been proved useless. Actually just one of many studies of heritability of cognitive ability was discredited, and heritability has little relevance to the use of tests in selection.

Failure

The 1960s also saw ambitious attempts to summarize validation research. Some used the *Psychological Bulletin* approach: 'tabular asterisks'—* for a result significant at the 5 per cent level, ** for the 1 per cent level, and *** for the 0.1 per cent level. Lent *et al.* (1971) carried this approach to its logical extreme, by calculating 'significance batting averages'; if a test–criterion correlation achieved significance at the 'p<0.05' level it scored a 'hit'. Aptitude tests scored 'hits' in 75

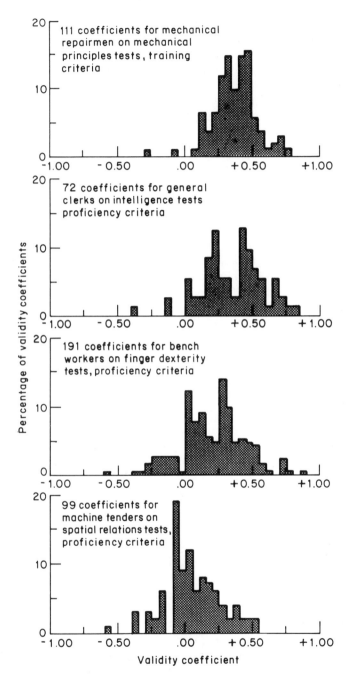

Figure 7.2. Four distributions of validity coefficients, for four combinations of test, and criterion (Ghiselli, 1966). (Reprinted by permission of John Wiley & Sons, Inc.)

per cent of published studies, whereas personality measures achieved only 10–27 per cent 'hit rates'. The 'tabular asterisks game' (Meehl, 1978) doesn't help psychology progress, because the end-result is invariably a mess; 25 studies say 'X predicts Y' and 25 say 'No it doesn't', and all attempts to find factors that distinguish one set from the other prove inconclusive.

Analysis by significance levels also ignores effect *size*, and gives little indication whether a measure has practical value. A test may show a highly significant *mean* difference between good and poor workers, especially if the samples are very large, but not be worth using because the two distributions overlap too much; a test that discriminates 90 per cent of good from bad workers is far more useful.

Meta-analysis

'Meta-analysis' pools studies to yield an estimate of effect size based on a sample of thousands, not tens (Glass, 1976). Variations in design and analysis of researches usually make pooling difficult, but most validation studies report correlations and sample size, so comparison across studies is possible. Ghiselli (1966, 1973) reports meta-analyses of validation research; his analysis weights each validity coefficient by its sample size, then calculates an average (median) for each test × job pair. Figure 7.2 presents distributions of validity coefficients for four test × job pairs.

Table 7.3. Dunnette's (1972) summary of validity of CA tests for four classes of job in the petroleum industry (decimal points omitted)

	O&P	M	Cl	T&QC	All
General intelligence	32	20	17	24	26
Quantitative tests	19	35	12	14	25
Verbal tests	—	29	22	16	23
Reading tests	13	38	—	34	27
Mechanical ability tests	20	38	—	18	30
Perceptual speed tests	—	16	15	—	18
Spatial aptitude	—	24	04	—	20
Job knowledge test	—	43	40	—	42

O & P — operating and processing; M — maintenance; CI — clerical; T & QC — testing and quality control

Dunnette (1972) similarly reviewed all the data he could find on the validity of tests for jobs in the American petroleum industry, and calculated median validities (Table 7.3). Overall these results appear fairly unpromising, but some ability tests did rather better. Army Classification Battery achieved a median validity of $r = 0.51$, while the despised Wonderlic Personnel Test (see Chapter 12) achieved a median validity of $r = 0.43$.

Ghiselli found reviewing the literature rather depressing:

> A confirmed pessimist at best, even I was surprised at the variation in findings concerning a particular test applied to workers on a particular job. We certainly never expected the repetition of an investigation to give the same results as the original. But we never anticipated them to be worlds apart. Ghiselli (1959).

Ghiselli's and Dunnette's distributions of validity coefficients had generally low averages—around $r = 0.30$. Critics were quick to argue that a correlation of 0.30 explains only 9 per cent of the variance in productivity, leaving 91 per cent unaccounted for. Is it worth using tests that appear to contribute so little information? Especially when they are beginning to get unpopular anyway. Critics overlooked Ghiselli's reminder that

> Averages of validity coefficients . . . are distorted by the fact that reliability of tests and criteria varies from one investigation to another. Furthermore . . . the workers used differ in range of talent, so that in cases of extensive restriction there is marked attenuation of the validity coefficient. Errors of these sorts . . . are likely to reduce the magnitude of the average validity coefficient. Therefore the trends in validity coefficients to be reported here may well be underestimates.

Two questions were asked: 'Why are these average observed validity coefficients so low? and why is considerable variability observed between similar predictor – criterion pairings?' (Burke, 1984). Two linked answers were given during the 1960s and early 1970s.

Moderator variables

Test–criterion correlation is 'moderated' by some third factor. Perceptual Speed may correlate well with Clerical Proficiency where work is routine and fast, but poorly or not at all where work is more varied and less rushed. Pace and complexity 'moderate' predictive validity of Perceptual Speed (the example is fictional.) Supposed moderator variables include: 'organisational climate, management philosophy or leadership style, geographical location; changes in technology, product, or job tasks over time; age; socioeconomic status; and applicant pool composition' (Schmidt *et al.*, 1981). Moderator variables are likely to be 'found' where the number of studies being reviewed is small; the handful that manage to achieve significance may chance to have some feature in common.

Situational specificity

A more pessimistic hypothesis, developed as the search for 'moderators' failed to find them reliably. The 'moderator' is the 'undifferentiated situation'. So many factors affect test validity so complexly that it's impossible to construct a model that predicts validity in any particular setting. The right tests for a particular job, in a particular organization, can only be found by trial and error—the *local validation study*. Reviewers are more likely to conclude validity is situationally specific when validation studies are many, because chance moderator variables are less likely to be 'found'. (Their existence in nevertheless presumed; Hunter and Hunter (1984) note that reviewers always piously conclude 'Further research is needed to find out what these moderator variables are.') Schmidt and Hunter (1978) conclude that 'personnel psychologists have a strong tendency, maybe even a psychological need, to interpret error variance as true variance'.

Job analysis

Job analysis (Chapter 3) enables the psychologist to choose the tests most likely to predict productivity. Note the contradiction inherent in believing in both situational specificity *and* the value of job analysis. If test–criterion relationships are so complex no-one can predict the outcome, what is the point of analysing the job? The only logical strategy is a comprehensive, all-purpose test battery— the 'shotgun' approach.

VALIDITY GENERALIZATION

'Meta-analysis' makes some sense of validation studies, but still leaves a fairly confused and depressing picture, because it fails to take account of the limits of the typical validity study.

1. *Sampling error.* The typical validity study tests a fairly small sample. Lent *et al.*(1971) report a median sample size of 68 in a survey of 406 studies. The influential (US) Equal Employment Opportunities Commission recommends sample sizes of 30–60 for validation studies. In fact correlations calculated on samples as small as 60 are very unstable; where the true correlation is 0.30, and $n = 68$, values of r below 0.18 or above 0.42 may be expected in one in three replications (see Figure 7.4).
2. *Criterion reliability.* The typical validity study takes no account of criterion unreliability—which *varies around* a mean of roughly $r = 0.60$ for supervisor ratings and $r = 0.80$ for training grades. Variations in criterion reliability will cause variations in validity coefficients. Suppose the criterion in study A has a reliability of 0.75, while the criterion in study B achieved a reliability of only 0.45 (because the criterion raters in study B weren't as careful, or as observant, or as keen to help the researcher as those in study A). Validity in study B can't exceed 0.45, whereas in study A it could be as high as 0.75.
3. *Restricted range.* The typical validity study takes no account of range

restriction, which also *varies from study to study*, causing further variations in validity coefficients.
4. *Test reliability*. Validity is limited by test reliability, which also *varies from study to study*, contributing a fourth source of variation in validity coefficients.

All four limitations of the typical validity study increase error variance in validity coefficients. All four limitations themselves vary from study to study, meaning the highest validity coefficient possible also varies.

Validity coefficients contain four sources of error. Suppose this error were sufficient to *explain all the variation about the mean*, so that, in a series of ideal validation studies, the validity coefficient would always be the same. Validity generalization analysis estimates how much variance in a sample of validity coefficients the four sources of error *could* account for, then compares this estimate with the actual variance to see if there's any 'residual variance' left to explain.

Sampling error can (usually) be calculated. Variations in range restriction and test and criterion reliability are estimated. Pearlman *et al.* (1980) give computational details.

Residual variance is the variance that would be observed among uncorrected ('observed') correlations across a large number of studies if:

1. *n* were infinite in each study;
2. criterion reliability were held constant *at its mean value*;
3. range restriction were held constant *at its mean value*; and
4. test reliability were held constant *at its mean value*." (Schmidt *et al.*, 1979a)

Zero residual variance means there's no variance left when the four sources of error have been subtracted. There is no true variation in validity. Validity is the same in every study included in the analysis. Validity only *appears* to vary because it isn't measured accurately. If residual variance is zero, the hypothesis of Situational Specificity can be rejected.

Validity generalization analysis also corrects mean validity for test and criterion unreliability, and restricted range, as recommended by Ghiselli, to find *estimated mean true validity*.

Table 7.4 applies validity generalization analysis to Ghiselli's data (see Figure 7.3). Column 6 of Table 7.4 shows that between 52 and 92 per cent of the *observed* variance in validity might be accounted for by the four artefacts. Corrected estimates of mean validity, with one exception, are far higher than the uncorrected estimates presented by Ghiselli (Schmidt and Hunter, 1977). As a rule of thumb, validity generalization analyses find 'true' validity is twice the uncorrected mean validity coefficient. (If validity is zero, as it is for spatial relations tests in machine tenders, twice zero equals zero.)

Table 7.4. Validity generalization analysis of the data of Figure 7.2. Based on data given by Schmidt and Hunter (1977)

Job	Ability	1	2	3	4	5	6	7	8	9
Mechanical repairman	Mechanical principles	114	0.39	0.21	0.19	0.02	90	0.78	0.75	0.70
Bench worker	Finger dexterity	191	0.25	0.26	0.14	0.12	54	0.39	0.24	-0.04
Clerk	Intelligence	72	0.36	0.26	0.17	0.09	65	0.67	0.50	0.40
Machine tender	Spatial relations	99	0.11	0.22	0.12	0.10	54	0.05	-0.03	-0.30

Column 1 gives the number of validity coefficients analysed (not the number of subjects); column 2 lists the raw median validity coefficient calculated by Ghiselli.

Column 3 lists the actual SD of the validity coefficients averaged in column 2; column 4 lists the estimate derived from validity generalization analysis of the size of SD that known artefacts could produce; column 5 lists the difference between columns 4 and 3, which is residual variance; column 6 lists what percentage proportion of observed variance could be accounted for by the artefacts.

Column 7 lists estimated mean true validity.

Column 8 lists 90 per cent credibility values; column 9 lists 97.5 per cent credibility values.

Uncorrected error and the 75 per cent rule

Sometimes residual variance *is* zero, but often it isn't. Sometimes validity generalization analysis concludes validity doesn't really vary—but not always; sometimes there's still some variation left, even after for correcting for sampling error, etc. Schmidt and Hunter argue there are three further sources of error in the validity coefficient that validity generalization analysis can't estimate:

5. *Criterion contamination.* Sometimes criterion ratings are made by people who know subjects' test scores, which may 'contaminate' or bias their ratings. Contamination too *varies from study to study.*
6. *Other errors.* Computational, typographical and data recording errors alter validity coefficients; some researchers are more careful than others.
7. *Factor structure.* DAT, GATB and the military test batteries all measure a *similar* set of abilities, but not an *identical* set; the number of abilities, and the correlations between them, vary.

Schmidt and Hunter propose the '75 per cent rule'. If four artefacts account for 75 per cent of the variance in validity, perhaps all seven could account for 100 per cent. Therefore Schmidt and Hunter propose rejecting Situational Specificity if error variance estimated by validity generalization accounts for at least 75 per cent of the observed variance in validity. In column 6 of Table 7.4 the '75 per cent rule' rejects Situational Specificity for mechanical comprehension tests of repairmen, but not for the other test × job pairs. There is no true variation in test validity for repairmen, but there may be true variation in test validity for clerks and bench workers. Intelligence and finger dexterity tests may really predict productivity more accurately for some clerical or bench jobs than others.

Credibility values

If there is residual variance, so Situational Specificity can't be rejected, validity can still be generalized, using 'credibility values'. The estimated standard deviation of corrected validity coefficients—square root of the estimated variance—summarizes their variability. The selector can extrapolate from previous research to new selections by calculating the value in the Estimated True Validity distribution above which 90 per cent of true validities lie. If 'true' validity is 0.52, and its variance is 0.022, then its SD is 0.148. (0.148 squared = 0.022). Ten per cent of a normal distribution lies 1.28 SDs below the mean, so the value above which 90 per cent of true validity coefficients lie is 0.52 minus 1.28 times 0.148, which is 0.33 (Figure 7.3).

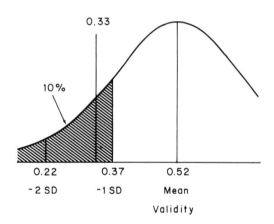

Figure 7.3. Credibility values for validity coefficients. 'Mean true validity' is 0.52, and its SD is 0.148. In such a distribution, 10 per cent of observed validity coefficients are below $r = 0.33$, so the 90 per cent credibility value is 0.33.

The test can be used with a nine in ten chance of achieving a true validity of at least 0.33. Column 8 of Table 7.4 gives 90 per cent credibility values for the four test × job pairs. Values for mechanical comprehension in repairmen and general intelligence in clerks are high, meaning these two tests will usually predict for these two jobs; the value for bench workers is rather lower. Linn *et al.* (1981)

note yet another rule of thumb: '90% credibility values are of about the same magnitude as the average observed [i.e. uncorrected] correlation'. More cautious selectors might prefer 95 or 97.5 per cent credibility values. Column 9 of Table 7.4 gives 97.5 per cent credibility values also, which fall below zero for *two* test–productivity pairs.

Variation without cause—the second proof

Situational Specificity implies that 'if the setting, job, organization, criterion, and applicant pool do not vary, observed test validity will not vary' (Schmidt and Hunter, 1984). Common sense also says an investigator who carries out two exactly similar studies should get the same result. Situational Specificity and common sense both overlook sampling error and fall into the Fallacy of Small Numbers. The 'Law of Large Numbers' states *large* random samples will be highly representative of the population from which they're drawn. The 'Fallacy of Small Numbers' holds that *small* random samples are also representative of the population from which they're drawn; they are not. Correlations calculated on small samples vary a lot. Bender and Loveless (1958) selected shorthand typists, using the same five tests, for four successive years. Tests that 'worked' one year didn't 'work' the next; the Minnesota Clerical Test (Names) correlated significantly ($p<0.05$) with proficiency the first year, but not for the next two, then achieved significance again in the fourth year. Perhaps each year's cohort of applicants differed, or perhaps the job changed subtly. Or perhaps the answer is in the sample sizes: 39, 41, 41 and 49—too small to produce stable correlations.

Schmidt *et al.* (1985b) demonstrate conclusively how small sample correlations vary in the absence of any possible 'real' cause. They randomly divided a very large sample (n = 1455) of US Postal Service letter-sorters into smaller groups. The validity coefficient of a clerical test for the whole sample was 0.22. Figure 7.4 shows the distribution of validity coefficients for 63 'pseudo-samples' of 68 each (the median sample size in validation studies reviewed by Lent *et al.*, 1971). Values ranged from –0.03 to 0.48; less than a third of the coefficients were statistically significant. The validity coefficients in Figure 7.4 only vary because of sampling error, which shows how misleading correlations calculated on small samples are, and shows that 68 is a small sample—*too* small.

If n = 68 is too small, how large does n have to be? Few researchers can aspire to n =1455. Schmidt *et al.* (1976) calculate a validation study needs an n of 172 to be reasonably sure of detecting a true validity of 0.50, given typical values of criterion unreliability and range restriction.

Every statistics text warns researchers of sampling error in the correlation coefficient; why do these warnings go unheeded? Why have psychologists 'effectively denied the real role of sampling error in small samples' (Schmidt and Hunter, 1984) so that 'By reading error variance like tea leaves, they have conjured up visions of complexity'? Expedience, perhaps. US government and

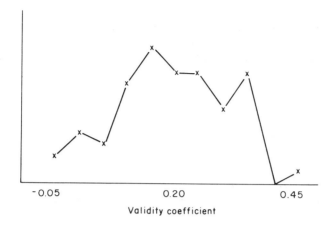

-0.05   0.20   0.45

Validity coefficient

Figure 7.4. Distribution of validity coefficients for 63 'pseudo-samples', each of 68, drawn randomly from a larger sample of 1455. Data from Schmidt *et al.* (1985b).

military psychologists have ready access to very large captive samples; psychologists selling local validation studies in the private sector must often settle for *n* = 68, or starve.

Schmidt *et al.* (1985a) liken faith in the local validity study to 'checking the accuracy of the powerful telescopes used in astronomy by looking at the night sky with the naked eye'.

APPLICATIONS OF VALIDITY GENERALIZATION

Schmidt and Hunter's (1977) first validity generalization analysis showed how limited or non-existent situational specificity was in four of Ghiselli's test × job validity distributions. Subsequent work explores the full potential of validity generalization analysis.

Clerical jobs

Validity generalization analysis first showed that tests could often be used for the same job in different places. Schmidt *et al.* went on to apply it to 'families' of jobs. Ability tests predict equally well for secretaries in different organizations (a single job), for secretaries, shorthand typists, typists, filing clerks and mailing room staff (a 'family' of clerical jobs), and for secretaries, cashiers and tellers, shipping clerks, telephone operators and 'transportation service clerks' (members of the five different clerical 'families').

Army trades

The Army Classification Battery's nine subtests have been validated for 35 very different army jobs, ranging from radar repair, through welder, dental laboratory technician, clerk, cook, to military policeman. Validity Generalization analysis does find reliable differences between jobs in ACB subtest validities—but the differences are too small to have any practical use (Schmidt and Hunter, 1978). Schmidt and Hunter calculate that sample sizes would need to be 1420 *in both jobs* for differences in ACB subtest validities to achieve significance. In other words the ACB predicts productivity equally well for any of the 35 trades—generalizable validity indeed!

Technicians and apprentices

Trattner (1985) reports very little information is lost by using the same test battery for 23 diverse 'semi-professional' occupations; the savings in time and cost are of course considerable. Similarly Northrop (1985) reports the same set of tests can be used for selecting 74 different types of apprentice, without losing information. The US government and armed services employ a wide range of technicians and 'aides', including such varied specialities as: metereological technician, geodetic technician, nuclear medical technician, pathology technician; the 24 jobs fell into two broad categories: health, science/engineering. Lilienthal and Pearlman (1983) conclude the same tests can be used to select for all 24 jobs with equal validity.

Computer Programmers

The Programmer Aptitude Test (PAT) achieves a very high 'true' validity: 0.73 for job proficiency, and 0.91 for training grades. PAT, which is no longer available, consisted of number series, figure analogy and arthmetic reasoning items; PAT is effectively a non-verbal intelligence test, which implies another such could serve the same purpose (Schmidt *et al.*, 1980a).

IMPLICATIONS of VALIDITY GENERALIZATION ANALYSES

Cognitive ability tests are not a waste of time

In the late 1960s and early 1970s critics scorned the 'typical validity coefficient', of 0.30, as too low to contribute any useful information about employee effectiveness. Hunter and Hunter (1984) re-analyse Ghiselli's data (Figure 7.3), and show Estimated True Mean Validity is generally much higher than 0.30. Table 7.6 shows general intelligence has higher validity for some classes of job, while psychomotor tests have higher validity for others. Validity of general intelligence and psychomotor tests tend to be inversely related across the nine groups of jobs, so the multiple correlation of all three tests is fairly constant at around $r = 0.50$.

Ability tests are transportable

If situational specificity is rejected, tests become 'transportable', and can be used without a local validity study. If GATB selects good clerical workers in Washington DC, it will also select good clerical workers in Boston, San Francisco and very probably in London. In the USA 'fair employment' Guidelines (Chapter 12) still favour local validation studies, although some courts have accepted that tests are 'transportable' (Schmidt *et al.*, 1985a)

There are no 'moderators' worth looking for

Faced with inconsistent results, researchers start a 'well intentioned search for moderator variables' (Pearlman, 1984)—and 'find' them. If enough researchers conduct enough studies of the moderating effect of organizational climate on the validity of the Watson Glaser Critical Thinking Appraisal for department store managers, then a lucky few will find results significant at the 5 per cent level— about 1 in 20 is Pearlman's estimate. Having found a moderator, 'any investigators worth their salt (or up for tenure) ... will publish a new model or theory'.

Job analyses aren't absolutely essential

Pearlman *et al.* (1980) found ability tests predicted productivity equally well for a wide range of clerical jobs, which implies job analysis need be no more complex and elaborate than categorizing it as 'clerical'. (This doesn't mean all job analyses are redundant; Chapter 3 lists other uses besides guiding choice of measures in selection.)

Selection tests can be used 'off the shelf'

For many years no self-respecting occupational psychologist would commit him/herself to advising an employer 'the best tests for this job are X, Y, and Z'. The psychologist would feel obliged to recommend a local validation study. But the local validation study can rarely include enough subjects to give a meaningful estimate of the test's validity. So might not the psychologist's experience, or knowledge of the literature on test validity, enable him/her to select an appropriate test?

Schmidt *et al.* (1983) asked 20 occupational psychologists to predict the validity of six subtests of the Navy Basic Test Battery for nine navy jobs. They then compared estimates with the actual (but unpublished) validities based on samples of 3000 to 14,000. The 20 experts disagreed amongst themselves enough about test validity to make an *individual* judgement fairly unreliable, but the *pooled* judgement of any four experts gave a generally fairly accurate estimate of validity. In fact four experts together made as accurate an estimate as would be obtained by actually testing a sample of 173 subjects. In other words, asking four experts what test to use will give as good an answer as actually doing a local validation study on a sizeable sample. It's also much quicker, and much cheaper.

Tests work for minorities

The hypothesis of *Single Group Validity* states that tests work for white Americans, but not for non-white, so test-criterion correlation is positive for whites but zero for non-whites. The hypothesis of *Differential Validity* states that tests are more valid for whites than non-whites, so test-criterion correlation is greater for whites than non-whites. Both hypotheses are 'tested' by comparing correlations for whites and non-whites, and finding the 'white' correlation higher than the 'non-white'.

But given that correlations based on small samples are unstable, 'white' and 'non-white' correlations will often differ by chance. Non-whites are often a minority in a workforce, being a minority in the USA as a whole, so non-white correlations are often calculated on smaller samples, and are less likely to achieve significance. Chapter 12 reviews research in greater detail, and concludes there's no evidence for single group validity or differential validity, which implies tests can be used for whites and non-whites equally well.

Ability tests are useful at all occupational levels

Most people accept the need to select managers, scientists, even sales staff, carefully, and many people will accept ability tests are useful for the purpose. But one often hears it said 'you don't need tests for ordinary jobs' and 'anyone with any common sense can do X'. The validity generalization analyses produced by Hunter and co-workers show ability tests predict productivity in *all sorts* of occupations, not just the 'high powered' (Table 7.5). Re-analysis of Ghiselli's comprehensive review shows the combination of general intelligence, perceptual ability and psychomotor validity achieved validities higher than $r = 0.40$ for all classes of work except sales clerks. Hunter's unpublished analysis (Hunter and Hunter, 1984) of 515 jobs found GATB validity around $r = 0.30$ even for the least complex jobs.

Differential batteries or general intelligence

The Schmidt-Hunter-Pearlman group tend not to mention intercorrelations between the eight to ten abilities. Intercorrelations between tests in aptitude

Table 7.5. Re-analysis by Hunter and Hunter (1984) of
Ghiselli's (1966) summary of validity coefficients for nine
classes of job, and three classes of test

	GI	PC	PM	GI+PC+PM
Manager	53	43	26	53
Clerk	54	46	29	55
Salesperson	61	40	29	62
Protective professions	42	37	26	43
Service jobs	48	20	27	49
Trades and Crafts	46	43	34	50
Elementary industrial	37	37	40	47
Vehicle operator	28	31	44	46
Sales clerk	27	22	17	28

GI = general intelligence, PC = perceptual, PM = psychomotor
(Reproduced by permission.)

batteries are usually fairly high, so it's unlikely all eight or ten tests need to be used. Schmidt and co-workers haven't—publicly, to date—asked how much information would be lost in selection by using general intelligence tests instead of aptitude batteries.

CRITICIMS OF VALIDITY GENERALIZATION

Computational details

Callender and Osburn (1980) find an error in Schmidt and Hunter's original validity generalization analysis, and develop their own equations by computer simulation. Hunter *et al.* (1982) see 'only trivial differences between [their] equations and the independent equation of Callender & Osburn'. Burke (1984) reviews six sets of equations for Validity Generalization analysis.

Reporting bias

Journals are notoriously reluctant to publish 'insignificant' results, so perhaps published studies are a very biased sample of validity research. Hence mean validities, whether raw or 'true', may be gross overestimates. However most validity generalization analyses include unpublished studies, and make careful enquiries to locate them. Validity generalization analyses reported by the Schmidt–Hunter–Pearlman group use US government or military research, which tests whole, large populations. Other validity data are drawn from *Personnel Psychology's* Validity Information Exchange, whose policy was to publish all validity information regardless of statistical significance.

It's also possible to calculate the likelihood of unreported studies that may change conclusions about test validity. The 'File Drawer' statistic 'allows one to calculate the number of unreported studies in researchers' file drawers, all with null results, that would be needed to bring the overall p level for reported studes down to the .05 level of significance' (Burke, 1984). Callender and Osburn (1981) report File Drawer values for their validity generalization analysis of petroleum industry employees; between 482 and 2010 unreported studies with insignificant results would have to exist to reduce to insignificance the pooled estimate of validity based on 25 to 38 reported studies. Callender and Osburn aren't likely to be unaware of over 400 validity studies in the petroleum industry, and it's wildly unlikely there could be 2000 unreported researches in a fairly centralized industry. Rosenthal (1979) describes how to calculate 'File Drawer'.

Correcting for test reliability

Critics say it's pointless estimating how much more accurate selection would be if tests were perfectly reliable—because they aren't. Validity is necessarily limited by test reliability. For most purposes, including routine selection, this is true. However, researchers testing a theory of *quantitative ability* and *job satisfaction* could regard both as constructs that could ideally be measured perfectly reliably, and might legitimately correct for reliability of both before calculating their true correlation (Hunter *et al.*, 1982).

Too many assumptions?

Validity generalization analyses *estimate* distributions of unreliability and range restriction, because neither are reported in most validation studies. Only sampling error can be calculated, because validity studies nearly always report sample size.

Schmidt and Hunter argue sampling error, which *can* be calculated, accounts for 90 per cent of artefact variance. They propose 'bare bones' validity generalization analysis, a conservative procedure that corrects validity variance for sampling error only, and needs make no assumptions about test or criterion reliability or range restriction. 'Bare bones' validity generalization analysis of the Programmer Aptitude Test increased *residual SD* by a trivial amount (Schmidt *et al.*, 1980), which implies that sampling error matters most, when assessing true validity of a selection test.

Hirsch *et al.* (1984) tried another approach; they found data on test and criterion reliability and range restriction for enough studies to *calculate* their effects. *Calculated* variance contributed by the four artefacts accounted for 79 per cent of observed variance, whereas *estimated* artefacts accounted for only 72.5 per cent, showing the assumptions are if anything conservative.

Arbitrary classifications

Validity generalization for clerical workers (Pearlman *et al.*, 1980) uses fairly broad categories: secretary, typist, filing clerk, duplicating machine operator. Critics (Algera *et al.*, 1984) argue such classifications are as arbitrary as generalizing validity across a study of intelligence and speed of learning in children, and a study of spatial relations and navigation skill in aircraft pilots. Finding a correlation of 0.40 in both studies doesn't prove measures or abilities have anything in common. But Pearlman *et al.*'s classifications aren't arbitrary. They classify jobs using the US Government's *Dictionary of Occupational Titles*; they use Ghiselli's (1966) classification of tests; they report high inter-judge reliabilities for their classifications. And if their categories were arbitrary, validity wouldn't generalize within them.

WHY ABILITY TESTS PREDICT PRODUCTIVITY

Personnel psychology often bemoans its lack of theory, and sometimes tries to make good the perceived deficiency. Ability testing has never pretended to any systematic theory. Binet's first test was written to screen out educationally subnormal children, and derived its items from the convenient fact that older children can solve problems younger ones can't. Ability tests ever since have mostly been written for particular practical purposes not as part of a general theory of human cognitive abilities.

Recent research asks *why* ability tests predict productivity so well, in such a wide range of jobs. Hunter (1983) found General Mental Ability didn't correlate

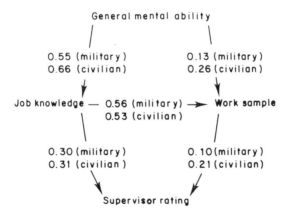

Figure 7.5. The relationships between general mental ability, supervisor ratings, job knowledge, and work sample performance, in civilian and military samples (Hunter, 1983). (Reproduced by permission of Lawrence Erlbaum Associates, Inc., Publishers)

directly with Supervisor Ratings. Ability did correlate with Job Knowledge and Work Sample Performance, which in turn correlated with Supervisor Ratings. An intelligent person learns quickly what he/she needs to know to do the job (Job Knowledge), and he/she learns how to do the job well (Work Sample), which causes supervisors to rate him/her highly. Figure 7.5 shows acquisition of knowledge is the more important route between Ability and good ratings, although there is some direct contribution of Ability to Work Sample performance. More intelligent people are better workers primarily because they learn more quickly what the job is about. In high-level work this may mean learning scientific method, scientific techniques, and a specific body of knowledge. In low-level work it may mean only learning where to find the raw materials, what to do with them, and where to put the finished product. Hunter (1983) found the 'paths' between Ability, Work Sample, and Supervisor Ratings weaker in military samples than in civilian ones. He suggests this reflects military emphasis on training and drill. Soldiers aren't left to work things out for themselves, or to devise their own ways of doing things; performance reflects training more than individual differences in cognitive ability.

Schmidt *et al.* (in press) confirmed Hunter's results, and found that Experience also improves Work Sample performance, and leads to better Supervisor Ratings *through* improved Job Knowledge (Figure 7.6). This implies Experience can 'substitute' for General Mental Ability; less able workers will learn enough about the job to work productively, but will take longer to achieve this. Meanwhile they cost the employer money by being less productive than their more able colleagues. Research has not yet directly confirmed the 'substitution' hypothesis.

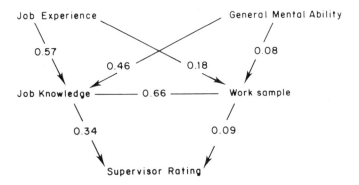

Figure 7.6. The relationships between experience, mental ability, supervisor ratings, job knowledge, and work sample performance, in civilian and military samples (adapted from Schmidt *et al.*, 1987). Copyright 1987 by the American Psychological Association. Reprinted by permission.)

CONCLUSIONS

Validity generalization analysis has proved again what we really always knew: test of cognitive ability predict productivity very well. For a vast range of jobs the more able worker produces more, produces better, produces faster.

The predictive validity of ability tests, for virtually all work, doesn't really need any further demonstration, although the American legal system (Chapter 12) is likely to continue demanding such proof, until the law is changed. What is worth researching, and has been neglected for 80 years, is *why* cognitive ability predicts efficiency to well. Knowing why may produce better tests, and may eventually satisfy the tests' critics.

Validity generalization analysis proves something we didn't know before, or were reluctant to admit. Tests can be used 'off the shelf'; it isn't really necessary to analyse the job in great detail, nor to conduct a local validation study, to know that tests of cognitive ability will select more productive workers.

Some other tests can predict as well as ability tests, but none are so cheap, nor so universally valuable. Assessment centres (Chapter 9) are very expensive: work samples (Chapter 10) are necessarily specific to the job, which makes them expensive also: peer assessments (Chapter 5) are unpopular and impractical.

The value of ability tests has been well known since the 1920s, so why do so many people so eagerly write them off? Why has it been necessary to invent a new way of analysing selection research, just to prove ability tests are worth using?

Perhaps the answer lies in percentiles: 99 per cent of the population feel threatened by ability tests because they're not in the top 1 per cent. Then there is the irrelevant (for our purposes) issue of heredity. There is also the problem of 'adverse impact' (Chapter 12).

CHAPTER 8

Personality Tests

'Total awareness of bottom line vitality'

Ghiselli's (1966) review of test validity lists intelligence as the best single predictor of selling ability. This always surprises personnel managers who say 'Surely personality is much more important'. Advertisements for sales staff, from the lowest level to the highest, list the traits essential for selling: commitment, enthusiasm, smartness, discipline, dynamism, flair, drive, resilience, acumen, self-motivation. 'Self-starting' is a phrase much in vogue. One advert for a sales manager created a series of bizarre, even indecent, images by specifying 'thrusters—pro-active and professional in interpersonal skills—with total awareness of bottom line vitality' (but neglected to say what the product was).

Defining personality

Everyone agrees the right personality is essential for selling. Then the *dis*agreements start. First define 'personality'. The layman usually means social presence—'Jill has a lot of personality'; personnel managers often mean the same. Psychologists' definitions are broader. Cattell (1965) defines it as: 'that which permits a prediction of what a person will do in a given situation'. Cronbach's (1984) definition is a little narrower: 'one's habits and usual style, but also ... abilities to play roles'. Allport (1937) defines personality as 'the dynamic organisation within the individual of those psychophysical systems that determine his unique adjustment to his environment'. Personality traits are 'neuropsychic system[s] ... with the capacity to render many stimuli functionally equivalent, and to initiate and guide consistent (equivalent) forms of adaptive and expressive behaviour'. Traits are mechanisms within the individual that shape how he/she reacts to *classes* of event and occasion.

Most occupational psychologists adopt, explicitly or implicitly, the trait model. A trait 'summarises past behaviour and predicts future behaviour'. A few psychologists prefer 'dustbowl empiricism', and reduce traits to scores that derive from personality tests and which might predict productivity.

Is there anything there to define?

In the late 1960s many psychologists began to question the very existence of personality. Mischel (1968) reviewed evidence, some of it by no means new, that seemed to show that behaviour wasn't consistent enough to make general statements about personality meaningful. Take the trait of honesty, which so many reference requests ask about. Hartshorne and May's Character Education Inquiry, in the late 1920s, found seven sets of measures of honesty virtually uncorrelated, so it's meaningless to describe someone as 'honest' unless one specifies when, where, with what, with whom. Mischel reviews similar evidence for other traits that often feature in job descriptions: extraversion, punctuality, curiosity, persistence, attitude to authority.

Personality theorists argue Hartshorne and May's tests of honesty, while very ingenious, were single-item tests, so it isn't surprising they intercorrelated poorly. Single-item tests are inherently extremely unreliable, and unlikely to predict anything. One question from an intelligence test wouldn't predict anything, so why should a single-item honesty test prove any more successful? Epstein (1979) averaged measures of extraversion, forgetfulness, mood and carefulness across 6 days, and found he got stable, useful measures.

Recently Kenny and Zaccaro (1983) re-analysed data on leadership, long regarded as the classic non-trait. Leadership research uses a 'rotation' paradigm, in which groups of people are re-combined, and emerging patterns of leadership studied. Conventional wisdom (among social psychologists) held that leadership wasn't an individual trait, but a *role* anyone could assume. Kenny and Zaccaro's re-analysis finds individual identity accounts for 49–82 per cent variance in leadership in 'rotation' studies and they conclude there *are* leaders. Earlier research found leadership correlates very modestly with intelligence, dominance and adjustment. The correlations are small ($r = 0.15–0.25$), but arguably not completely useless (Chapter 13).

To adapt a remark first made about schizophrenia, 'if personality is a myth, it's a myth with a genetic component'. Research finds scores on many inventories to be heritable; people are born predisposed to be anxious, introvert, aggressive, or 'just weird' (Cook, 1984).

Measuring personality

Layman and personnel manager alike express scorn at most personality measures: 'But surely *that* doesn't really measure personality?' Personality measures divide into:

(a) *Observation.* The Thought Police, in Orwell's *1984*, could watch everyone all the time. 'You had to live ... in the assumption that every sound you made was overhead, and, except in darkness, every movement scrutinized'. Personnel managers can only observe a limited, carefully edited performance, lasting between the 30 minutes of a typical interview and the 3 days of an assessment centre. Nor can they observe applicants' thought and feelings.

(b) *Situational tests.* Waiting for behaviour to occur naturally is very time-consuming; the 'situational test' saves time by contriving an occasion for significant behaviour to occur. Hartshorne and May gave children opportunities to cheat, take money, lie about their strength etc. The War Office Selection Board introduced 'command tasks'.

(c) *Questionnaire/inventory.* Observation is time-consuming; it can easily take 15 minutes to observe a single act by a single person. Psychologists looked for short cuts: ways of getting more information more quickly. One short cut is the questionnaire or 'inventory'; instead of watching the person to see if he/she talks to strangers, one asks 'Are you afraid of talking to strangers?' Questionnaires are very economical; in 15 minutes one can ask 100 questions to as many people as one can assemble. The questions can tap thoughts and feelings, as well as behaviour: 'Do you often long for excitement?', 'Are you sometimes troubled by unusual thoughts?'. (Questionnaires are justified as a quick and easy substitute for observation, but historically their true origin lies in the medical interview.)

(d) *Ratings, checklists.* The second short cut is to ask someone who knows the subject well to describe him or her: references, ratings, checklists (Chapter 5).

(e) *Projective tests.* People react to be observed, and may not tell the truth about themselves or others; projective tests are supposed to by-pass people's defences, and measure their personality despite themselves.

(f) *Miscellanous*, including Kelly's (1955) Role Repertory Grid ('rep grid'), and 'self-characterizations'.

Different theories of personality (Cook, 1984) favour different approaches to measurement. Psychoanalysis relies on dreams and free associations. Motive/need theories favour projective tests. Trait theory accepts questionnaires and inventories. Behaviourists prefer behavioural measures, such as work samples. Phenomenal approaches use 'repertory grids', and 'self-characterizations'. In practice distinctions are blurred; questionnaires are used to test all sorts of personality theory, even psychoanalysis. Questionnaire measurements of different traits often correlate very highly; similarly ratings of different traits often correlate very highly. This effect—called *method variance*—means assessors should ideally measure every trait by two *different* types of measure—*multi-trait multi-method measurement*—but it's rarely possible in practice.

PERSONALITY INVENTORIES

Most use 'endorsement' items:

My eyes are always cold.	TRUE FALSE
My parents are older than me.	TRUE FALSE
Do you trust psychologists?	YES ? NO

'Endorsement' format is quicker and easier for subjects, but encourages 'response sets': consistently agreeing, consistently disagreeing, being consistently evasive or non-committal (by checking '?'). Kline (1976) says 'on careful reflection, many [endorsement items] are unanswerable, although they evoke an immediate natural response'.

'Choice' format can equate the attractiveness of the alternatives, to try to limit faking:

Would you rather be Dr Crippen or Jack the Ripper?

Choice format needs more thought and takes longer. Cattell (1986) thinks it creates 'cumulative antipathy'. The 'Crippen or Ripper' example, which comes from a real inventory, shows why; it offers subjects an extraordinarily difficult and unpleasant choice: *either* a poisoner *or* a maniac, and both long dead. Forced choice also *creates* correlations between the scales, which can give very misleading results.

Keying and *validation* distinguish a list of questions thrown together, like an 'Is your husband a good lover?' quiz in a magazine, from a proper personality test. A proper personality test is validated, and standardised. There are four main ways of validating personality tests:

1. *Acceptance.* People accept the test's results. Stagner (1958) gave personnel managers a personality test, pretended to score it, then handed each manager a profile; all were convinced the test had described them perfectly, even though Stagner gave *every* manager the *same* interpretation. People are very ready to be taken in by all-purpose personality profiles—the so-caled 'Barnum effect'. (So long as the profile's not *too* harsh—people often indignantly reject the less flattering parts of California Psychological Inventory reports.)

2. *Content.* The inventory looks plausible. The first personality inventory, Woodworth's Personal Data Sheet, gathered questions from lists of neurotic and psychotic symptoms in textbooks and from discussions with psychiatrists, to ensure item *content* was plausible and relevant. The *first* stage in writing any inventory is choosing the questions, but a good

inventory doesn't leave it there. The *second* stage, deciding which questions to keep, uses factorial or empirical validation.

3. *Factorial.* The questions hang together. The author of the inventory chooses questions that look similar, and tests his/her hunch by correlation and factor analysis. Questions that don't fit are discarded. If the questions measure two things, the scale may have to be split. Cattell's (1965) research is the most ambitious use of factorial validation.

4. *Empirical.* The questions are included because they predict. The inventory is 'empirically keyed', using 'criterion groups'. The questions may be very diverse, and the link between the question and what it measures may be obscure. In theory questions might appear totally irrelevant; playing tiddly-winks every Sunday afternoon might help identify mass murderers. In practice items on the MMPI Psychopathic Deviance scale (nearest thing to a mass murderer scale) aren't that subtle; they consist mostly of expressions of fondness for hurting people, or disregard for law or social norms.

Answers to inventory questions are 'signs', not 'samples'; the psychologist wants an answer to 'I sleep pretty soundly most nights' for what he/she can *infer* from it. If the psychologist wanted precise information about the subject's sleep patterns, he/she wouldn't use vague phrases like 'pretty well' or 'most nights'.

Empirical keying can produce inventories that are almost completely atheoretical, that postulate no traits, drives, complexes, etc., but simply generate scores that predict outcomes. Examples include: Strong Vocational Interest Blank, Jurgensen's Classification Inventory (see below), as well as Biodata inventories (Chapter 6).

New scoring keys can be written for inventories such as SVIB and MMPI. Twenty-three pairs of new keys were added to SVIB in 1985, including: travel agents; broadcaster; chef; carpenter; electrician; R&D manager; bus driver; funeral director; army, navy, airforce and marine 'enlisted personnel' (other ranks). MMPI too has a multiplicity of special keys.

What to measure

There's an almost infinite range of possibilities, depending on one's personality theory: traits, needs, motives, values, cognitive styles or self-concepts. In practice any characteristics measured by a questionnaire have that very important fact in common, regardless of the measure's title and rationale.

How many to measure?

An empirically validated inventory measures as many different things as its author succeeds in measuring. A factorially validated inventory finds an empirical answer to the question 'how many things to measure'. Cattell found sixteen personality factors; Guilford found ten. Factor analysis doesn't finally answer the question—How many? Eysenck thinks there are only two or three fundamental dimensions of personality, not sixteen, but there isn't a real disagreement between Eysenck and Cattell. Cattell's sixteen factors intercorrelate to some extent; factor analysis of the factors reveals 'higher-order' factors—exvia/invia and anxiety—which resemble Eysenck's Extraversion and Neuroticism (Figure 8.1). Sixteen scores look more useful than two or three, and 16PF is much more widely used for selection than Eysenck's measures. However critics argue the 16PF is too short to measure sixteen factors reliably, and that it's 'over-factored': some of the factors don't appear in every analysis, and may not really exist.

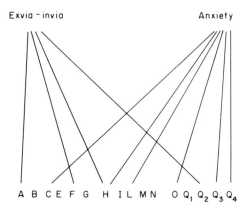

Figure 8.1. Higher-order factors, 'exvia-invia' and anxiety, in Cattell's sixteen personality factors.

Interpreting inventory scores

A raw score on a personality inventory, like a raw score on a cognitive ability test, is meaningless; it must be related to a population—people in general, managers, students, etc. Many inventories use T scores, in which the mean is set at 50, and the standard deviation at 10. Profile sheets for MMPI and California Psychological Inventory convert raw scores into T scores, and allow scores on different scales to be compared (Figure 8.2). Cattell's 16PF uses 'sten' scores, and Guilford's inventories use 'C scores', which differ only in detail from T scores. CPI or 16PF profiles are a neat, quick way of presenting the data, but encourage over-interpretation. The reliability of individual scales is often low; the difference between two unreliable scores is doubly unreliable, so the difference between points on a CPI or 16PF profile has to be quite large to merit

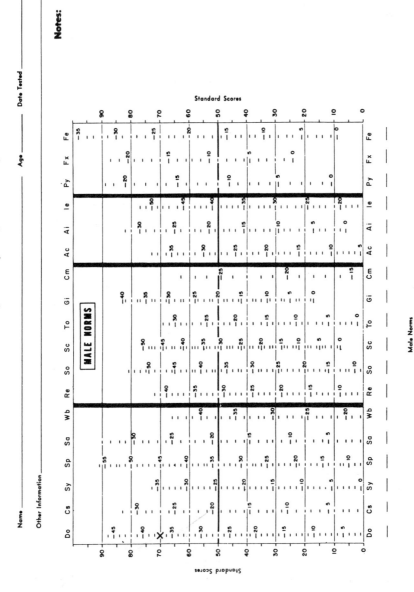

Figure 8.2. The profile form used for the California Psychological Inventory, illustrating the T score system. A raw score of 37 for Dominance converts into a T score of 70, which is two standard deviations above the male average. Female scores are plotted on the other side of the form. Reproduced by special permission of the Publisher, Consulting Psychologists Press Inc. Palo Alto, CA 94306, from the California Psychological Inventory by Harrison Gough, PhD. © 1958. Further reproduction is prohibited without the Publisher's consent.

interpretation. For example, on 16PF Forms A and B, a difference of two 'stens' between Factor A 'Affectothymia' and Factor B 'Intelligence' falls well within the error of measurement. Only a difference of four 'stens' can be confidently taken as 'real'. There are only ten 'stens' in all, so only very gross differences within 16PF profiles can be safely interpreted.

Some inventories contain *infrequency keys* —sets of questions where most subjects say True or most say False. People answering at random are as likely to give the infrequent answer as the frequent one, so accumulate a high Infrequency score, which means they're answering carelessley, or don't understand the procedure, or don't speak Engish very well, or are being deliberately unco-operative.

SURVEY OF (SOME) INVENTORIES

Woodworth's PDS was written too late to be used in the First World War, but created so much interest that several hundred inventories were in use in the USA by 1935. Most were fairly bad, so people soon became wary of them. Inventories are listed and reviewed in the *Mental Measurements Yearbooks* (Buros, 1970); *MMY* reviews discuss size and adequacy of standardization sample, reliability, validity, and whether the manual is any good. *MMY* reviews are very critical even of major tests.

Major inventories such as CPI or 16PF are used for clinical diagnosis, career guidance and counselling, as well as for selection. Large new inventories are hard to launch because so much is invested in existing ones; Gough (1962) lists nearly 800 books, chapters or papers on the CPI. Nearly all major inventories originate in the USA, because no-one else has the money, access to large populations or general acceptance of the inventory's value. Nevertheless, personality inventories haven't been used, even in the USA, on anything like the scale of cognitive ability tests, which may be why they haven't proved so reliable and accurate. (On the other hand, perhaps people don't use them, precisely *because* they're less reliable and accurate).

Minnesota Multiphasic Personality Inventory (MMPI)

The first major multi-score inventory, dating from the late 1930s. MMPI asks 550 questions, answered 'True', 'False', '?', and measures nine psychiatric syndromes. MMPI was the first inventory to be empirically keyed against (rather small) criterion groups. MMPI can be used for screening, but is rather long and offends some subjects by asking too many intrusive questions. MMPI is the classic inventory everyone criticizes—'long and inefficient', 'dimensions used . . . relics of an antiquated psychiatry' (Cronbach, 1984)—but goes on using, because they're used to it, or can't find anything better.

Table 8.1. Cattell's sixteen personality factors, as measured by the 16PF inventory. Adapted from *The 16 PF Test Profile*. Copyright © 1956, 1957, 1961, 1962, Institute for Personality and Ability Testing, 1602-04 Coronado Drive, Champaign, Illinois, U.S.A. Reproduced by permission.

Factor	
A	Cool — Warm
B	Concrete-Thinking — Abstract-Thinking
C	Affected by Feelings — Emotionally Stable
E	Submissive — Dominant
F	Sober — Enthusiastic
G	Expedient — Conscientious
H	Shy — Bold
I	Tough-Minded — Tender-Minded
L	Trusting — Suspicious
M	Practical — Imaginative
N	Forthright — Shrewd
O	Self-Assured — Apprehensive
Q1	Conservative — Experimenting
Q2	Group-Oriented — Self-Sufficient
Q3	Undisciplined Self-Conflict — Following Self-Image
Q4	Relaxed — Tense

16 PF

Measures sixteen personality 'source traits', derived from factor analysis. Cattell originally referred to his factors by letter and neologism, to emphasize his factor analysis yielded an entirely new account of human personality, but soon had to compromise and give 'plain English' descriptions (Table 8.1).

16PF is very popular in the UK, partly because tradition allows non-psychologist personnel managers to be trained to use it. 16PF is also used by 38 per cent of UK occupational psychologists, not necessarily for selection, and not necessarily without reservations. Parry (1959) says 16PF was considered for inclusion in CSSB, but rejected, because there are only ten or thirteen questions measuring each factor, although 'a reliable paper test with less than 20 items is almost unknown'. 16PF has four forms; forms A and B are parallel 'long' forms, each asking 187 questions. Forms C and D are parallel 'short' forms, each asking 105 questions. Critics say forms A and B are too short in the first place, making a shorter form undesirable. 16PF is widely criticized for poor reliability—'correlations between forms (even pairs of forms) are so low that data gathered with one form or pair of forms may simply not be generalisable to all forms' (Buros, 1970).

16PF is popular with personnel managers, because the handbook (Cattell *et al.*, 1970) gives 'specification equations' for over 50 occupations. The equation for psychiatric technicians reads:

Rated Performance = 0.12A + 0.31C - 0.12E + 0.19G + 0.16H -0.19M - 0.12O - 0.19Q1 + 0.19Q3 - 0.12Q4 + 4.07.

People who make good aides in psychiatric hospitals have high scores on factors, A, C, G, H and Q3, and low scores on factors E, M, O, Q1 and Q4. Cattell says:

> The emphasis on emotional stability, superego strength, and self-sentiment development is to be expected in an occupation requiring calm, objective, and considerate treatment of irrationality in others. It is interesting to note also that high ... H is also favourable, presumably meaning a sympathetic autonomic nervous system which can take disturbing impacts without over-reacting.

Specification equations can be very misleading if they are calculated on small samples; they should be cross-validated on a second sample before they're used for selection. Most of the specification equations in the 16PF Handbook don't appear to have been cross-validated, and should be viewed with caution.

Guilford Zimmerman Temperament Survey (GZTS)

Developed factorially from intercorrelations between answers to inventory questions (whereas Cattell's factors were first calculated from intercorrelations of ratings.) GZTS asks 300 questions, to measure ten factors (Table 8.2), asking 30 questions for each factor. Interpretation of GZTS emphasizes interactions between scales. A high score on Emotional Stability (E) is desirable if accompanied by high General Activity (G); but high E with *low* G means the subject is likely to be sluggish, lazy and phlegmatic. Like 16PF, GZTS isn't all that reliable, but high reliabilities for individual scales are essential for reliable interpretation of differences between scales.

Table 8.2. Ten personality factors measured by the Guilford Zimmerman Temperament Survey

Factor	
G	General activity
A	Ascendance (dominance)
S	Sociability
E	Emotional stability
O	Objectivity ('thick-skinned'–over-sensitive)
F	Friendliness (absence of belligerence, hostility)
T	Thoughtfulness ('thinking introversion')
P	Personal relations (tolerance of others–critical, suspicious)
M	Masculinity

California Psychological Inventory (CPI)

CPI asks 480 endorsement format questions, to measure 22 traits (Table 8.3) CPI takes 45–60 minutes to complete (less if computer-administered). All 22 scales are written so that high scores are 'good' scores; Gough regards the average of all 22 scores as an index of the individual's social and intellectual efficiency. CPI contains about half the MMPI—the less 'intrusive' questions—and is often called the 'sane man's MMPI' (Megargee, 1972). Despite its derivation from MMPI, CPI hasn't seen the same proliferation of special scales. Instead Gough prefers to devise new indices using regressions. 'Type A' (coronary heart disease-prone) personality can be estimated using the formula:

$$44.93 + 0.22\text{Do} + 0.62\text{Sa} + 0.32\text{Sc} - 0.35\text{Re} - 0.39\text{So} - 0.39\text{Ai} - 0.26\text{Fx}$$

CPI has larger and better normative samples than MMPI. CPI's main defect is redundancy; all but four scales correlate quite highly ($r = 0.50+$) with one or more other scales. The new Form 462 reduces overlap between scales.

The major inventories—CPI, 16PF, GZTS—are 'all-purpose'; they were written, and are used, for counselling and clinical diagnosis as well as selection. Yet the two purposes are quite different, and may need quite different measures.

Table 8.3. Twenty-two personality traits measured by California Psychological Inventory

Do	Dominance
Cs	Capacity for Status (personal qualities that underlie and lead to high status)
Sy	Sociability
Sp	Social Presence
Sa	Self-acceptance
Wb	Sense of Well-being (absence of worries and complaints)
Re	Responsibility
So	Socialization (social maturity, integrity)
Sc	Self-control
To	Tolerance
Gi	Good Impression (concern with others' opinions)
Cm	Communality (a control scale)
Ac	Achievement via Conformance (interest and motivation to achieve where conformity helps)
Ai	Achievement via Independence (interest and motivation to achieve where independence helps)
Ie	Intellectual Efficiency
Py	Psychological Mindedness
Fx	Flexibility
Fe	Femininity
Em	Empathy
In	Independence
Mp	Managerial Potential
Wo	Work Orientation (strong work ethic)

Several inventories have been written specifically for selection work—but none has really caught on, because they proved no more successful than long all-purpose inventories.

Classification inventory (JCI)

This was written by Jurgensen (1944). JCI used forced-choice format: triads and paired items, equated for desirability:

People who have little control over their tempers.
People who think they are better than other persons.
People who crow over winning a game.

People who always interrupt when you are talking.
People who pick their teeth.

JCI was standardized on applicant populations, not college students or psychiatric patients. JCI abandons traits as intervening variables. Typically the occupational psychologist argues: this job needs dominant people; this inventory measures dominance; therefore high scores will be better for the job. Either assumption can be false, and both invoke the nebulous concept 'dominance'. Jurgensen inferred directly from inventory to performance, by keying JCI directly to specific jobs like SVIB and Biodata inventories (Chapter 5). Unfortunately JCI failed: the keys didn't cross-validate, and the inventory proved easy to fake.

Table 8.4. Abilities, traits and needs measured by Ghiselli's Self-Description Inventory

Abilities

  Supervisory ability
  Intelligence
  Initiative

Traits

  Self-assurance
  Decisiveness
  Masculinity–femininity
  Maturity
  Working-class affinity

Needs

  Occupational success
  Self-actualization
  Power
  Financial reward
  Job security

Self Description Inventory

This was written by Ghiselli (1971). It uses 64 pairs of adjectives, equated for desirability, to measure thirteen traits (Table 8.4). SDI has been quite well validated; the Power scale was written using the answers of students who described themselves as having a very strong need for power, or very little need, then cross-validated by comparing line managers with staff managers, and by showing that need for power correlated with success in authoritarian organizations, but not in democratic climates. SDI measures abilities as well as personality, so is especially suitable for a brief assessment.

Strong Vocational Interest Blank

SVIB (formerly 'Strong Campbell Interest Inventory') was written in the 1920s, and has been through seven editions. The core of SVIB are the 209 Occupational Interest Scales, which compare subjects' answers with keys derived from *criterion groups* of people successful in various vocations. Critics say SVIB's occupational keying is mindless empiricism: '[tests like SVIB] have no psychological meaning. Practically, they are useful; theoretically they are almost valueless' (Kline, 1976). Kline also thinks SVIB redundant: 'we would probably do as well to ask our clients 'What are you interested in?' as to give them the elaborate ritual of the SVIB! [It's] really an elaborate and technically wonderful steam hammer with which to crack an egg.' However SVIB also contains scales based on factor and cluster analysis: 23 *Basic Interest Scales*, and six *General Occupational Themes*: Realistic, Investigative, Artistic, Social, Enterprising and Coventional. The General Occupational Themes derive partly from factor analysis, and represent six types of people, each suited for a very general class of work.

Occupational Personality Questionnaires (OPQ)

A family of nine inventories, varying in *length*, and *format*. The longest versions measure 30 *Concepts*; the shorter *Factor, Octagon* and *Pentagon* versions measure 17, 8 and 5 higher-order factors derived from the 30 *Concepts* (Figure 8.3). OPQ uses three formats: '3', '4', and '5'. '3' is 'endorsement' format: 'Yes', 'Uncertain', 'No'; '5' is a five-point rating from 'strongly agree' to 'strongly disagree'; '4' is a forced-choice format, in which sets of four statements are rank-ordered. The Manual recommends pairs of formats be used, e.g. *Factor Model 3* should be used with *Factor Model 5*. The various forms of OPQ have good internal consistency, but data on re-test reliability are rather limited (Saville & Holdsworth Ltd, 1985). Validity data are also limited as yet: SHL report moderate correlations between *Concept 4* and appraisal ratings for 440 managers. OPQ illustrates the expense of launching major new inventories; to

OPQ FACTOR MODEL	OCTAGON MODEL	PENTAGON MODEL
PEOPLE		
Influence	Assertive	
Social confidence		
Empathy	Empathy	Extroversion
Gregarious	Gregarious	
Social desirability		
COGNITIVE STYLE		
Imaginative	Abstract	Abstract
Conservative		
Planful	Methodical	Methodical
Detail conscious		
EMOTIONS		
Relaxed	Relaxed	Emotional
Phlegmatic		stability
Optimistic	Self-controlled	
VIGOUR		
Contesting		
Active	Vigorous	Vigorous
Decisive		

Figure 8.3. The three forms of the Occupational Personality Questionnaires: Factors, Octagon and Pentagon, which measure fifteen, eight and five traits (Saville and Holdsworth ltd, 1985). (Reproduced by permission.)

recover their R&D costs, SHL have to charge OPQ users an annual licence fee of £960 (on top of the cost of materials and training).

Computer interpretation

Most inventories can be administered, scored and interpreted by computer (Fowler, 1985). Computer administration is twice as fast as paper-and-pencil testing; computer scoring is 50 times faster. Fowler reports that 80 per cent of subjects preferred computer administration, while none preferred the paper form (which isn't surprising, given that most answer sheets are designed to be read by scoring machines, not people); he concludes that 'fear of computing is a malady that affects professionals much more than their patients'. Computer interpretations can be faster still. Figure 8.4 shows an extract of a computer interpretation of a CPI profile, printed 5 minutes after the subject answered the last question.

Psychological Systems Questionnaire (PSQ)

Adapting an existing questionnaire to computer administration and scoring isn't particularly difficult, and doesn't fully exploit the computer's powers. PSQ is an

OVERALL LEVEL of the PROFILE

The overall elevation of Ms Example's profile is average. This means she is averagely well adjusted, and presently able to function socially and intellectually averagely well. There is however fairly wide variation between individual scales.

SECTOR I

Ms Example's overall score for Sector I is average. This means she will show an average level of poise, ascendancy, self-assurance and ability to deal with others. There is however fairly wide variation between individual scales.

SECTOR II

Ms Example's overall score for Sector II is low-average. This means she will show a low-average level of socialisation, maturity, responsibility, and intrapersonal structuring of values.

Dominance

Ms Example's Dominance score is average; she displays an average level of leadership ability, persistance and social initiative.

Capacity for Status

Ms Example's Capacity for Status score is high-average. She will tend to possess the qualities of ambition and self-assurance needed to achieve a high social standing. High Cs scorers describe themselves as socially poised and self-confident, as secure and free from fears and anxieties, as having literary and aesthetic interests, as having a strong social conscience, and as being interested in belonging to many groups. The Cs scale is an index of level of income, education, prestige and power. High Cs scorers are more likely to go to college than their level of ability would otherwise predict. High scorers tend to be upwardly socially mobile. Other people will tend to see Ms Example as slightly more than usually ambitious, active, forceful, insightful, resourceful and

Centre for Occupational Reseach Ltd
14 Devonshire Place, LONDON W1N 1PB

Figure 8.4. Part of a computer-generated interpretation of a California Psychological Inventory profile.

'interactive' programme, that selects from a pool of 700 questions, instead of asking a fixed sequence (Johnson *et al.*, 1979). Questions can be reworded to fit individuals. The first questions check 'faking good'; subjects are encouraged to be more candid if necessary. If the subject's depression score gets very high the programme asks an open-ended question: 'Mr Jones, your test responses seem to indicate that you are very depressed. Would you care to make any comments about this?'

Table 8.5. Retest reliability of the original eighteen CPI scales, for 234 men and women retested at an interval of 1 year (Megargee, 1972). (Reproduced by permission.)

Do	Dominance	0.63
Cs	Capacity for Status	0.68
Sy	Sociability	0.68
Sp	Social Presence	0.65
Sa	Self Acceptance	0.65
Wb	Sense of Well-being	0.71
Re	Responsibility	0.71
So	Socialization	0.72
Sc	Self-control	0.72
To	Tolerance	0.66
Gi	Good Impression	0.66
Cm	Communality	0.41
Ac	Achievement via Conformance	0.69
Ai	Achievement via Independence	0.60
Ie	Intellectual Efficiency	0.76
Py	Psychological Mindedness	0.48
Fx	Flexibility	0.63
Fe	Femininity	0.85

GENERAL VALUE OF INVENTORIES

Stability

Test–retest reliability of inventories is often disappointingly poor. Table 8.5 lists retest reliabilities for 18 CPI scales, for 234 men and women, tested twice at an interval of 1 year. Individual profiles do change considerably over fairly short periods of time; Figure 8.5 shows two CPI profiles produced at an interval of 6 months by one woman. On the other hand, inventories have shown impressive long-term stability. Strong (1955) reports high median retest correlations (r = 0.75) in SVIB profiles over 22 years; 'those who had interests most similar to engineer, lawyer, or minister on the first occasion were ones who had scores most similar to those criterion groups on the second occasion'.

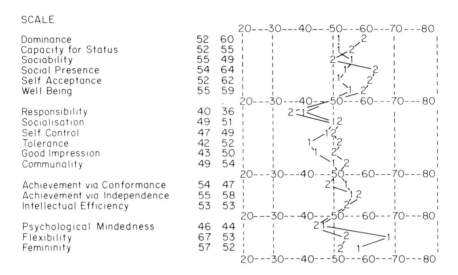

SCALE

Scale		
Dominance	52	60
Capacity for Status	52	55
Sociability	55	49
Social Presence	54	64
Self Acceptance	52	62
Well Being	55	59
Responsibility	40	36
Socialisation	49	51
Self Control	47	49
Tolerance	42	52
Good Impression	43	50
Communality	49	54
Achievement via Conformance	54	47
Achievement via Independence	55	58
Intellectual Efficiency	53	53
Psychological Mindedness	46	44
Flexibility	67	53
Femininity	57	52

Figure 8.5. Two CPI profiles from the same person, completed 6 months apart. (Reproduced by special permission of the Publisher, Consulting Psychologists Press, Inc., Palo Alto, CA 94306, from the California Psychological Inventory by Harrison Gough, PhD. © 1958. Further reproduction is prohibited without the Publisher's consent.)

Faking

There are three basic questions in selection:

1. What *have* you done?
2. What *can* you do?
3. What *would* you do?

CVS, WABs and Biodata answer Question 1. Ability tests answer Question 2. Personality tests would answer Question 3, if it were a sensible one to ask, which many critics think it isn't. Why not? Partly because applicants can tell lies, and the employer can't check the answers.

Most inventories are fairly transparent. No-one applying for a sales job is likely to say TRUE to 'I don't much like talking to strangers'; nor is someone trying to join the police likely to agree that he/she has 'pretty undesirable acquaintances'. Faking good isn't a problem with ability tests; the only ways to get a high score on Raven's Progressive Matrices are to work out the correct answers, or cheat.

Faking may be deliberate lying or half-conscious distortion. An inventory necessarily measures the individual's self-concept which, in well-adjusted people, is usually fairly favourable. Cronbach (1984) likens a completed inventory to a 'statesman's diary': 'the image the man wished to leave in history', 'the reputation the subject would like to have'.

Personality inventories are fakeable. Figure 8.6 shows two average CPI

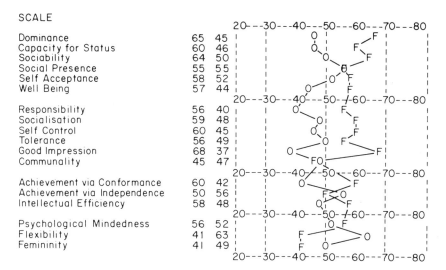

Figure 8.6. Two composite CPI profiles produced by a group of 25 students. The 'own' ('O') profile was completed as an anonymous lab class exercise; the 'fake-good' ('F') profile was completed to maximize the subjects' chances of getting on a management training scheme with a major employer. (Reproduced by special permission of the Publisher, Consulting Psychologists Press, Inc., Palo Alto, CA 94306, from the California Psychological Inventory by Harrison Gough, PhD. © 1958. Further reproduction is prohibited without the Publisher's consent.)

profiles, from a group of 20 students who completed CPI twice, once as an anonymous practical class exercise, the second time giving the answers they thought would maximize their chances of getting a job they really wanted. The 'job' profiles are consistently more favourable than the 'own' profiles.

But do real applicants fake inventories? GZTS profiles completed by job applicants are 'better' than profiles completed by people seeking counselling or taking part in research (Herzberg, 1954), but nowhere near as 'good' as faked good profiles. This implies real applicants are relatively honest, compared with subjects in fake-good studies. Dunnette *et al.* (1962) estimated one in seven applicants for sales jobs faked, and even they faked less than subjects in fake-good studies. People already employed 'fake' less than applicants (which means tests validated on existing staff may not work so well for applicants).

There are many lines of defence against faking.

Rapport

The tester can persuade the subjects it's not in their interests to fake, because getting a job for which one's personality isn't really suited will ultimately cause unhappiness, failure, etc. This argument may have limited appeal to those who haven't any job, ideal or otherwise.

Subtle questions

'Do you like meeting strangers' is clearly a crass question when selecting a door-to-door salesman. Is it possible to find subtler questions? Authors of empirically keyed inventories like to think so. Gough (unpublished) argues many CPI items are too subtle to be faked easily; 'There are times when I act like a coward' is keyed *true* for Dominance because, Gough argues, dominant people can admit to feeling fear occasionally. Critics say inventory questions can be divided into the unsubtle that work, and the subtle that don't.

Control keys

Many inventories contain 'lie scales', politely known as 'social desirability' scales. Lie scales are lists of answers that deny common faults, or claim uncommon virtues, or both. CPI's lie scale, called 'Good Impression', was written by choosing questions sensitive to instructions to 'fake good'. In the 'fake good' experiment in Figure 8.6, 95 per cent of faked profiles had Good Impression scores over 60. However Lie scales aren't always all that subtle. Subjects who know the Eysenck Personality Inventory has extraversion, neuroticism and lie questions can tell which is which (Power and MacRae, 1971). But do naive subjects know about lie scales?

Correcting for defensiveness

A high lie score reveals the subject's answers can't be trusted, which is clearly worth knowing. However the assessor is then left without an interpretable personality profile. MMPI's K key measures defensiveness, then 'corrects' the profile by adding varying proportions of K. Cattell (1986) suggests inventories need a 'distortion matrix', of different sets of corrections for different purposes: counselling, selection, clinical diagnosis, military screening, etc. Cronbach (1984) is sceptical: 'if the subject lies to the tester there is no way to convert the lies into truth'.

Forced-choice

Choice format questions can be equated for desirability, so the subject must choose between pairs of equally flattering or unflattering statements:

I am very good at making friends with people.
I am respected by all my colleagues.

I lose my temper occasionally.
I am sometimes late for appointments.

Forced-choice format has several snags:

(a) It's slower.
(b) Subjects don't like it.
(c) It *creates* correlations between scales. Every subject's scores on the Allport–Vernon–Lindzey Study of Values must total 180, so the subject who wants to express a strong preference for one Value has to express less interest in others. Grimsley and Jarrett (1973) found 'top' managers less Religious than 'middle' managers on AVL. Are 'top' managers really less Religious? Or do they value something else more—Theoretical, Economic, Social, Political, Aesthetic.

   The Myers Briggs Type Indicator—a 126-item measure of Jungian typology—uses forced-choice in which *both* choices relate to the same trait, hence avoiding the interdependence problem.
(d) Forced-choice format doesn't prevent faking. EPPS is still fakeable, because pairing questions for *general* desirability doesn't make them equally desirable for every *specific* purpose.

Change the questionnaire's format

Cattell's Motivation Analysis Test uses several novel question formats, some of which are probably quite hard to fake:

(a) *Uses*—forced-choice between two ways of spending time, money or effort. Cattell argues subjects will choose the alternative that satisfies the stronger need.
(b) *Estimates*—some objective, such as the quarantine period after rabies; some subjective, such as the relative importance of money and sex appeal. Cattell assumes people's needs shape the replies they give, so a person motivated by fear thinks quarantine periods *are* longer, because he/she thinks they *ought* to be longer.
(c) *Paired words*—a forced-choice word association, paced by the tester. People form associations that reflect strong needs, so a person motivated by fear associates 'hooligan' to 'football', not 'cup'.
(d) *Information*—factual questions, with verifiable answers. People know more about things that matter to them. An aggressive person is more likely to know which of the following *isn't* a type of firearm: Gatling, Sterling, Gresley, Enfield, FN.

Don't use questionnaires

There are other ways of assessing personality: projective tests, behavioural tests, ratings and checklists, observations, Biodata, and assessment centres.

Accept the inevitable

Elliott (1981) suggests faking good shows the applicant knows what's expected, whereas the person who produces an honest but bad profile either doesn't know what's expected at work, or isn't prepared to deliver. Faked responses on the Gordon Personal Inventory correlate quite well with clerical performance, whereas scores corrected for faking have no predictive value.

USING INVENTORIES IN PERSONNEL SELECTION

Inventories answer three main questions:

1. Has the applicant the right personality for the job?
2. Will he/she be any good at the job?
3. Is there anything wrong with him/her?

Questions 1 and 2 look very similar, but differ subtly. Question 1 is answered by comparing bank managers with people in general; question 2 is answered by comparing _good_ and _poor_ bank managers. Question 1 uses the survival or 'gravitational' criterion of success; people _gravitate_ to jobs they can do well, and then _survive_, so anyone who has been a bank manager for 10 years must be reasonably good at it. But suppose there are jobs where no-one is ever sacked, or even criticized, for inefficiency? 'Survival' then proves nothing.

Question 1: The right personality?

Miller (1976) is conscious of a 'strong demand for personnel officers, or their managing directors, ... for a profile involving all of the traits assessed by the questionnaire'. Employers would really like a book of ideal personality profiles for Manager, Salesman, Engineer, Computer Programmer, etc. Manuals for some tests meet this demand; 16PF and CPI manuals both give norms for different occupations. 16PF's Handbook suggests matching profiles. For some occupations the Handbook gives detailed specification equations; for others it suggests which scales should be above average, and which below: e.g. naval officer cadets are 'able (B+), rather adventurous (E+, H+), and active (F+) ... with practical realism (I–, M–, N+) and have good control mechanisms (C+, Q3+)' (Cattell _et al._, 1970).

The 'Perfect Profile' approach has several limitations.

(a) The sample sizes in the Occupational Profiles table of 16PF's Manual range from 18 to 1707, with a median of 90, which probably isn't big enough.
(b) Cross-validation information is rarely available. Ideally a Perfect Profile for a cost accountant will be based on two or more separate, large samples.

(c) The Perfect Profile is an average, about which scores usually vary a lot.
(d) Most Perfect Profiles derive from people doing the job, taking no account of how well they do it, nor how happy they are.
(e) The Perfect Profile may show how well the person has adapted to the job's demands, not how well people with that profile will fit the job.

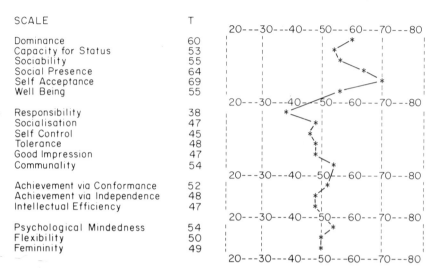

SCALE	T
Dominance	60
Capacity for Status	53
Sociability	55
Social Presence	64
Self Acceptance	69
Well Being	55
Responsibility	38
Socialisation	47
Self Control	45
Tolerance	48
Good Impression	47
Communality	54
Achievement via Conformance	52
Achievement via Independence	48
Intellectual Efficiency	47
Psychological Mindedness	54
Flexibility	50
Femininity	49

Figure 8.7. Composite CPI profile for 20 sales managers. (Reproduced by special permission of the Publisher, Consulting Psychologists Press, Inc., Palo Alto, CA 94306, from the *California Psychological Inventory* by Harrison Gough, PhD. © 1958. Further reproduction is prohibited without the Publisher's consent.)

Figures 8.7 and 8.8 show two composite CPI profiles, for two occupations, showing how each deviates from Men in General. Sales Managers score above average on Dominance, Sociability, the Social Presence, whereas Security Van Crewmen score below average on Capacity for Status, Responsibility, Tolerance, both forms of Achievement, Intellectual Efficiency and Empathy.

SVIB's Occupational Interest Scales are based entirely on gravitation and survival. SVIB occupational samples are drawn from people who have been in their work at least 3 years, and who have achieved some success, most typically in the form of membership of their professional body. Personnel managers, for example, were all Members of the American Society for Personnel Administration. SVIB scores predict career choice and satisfaction very accurately; Strong (1955) reports an 18-year follow-up of Stanford students. Those with 'A' ratings (interests very similar) for a profession had a 3.6 to 1 of entering that profession, whereas students with 'C' ratings (interests very dissimilar) had a 5 to 1 chance of *not* entering that profession. Students who had entered careers their interests suited them for were happier in their work.

Personnel Selection and Productivity

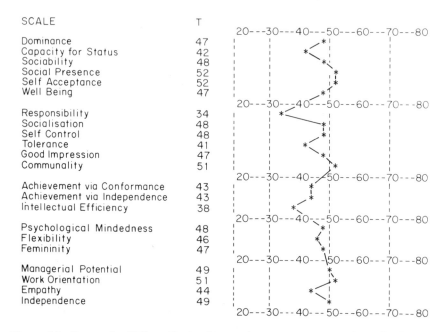

Figure 8.8. Composite CPI profile for 30 security van crewmen. This profile includes the more recently added Mp, Wo, Em and In scales. (Reproduced by special permission of the Publisher, Consulting Psychologists Press, Inc., Palo Alto, CA 94306, from the *California Psychological Inventory* by Harrison Gough, PhD. © 1958. Further reproduction is prohibited without the Publisher's consent.)

Question 2: Will he/she be successful?

A number of quite ambitious studies have used inventories to predict creativity, effective management, or just 'success'.

Creativity

A battery of seven inventories predicted creativity in architects, with varying success (Hall and MacKinnon, 1969). CPI did fairly well—achieving a cross-validated R of 0.47. SVIB did very well—achieving a cross-validated multiple R over 57 scales of 0.55. Other personality measures—Gough ACL, Myers Briggs Type Indicator, FIRO-B, and AVL—also achieved moderately high cross-validated multiple Rs. Only MMPI failed to predict creativity.

Effective management

Mahoney *et al.* (1960) divided 468 managers into two parallel sets of effective and ineffective. The managers were tested with CPI, SVIB, Wonderlic Personnel Test, and a Biodata inventory; cut-off points that distinguished effective from ineffective were calculated on Sample I, then cross-validated on Sample II. The effective manager is:

> somewhat more intelligent than the 'less effective' manager; his vocational interests are more similar to the interests of sales managers, purchasing agents, and manufacturing company presidents; and they are less similar to the interests of men engaged in biological sciences and technical crafts ... he tends to be more aggressive, persuasive, and self-reliant; he has had more educational training and was more active in sports and hobbies as a young man; and his wife also has had more educational training and worked less after marriage.

Success

In Stanford MBAs, 5 years after graduation, GZTS Ascendance predicts higher income, as does the Decision Making score of Ghiselli's SDI (Harrell, 1972). The differences are fairly small—corresponding to correlations of roughly 0.2. In MBAs working for *large* firms (1000+ employees), GZTS Social Interest and General Energy Level, MMPI Mania, SDI Self-Assurance and Initiative also predicted success. Harrell thinks success in large firms requires high, almost manic, energy levels. (However validity generalization analyses of ability tests (Chapter 7) make one wary of suggesting organizational climate 'moderates' predictive validity, on the strength of just one study.).

Fighter pilots and clerical workers

The Eysenck Personality Inventory is much shorter than most inventories: 57 items, measuring extraversion and neuroticism. EPI was written to test Eysenck's experimental and biological theory of personality, not for personnel work. Nevertheless Bartram and Dale (1982) found men who failed flying training were less stable and more introvert. The correlations weren't very large, but EPI takes only 10 minutes to complete, and pilot training is extremely expensive, so any increase in predictive validity is worth having. Eysenck's personality theory generates many predictions with direct relevance for work. He predicts extraverts lack persistence in repetitive tasks, which in turn implies they will be bored by routine clerical work; Sterns *et al.* (1983) found extraverts less satisfied in clerical jobs, and Cooper and Payne (1967) found extraverts tended to leave jobs sooner.

Police

Inwald Personality Inventory is a 310 true–false questionnaire designed specifically to predict effectiveness in police and 'corrections' officers. Shusman *et al.* (1984) report scores predict lateness, absenteeism, being injured, being disciplined, and getting bad reports in samples of American police officers, and correctly assign 60–82 per cent of officers to the categories 'effective' and 'ineffective', with some 'shrinkage' on cross-validation.

Unskilled workers

Inventories such as 16PF and CPI are too long and difficult for unskilled workers; Johnson *et al.* (1984) describe a short inventory designed specifically for low-income workers. The Work Opinion Questionnaire has only 35 items, all fairly short—'Supervisors are too bossy', 'If something goes wrong on the job, I get blamed'; scores correlate moderately well with supervisor ratings.

Summaries of validity of personality inventories

Guion and Gottier (1965) tabulated published studies of the concurrent and predictive validity of personality inventories: Bernreuter, CPI, EPPS, Kuder Preference Record and Occupational Interest Surveys, GZTS and its ancestors, Gordon Inventory, MMPI, SVIB, and Study of Values. The table makes depressing reading—low correlations and insignificant differences being the usual outcome. Only 12 per cent of the correlations summarized achieved statistical significance. No measure stands out as better or worse. Most studies use small samples; the largest is 603, the median 50.

Lent *et al.* (1971) report 'Significance Batting Averages' for personality and interest tests of 31 and 41 per cent; more often than not personality and interests failed to predict productivity. Dunnette (1972) summarized 134 validity coefficients for the American petroleum industry. Interest and personality inventories both achieved near zero median validity; however the best 25 per cent of coefficients of personality tests exceed $r = 0.37$, suggesting perhaps tests can predict productivity if used properly. Interest inventories were mostly used—with a singular lack of success—for maintenance jobs, whereas personality inventories were mostly used for clerical jobs.

Muchinsky and Tuttle (1979) review fourteen studies in which inventories were used to predict turnover. Only four studies included cross-validation, and only one found a consistent result; Bernardin (1977) found salesmen who left soon had higher anxiety and lower conscientiousness scores on the 16PF. Interest inventories fared slightly better, with three studies finding consistent cross-validated links between lack of interest in a job and high turnover.

Ghiselli (1973) reviews pooled validities across eight broad classes of job, for training and proficiency criteria. Table 8.6 shows validity averaged at or below $r = 0.20$ for most jobs, but reached $r = 0.30$ for executives and sales staff (as high as cognitive ability measures). Personality and interest tests were rarely used for industrial workers, and weren't very widely used for trades and crafts workers.

However, Ghiselli's review did *not* correct for sampling error, range restriction and test or criterion (un)reliability. Validity generalization analysis (Chapter 7)

Table 8.6. Validities of personality and interest inventories for twelve categories of job (Data from Ghiselli, 1973)

	Personality Training	Personality Proficiency	Interest Training	Interest Proficiency
Executive and administration	—	28	53	30
Foremen	—	15	—	17
All Managers	—	21	53	28
General clerks	—	30	17	—
Record clerks	—	18	—	-01
Computational	—	17	—	23
All clerks	—	24	17	12
Sales clerks	—	36	—	34
Salesmen	—	29	—	31
All sales	-11	31	—	32
Protective	—	24	—	-01
Service occupations	—	16	—	16
Vehicle operators	—	26	—	26
Trades and crafts	—	29	16	17
Industrial	—	50	—	14

showed ability tests' validity much higher than Ghiselli had supposed, so perhaps *validity generalization* analysis could similarly change the picture for personality inventories. Perhaps—but the only two validity generalization analyses of inventories reported so far have been very disappointing. Hunter and Hunter (1984) found SVIB performed very poorly—ninth equal of eleven measures, with an estimated 'true' validity of only $r = 0.10$. However SVIB isn't primarily a *selection* test, and the analysis of SVIB presented—rather sketchily—by Hunter and Hunter includes only three studies. Schmitt *et al*'s (1984) meta-analysis of 62 published validity finds an averge 'true' validity of $r = 0.15$, the worst of eight predictors analysed.

Predictive and concurrent validation

Most research estimates *concurrent* validity, rather than *predictive* validity. In concurrent validation, people presently doing a job complete the inventory, and get a criterion rating. In predictive validity, people are assessed *before* the criterion data are collected; ideally they are assessed before they start doing the job. What's the difference? Suppose a concurrent validity study shows that unsuccessful teachers are anxious, and unsure of themselves. Are they ineffective as teachers because they're anxious and unsure, or are they anxious and unsure because they're beginning to realize they're ineffective teachers? Concurrent validation can't prove direction of cause; whereas a predictive validation study which showed that 20-year-olds who were anxious and unsure of themselves made bad teachers 10 years later proves personality matters in teaching.

Concurrent studies are obviously a lot cheaper and easier to do. Guion and Gottier (1965) found only 37 per cent of studies 'could be considered studies of predictive validity, and this is an overestimate'.

Grimsley and Jarrett (1973) compared 'top' and 'middle' managers, concurrently, but argue the differences they find aren't artefacts. Younger 'top' and middle managers differed more than older, suggesting 'increased time spent in middle management positions does not cause middle managers to develop "middle manager responses" to test items'. Brousseau and Prince (1981), however, disagree. They tested 176 employees twice with GZTS at average intervals of 7 years, and found *changes* in GZTS scores correlated with five dimensions of the Job Diagnostic Survey. People doing work with 'High Task Identity'—doing a job from start to finish with a visible outcome—increased their scores on seven GZTS scales. People doing jobs with 'High Task Significance'—impact on lives and work of others—increased their scores on eight scales. Brousseau and Prince's data prove the work people do can cause systematic changes in their personality profiles, and prove that doubts about concurrent validation of personality inventories are justified.

Question 3: Is there anything wrong with him/her?

Personality inventories can be used like the driving test: not to select the best, but to exclude the unacceptable. Some employers use personality assessment as an insurance policy or safety net, and send applicants to the psychologist as a final check. Employees are most typically screened for (mal)adjustment, or (dis)honesty. Screening for 'burnout' is becoming popular in some professions.

Adjustment

Anderson's (1929) survey of staff at Macy's department store in New York found 20 per cent of employees fell into the 'problem' category—can't learn, suffer chronic ill-health, are in constant trouble with fellow-employees, can't adjust satisfactorily to their work. Culpin and Smith's (1930) survey of over 1000 British workers found 20–30 per cent suffering some measurable level of neurosis. These figures may seem improbably high, but are confirmed by 'community surveys' of mental health; if psychologists go out looking for maladjusted people, instead of waiting for them to be referred, one in five is the typical ratio they discover.

Anderson used a clinical interview—time-consuming, and expensive. Culpin and Smith used interviews and the McDougall–Schuster dotting task: subjects try to make marks in small circles on a paper disc that rotates faster and faster, which requires good motor control, good attention and freedom from panic. Good performers had few neurotic symptoms.

Screening is currently very widely used in the USA for 'law enforcement and corrections officers'; 42 states screen to identify people who are emotionally or psychologically unfit for the police. MMPI is the favourite test, with CPI and 16PF the runners-up. British police forces are beginning to consider screening. Officials in the American nuclear power industry were able to list over 150 cases of 'disturbing behaviour' in nuclear power plant operators. Psychologists advised the industry to test all operators on hiring with MMPI and CPI, and to retest periodically (Dunnette *et al.*, 1981, cited in Cronbach, 1984). Dunnette thought MMPI *49* types likely to be a risk—because they are prone to 'argumentative hostility' and 'impulsive action'.

Military screening

Very large numbers of US servicemen were screened during the Second World War; Ellis and Conrad (1948) conclude 'in the overwhelming majority of studies the instrument in question proved to have some value for screening or diagnostic purposes'. MMPI and shorter inventories were 'sieves separating the recruits into ... those who had to be screened further by a clinician ... and those who needed no further screening'. Some studies reported very high correlations between inventory scores and adjustment—as high as $r = 0.80$. Other studies reported cutting points of amazing efficiency—anyone scoring over 25 on Cornell Selectee Index 'invariably fell into the category of severe psychoneurotics', while anyone with a Cornell score under 15 'could be almost as readily as accepted for employment'.

Some military screening results *were* too good to be true. Many studies suffered 'criterion contamination', which means the psychiatrist making the diagnosis knew the man's test score. Faking was less likely in military testing, because many men didn't *want* to get good scores, because many weren't intelligent enough to fake, and because the military could issue dire threats about what would happen to anyone who found to have given untrue answers. Military testing reached men other test programmes never saw: 'unemployables, tramps, loafers, "bums", alcoholics, frank neurotics', so it suffered an unusual statistical problem—*excessive* (as opposed to *restricted*) range. There's a *wider* range of individual differences in conscript samples than in typical applicant samples, so the test can correlate better. It's useful to know how a test performs ona complete cross-section of American men, but not all that relevant to civilian employers who aren't interested in screening out people who'd never apply anyway, or wouldn't get past the receptionist if they did.

Callan (1972) describes a more recent US military screening, again using the MMPI (in a slightly unorthodox way; groups of 200 men at a time listened to the questions being played by a tape recorder over a public address system—answering 'by numbers'?). Callan first wrote a key that predicted discharge, absence without leave, malingering and disciplinary problems, then cross-validated it on 3328 recruits. Table 8.7 shows his best results (he tried several scoring methods). Callan—unlike Ellis and Conrad—didn't think screening cost-effective.

Table 8.7. Best results achieved (on cross-validation) by Callan's (1972) military delinquency MMPI key

	Problem	Not problem
MMPI key's prediction		
Problem	80 (True positive)	156 (False positive)
Not problem	232 (False negative)	2,860 (True negative)

Screening has four possible outcomes (Table 8.7):

(a) *True positives* are maladjusted individuals, picked out by the screening. Also known as *Hits*.
(b) *False positives* are well-adjusted individuals, falsely identified as maladjusted by the screening.
(c) *False negatives* are maladjusted people the screening classifies as well-adjusted. Also known as *'misses'*.
(d) *True negatives* are well-adjusted people the screening classifies as well-adjusted.

The more efficient the screening, the fewer misses and false positives it makes. A false positive is a potentially useful recruit turned away; a miss is an ineffective, potentially disruptive recruit admitted. True positives are usually a minority of applicants, so screening will often make more false positives than true positives, even though *percentage* True and False positives might look very promising. In Callan's data, screening correctly identified 34 per cent of true positives, with 'only' 4.7 per cent false positives—but this means 156 acceptable recruits were wrongly rejected, along with only 80 true positives. Overall Callan's screening achieved 88 per cent correct classification—but mostly derived from the 2860 true negatives.

The value of screening depends on:

(a) Whether it's accurate.
(b) *Base rate*—what proportion of applicants are maladjusted, dishonest or indisciplined. In Callan's data base rate was only 9 per cent whereas in the earlier surveys of Anderson and Culpin it was nearer 30 per cent.
(c) *Selection ratio*—if the applicant pool is limitless, the number of false positives doesn't matter.
(d) How serious are the consequences of a miss. A dishonest bus conductor is less of a threat than an unstable armed police officer.
(e) What happens to positives—true or false. In US military screenings all

positives were seen by a psychiatrist, so weren't necessarily 'lost'. A civilian employer who screened the workforce for signs of stress could arrange counselling or treatment for those appearing to need it.

The use of MMPI to assess ability to withstand stress in fire-fighters was challenged as an invasion of privacy, but was ruled acceptable 'in the public interest'. Similarly the right of law enforcement agencies to use psychological tests has also been upheld; in fact in one case a plaintiff won substantial damages when a police officer shot and crippled his wife, because he *hadn't* been screened.

Honesty testing

Questionnaires are widely used in the USA to screen out staff thought more likely to steal money or goods (Sackett and Harris, 1984). These measures used indirect questions that assume dishonest people see crime as more frequent, easier, meriting less punishment or more easily justified (by low wages, etc.). Honesty tests have been validated against polygraph assessments, by comparisons of convicted criminals and control subjects, or by comparing scores with admissions of past dishonesty. (Why should people tell the truth about past dishonesty? Researchers solve this problem—up to a point—by validating the test on people who aren't applying for a job.)

'Honesty' tests should *ideally* be validated by testing all employees when recruited, then later comparing the scores of those proven or presumed dishonest with the rest. The number of actual thieves caught is usually too small, so researchers look for indirect methods. One study reported high correlations between honesty scores and how often the employee's till was more than $5 short. Another study correlated honesty scores with the amount collected by paid charity collectors, on the assumption low takings meant the collector was helping/herself; a modest correlation resulted. Honesty testing, like the polygraph, gives a high rate of 'false positives'—about one in four, many of whom would have been perfectly honest. Sackett and Harris suggest it's not unreasonable to reject *applicants* on the strength of honesty tests, given that all selection is imperfect and that all job applicants face rejections. They argue equally strongly it would be very wrong to use honesty tests on *established employees*.

Burnout

People in some professions—counsellors, police officers, teachers, child-care workers, nurses, lawyers—experience 'emotional exhaustion resulting from chronic tension and stress in people-helping work' (Meier, 1984). 'Burnout' is caused by lack of reward and encouragement, frequent 'punishment', and the feeling that one has no control over whether people are pleased or displeased with one's work. 'Burnout' can be assessed by Maslach Burnout Inventory.

Cynics note that 'burnout' seems to occur almost exclusively in the public sector; 'burned out' managers and salesmen, if such exist, are dismissed.

INVENTORIES AND THE LAW

'Fair' employment

Inventories have come in for surprisingly little criticism—given their generally poor validity, and the ease with which they can be ridiculed. The Psychological Corporation's (1978) review of 'fair' employment cases between 1968 and 1977 mentions only one case, from 112, in which a personality test—16PF—featured.

Sex differences

SVIB originally had separate male and female forms, appropriately printed on pink and blue paper. The questions were merged into a common form in 1966, but SVIB still retains different scoring keys for the Occupational Interest scales. Virtually every occupation has a pair of separate male and female keys. Great effort has gone into finding samples of female farmers and male beauticians, etc.

Other vocational interest inventories prefer to devise *common* keys for male and female soliders, travel agents, bus drivers, etc., partly to simplify scoring and interpretation, partly to head off criticism. Hansen (1976) argues it's unrealistic to seek common keys at present, because men and women doing the same job often do it for different reasons, and have different outlooks; male pharmacists are typically entrepreneurs, whereas female pharmacists have a more scientific interest in their work. Common scoring keys eliminate questions that create sex differences, which shortens the scoring key, and reduces its reliability.

Privacy

Inventories were criticized for invasion of privacy during the 1960s. The US Senate voted that 'no [guidance] program shall provide for the conduct of any test . . . to elicit information dealing with the personality, environment, home life, parental or family relationships, economic status, or sociological and psychological problems of the pupil tested'. It's difficult to see how you can 'guide' someone if you aren't allowed to know anything about them.

ALTERNATIVES TO THE INVENTORY

'Across the front of each test and each manual, there should be stamped in large, red letters (preferably letters which will glow in the stygian darkness of the personality measurement field) the word EXPERIMENTAL' (Gustad, 1956).

Everyone agrees inventories have limitations, but what can replace them? Guion (1965a) argued *objective* measures of personality are needed. Objectivity means 'freedom from distortion'; distortion has three dimensions.

1. Distortion happens when the purpose of the assessment is clear to the subject.
2. Distortion happens when subjects have to use a forced-choice format and can't give their own answers.
3. Distortion happens when information can't be checked. Guion cites drinking habits: there are ways of finding out exactly how much alcohol someone drinks but the inventory item 'Do you drink a lot?' isn't one of them.

Personality inventories score low on all three dimensions: information is distorted by being forced into 'Yes/No' answers to ambiguous questions; information is distored because the subject can guess what the investigator wants to hear; information is distorted because there's no way of verifying answers. So what measure would be objective, verifiable, have an open-ended response and not betray its purpose? Guion nominates the 'tautophone': which 'plays an indistinct recording, and the subject reports what he has heard'. An interesting idea—which never caught on.

Projective tests

Projective tests assume everything a person does, says, writes, thinks, paints or even dreams reflects his/her personality. If people don't know they are revealing their personalities, they can't censor themselves, and then consciously or unconsciously 'fake good'. Projective tests are even more numerous and vastly more varied than questionnaires/inventories. Kinslinger's (1966) review covers six tests widely used in the US personnel research:

Rorschach (and several variants);
TAT and variants, including Vocational Apperception Test;
Worthington Personal History;
sentence completion tests;
Tomkins Horn Picture Arrangement Test;
Rosenzweig Picture Frustration Study.

Rorschach

Subjects describe what they see in a set of 'inkblots'. The Rorschach is classically scored by deciding if the response is based on detail or the whole blot, on colour or form, etc. Multiple-choice scoring has also been used.

Rorschach scores are very poor at differentiating physical scientists, technicians, biologists, anthropologists, psychologists and artists. Other studies reviewed by Kinslinger found Rorschach unable to distinguish production engineers, research engineers, lab. technicians and administrators. Rorschach is similarly unable to predict success at work. Early studies, described by Dorcus and Jones (1950), thought TAT and Rorschach the ideal way to predict turnover or accident-proneness in tram (streetcar) drivers in Southern California; neither test predicted anything. Kelly and Fiske's (1951) study found Rorschach scores unable to predict success in clinical psychology. Other studies reviewed by Kinslinger similarly failed to find Rorschach reliably predicted any aspect of productivity.

Thematic Apperception Test (TAT)

A set of pictures carefully chosen both for their suggestive content and their vagueness. The subject describes 'what led up to the event shown in the picture, what is happening, what the characters are thinking and feeling, and what the outcome will be'. The subject 'projects' into the story his/her own 'dominant drives, emotions, sentiments, complexes and conflicts'.

Most research with TAT has used it to assess 'need for achievement (nAch) (Chapter 11). Rodger (1959) found 'route' salesmen, tested by Rorschach and TAT, showed 'markedly rigid personality structures and personality impoverishment'; the salesmen had no strongly held opinions of their own, but were skilled at taking the lead from what others thought; they were materially oriented, to the point of being 'less inhibited by concepts of rights and wrong'; their relations with others were superficial, to the point of 'conceal[ing] distrust behind a facade of congeniality'.

Tomkins-Horn Picture Arrangement Test (PAT)

Sets of three pictures, which can be arranged in various sequences. If the subject chooses a sequence that ends with the hero in others' company, the choice scores for 'General Sociophilia'. Critics say the test has too many scoring keys, many of which are too short.

Miner (1971) used PAT for selecting management consultants, concurrently validated against management ratings. PAT showed the successful consultant is: drawn to authority figures, doesn't want to be alone when away from work, prefers physically close relationships and moves toward supportive relationships. Such people can act independently, want to be with more powerful people, and don't want to be with peers. The results make sense, given that management consultants spend a lot of time with bosses of large companies. A composite PAT score correlated very well with success.

Sentence completion tests

These are more 'structured', and easier to score, but not necessarily very subtle:

My last boss was . . .
I don't like people who . . .

The Rotter Incomplete Sentences Test has some scope for screening out disturbed persons. The Miner Sentence Completion Scale is written for selecting managers; it measures: attitude to authority, competitive motivation, masculine role, etc. According to Miner (1978), the test can predict promotion in marketing and other managers. American Telegraph and Telephone's Management Progress Study used two sentence completion tests, and the TAT, from which 'composite' scores were drawn by a clinical psychologist. The projective tests predicted salary increase rather less successfully than assessment centre ratings.

Worthington Personal History Blank

A specially designed four-page application form, that gives the applicant the fullest scope for revealing his/her personality. The space for name is just that—a space, with no indication whether to put surname first, use full initials, titles or whatever. An applicant who wrote 'Jonathan Jasper Jones Jnr' stood out because men usually use initials; exceptions tend to be 'young men who haven't yet made their way in the world' (Spencer and Worthington, 1952).

Early research suggested Worthington PH was very promising; *qualitative* scoring predicted output in factory workers very well. Other studies, described by Kinslinger, found the Worthington PH could predict supervisory potential, and characterize workers in ways supervisors and managers agreed with. Owens, however (Clark and Owens, 1954), found the Worthington PH of little value. Owens went on to develop Biodata methods (Chapter 6)—the exact opposite of the PH. The Worthington PH is intentionally open-ended and subjectively scored, whereas WABs and Biodata was highly structured and quantitatively scored.

Miscellaneous

Personal construct theory (Cook, 1984) argues the way people *see* or 'construe' the world, the people in it, determines how they act, so assessment of 'personal constructs' is central to understanding people. Personal construct theory (Kelly, 1955) provides two ways of assessing personal constructs: 'self-characterization', and the Role Repertory Grid Test ('Rep' test).

Self-characterisation.   Kelly (1955) says a sketch written in the third person, as if by a close, sympathetic friend, is a good way of finding out about someone. Self-characterizations typically use four headings:

(a)   What I most like about the world in which I live.
(b)   What I most dislike about it, and what I do about, these dislikes.
(c)   What I most like about myself.
(d)   What I most dislike about myself, and how I hope to change.

There's no systematic evidence the method predicts anything, including productivity.

Repertory grid.   As originally conceived by Kelly, an elaborate procedure, in which:

1.   the subject writes the initials of people filling significant roles in his/her life: father, mother, spouse, teacher, boss, etc.;
2.   the subject 'sorts' three roles—e.g. self, father, mother—stating which one differs from the other two, e.g. self and father differ from mother;
3.   the subject names the 'construct' used to 'sort' the three roles, e.g. male/ female;
4.   the subject applies the 'construct' to the other roles, i.e. saying which are male, which female;
5.   the subject repeats steps 2 to 4 a number of times for different sets of three roles.

The 'Rep' test reveals how the subject groups people, what concepts he/she uses to group them, and how many independent ways of understanding others the subject has. The 'Rep' test has been very popular, especially in Britain, but has never proved to predict much, including productivity.

CONCLUSIONS

'Personality test' means, in practice, personality *inventory*; other methods are cumbersome and ineffective.

   Research on validity of inventories has proved disappointing. The earlier narrative reviews found validity coefficients very inconsistent, but tending to be small. Perhaps validity generalization will make sense of the literature, as it did so well for ability tests; the first two analyses, however, confirmed the conclusions of the narrative analysis—very limited validity.

   Inventories emerge as definitely less useful than Weighted Application Blanks and Biodata (Chapter 6), or than peer assessments (Chapter 5). Inventories are also less useful than assessment centres, although research has not yet discovered what aspect of the AC contributes its predictive validity.

On the other hand, inventories prove to have no *less* predictive validity than the interview, while having the advantage of being cost-effective and standardized.

Selectors still lack a good way of identifying people who *could* do well, but *won't*, because they're too anxious, because they don't get on well with people, because they're inconsistent or distractible, or because they don't like being told what to do.

CHAPTER 9

Assessment Centres

Does his (or her) face fit?

An assessment centre isn't a place; it's a method. It's not a cut-and-dried copyright method, like the Wonderlic Personnel Test, or McMurray's programmed interview; it's a very broad class of method. Assessment centres were invented simultaneously on both sides of the Atlantic: War Office Selection Board (WOSB) in Britain, and Office of Strategic Services (OSS) programme in the USA.

War Office Selection Board

Before 1943 the British Army selected its officers by conventional, *short* tests: recommendation and interview. The most striking feature of WOSB was *length*, so it became known as the 'country house weekend'. Candidates were assessed by a variety of methods. Tests included group discussions and group tasks, such as planning how to 'escape' over an electrified wire entanglement. Typical topics for discussion included: 'Is saluting a waste of time?'. WOSB included group exercises, 'to assess the subject's ability to get on with and influence his colleagues, to display qualities of spontaneous leadership and to think and produce ideas in a real life situation' (Parry, 1959). WOSB assessors included: board president, visiting member, psychiatrist and Military Testing Officer.

Office of Strategic Services

In the USA psychologists, led by Henry Murray, were advising the OSS, forerunner of the CIA, how to select agents to be dropped behind enemy lines, collect intelligence and return it to HQ. Murray's team identified nine dimensions to effective spying: practical intelligence, emotional stability, leadership, physical ability, propaganda skills, maintenance of cover, etc.— 'maintenance of cover' required each candidate to pretend to be someone else throughout the assessment—'to have been born where he wasn't, to have been educated in institutions other than those he attended, to have been engaged in work or profession not his own, and to live now in a place that was not his true

156

residence' (Mackinnon, 1977). The OSS programme must be unique in regarding systematic lying as a virtue.

Post-war developments

The first modern, peacetime AC was American Telegraph and Telephone's (AT&T) Management Progress Study. The AT&T programme included: a business game, leaderless group discussion, and 25-item 'In-Basket' test, 2-hour interview, an autobiographical essay and personal history questionnaire, projective tests, personality inventories, a Q sort (a variant on the inventory, in which the subject sorts cards, on which inventory-type statements are typed, into a forced distribution), and a high-level intelligence test. The programme included far more individual tasks and psychological tests than contemporary ACs. So did CSSB, which in its earliest form included seventeen cognitive ability tests.

The original AT&T study assessed over 400 candidates, who were followed up, 5–7 years later; AC ratings predicted success in management with an accuracy that came as a welcome surprise to psychologists who were finding most other methods so fallible they were hardly worth using (Bray and Grant, 1966). AT&T now run ACs on a very large scale, with 50 centres passing 10,000 candidates a year.

ACs have become very popular in North America since the 1960s; over 1000 organizations were using them by the mid-1970s, including a high proportion of public bodies. Britain has been slower to adopt ACs, the current interest in British industry owes its inspiration more to US practice than to WOSB and CSSB. A survey of IPM members in 1973 found only a handful (4 per cent) used ACs. By 1986 over 20 per cent of top UK employers were using ACs to select at least some managers (Robertson and Makin, 1986). ACs are mostly used in Britain for selection, whereas in North America they're used more for 'development'—deciding who to promote, and what training people need.

The present shape of ACs

The 1979 'Task Force on Assessment Centre Standards' defined the AC as 'standardised evaluation of behaviour based on multiple inputs. Multiple trained observers and techniques are used.' Simulation exercises are the core of the American AC.
To elaborate the definition, ACs:

(a) use multiple techniques, at least one of which should be a simulation (of the job),
(b) use multiple trained assessors,
(c) use assessors who pool information to arrive at an 'executive decision'—

Cohen (1978) sees arriving at a *consensus* about candidates as the most central aspect of the AC,
(d) use assessors who separate *evaluation* of behaviour from *observation*,
(e) use dimensions that are determined by job analysis.

Assessing candidates in groups has several advantages. It allows group psychological testing, which saves time. It creates group dynamics, which allow aspects of the individual to be studied that can't be measured by other means. People may *describe* themselves as dominant and forceful in their application, or when completing a personality inventory, but can they *actually* dominate a group and persuade others to accept their views? Purists argue every group is unique, so no two ACs are comparable; recombining candidates in differing subsets for different exercises meets this criticism, up to a point.

The length and intensity of some ACs can 'get behind' any 'front' the candidate is presenting, to give a clearer idea what he/she is really like. Sociologists will argue the distinction between a 'front' and what 'someone's really like' is false. Everyone, everywhere, is playing a role. Only hermits and idiots don't change their behaviour to suit the occasion. But some roles are easier to play than others, and some can only be played for a short time. Many people can bluff their way through a half-hour interview; acting the part of a good manager for two or three days is more of a test.

AC exercises

ACs use both *group* and *individual* exercises. *Group* exercises further divide into *assigned role* and *unassigned role* exercises.

(a) *Assigned role* exercises, in which each person has an individual brief, competing for a share of a single budget, or trying to 'push' his/her candidate for a job. Assigned role exercises are used to assess negotiating skills, persuasiveness and ability to compromise. Military ACs often use 'command exercises', simulating the task of controlling a group of men solving a practical problem. The OSS programme included the famous 'Buster and Kippy' Command Task, in which candidates tried to erect a prefabricated structure, using two specially selected and trained 'assistants', one aggressive, critical and insulting, the other sluggish and incompetent.
(b) *Unassigned role* exercises, such as running a simulated business, in which decisions must be made rapidly, with incomplete information, under constantly changing conditions. Unassigned role exercises assess: tolerance of uncertainty, tolerance of stress, ability to provide one's own structure, and ability to adjust in changing circumstances. The *unassigned role* category also includes leaderless group discussions.

(c) *Team exercises*, in which half the group collectively advocates one side of a case, and the other half takes the opposing viewpoint. Team exercises assess negotiating skill, teamwork, analytic skill and problem-solving ability.

Individual exercises divide into:

(a) *'In-Basket' (or 'In-Tray')* which assesses: planning, organizing, quality of decisions, decisiveness, management control and delegation (Chapter 10). Candidates can be interviewed about their actions and asked to account for them.
(b) *Irate customer/employee.* The candidate handles a visit or phone call from a dissatisfied customer, or from an employee with a grievance. Used to assess: analystical skills (getting the facts, interpreting them), and interpersonal skills. The OSS programme included an exercise in which the candidate tried to explain why he had been found in Government offices late at night searching secret files, and was searchingly cross-examined by a trial lawyer.
(c) *Sales presentation.* Candidate tries to sell goods/services to an assessor briefed to be challenging, sceptical, unsure the product is necessary, etc.

Surveys shows the 'In-Tray' test, the business game, and the leaderless group are used in nearly all ACs, whereas interviews and psychological tests were included in only two-thirds.

RELIABILITY

Overall

Wilson (1948) quotes a fairly good retest reliability for CSSB as a whole, apparently based on candidates who exercised their rights to try CSSB twice; the report is otherwise rather vague. Morris (1949) gives details of two retest reliability studies with WOSB. In the first, two parallel WOSBs were set up specifically to test 'inter-WOSB' agreement; two 'batches' of candidates attended both WOSBs, group 1 going to WOSB A first and WOSB B second, while group 2 went first to B, then A. There were major disagreements over 25 per cent of candidates. In the second study two parallel Boards simultaneously but independently observed and evaluated the same 200 candidates, but didn't communicate with each other at all; the parallel WOSBs agreed very well overall, as did their respective Presidents, psychiatrists, psychologists and Military Testing Officers.

Later Moses (1973) compared 85 candidates who attended long and short assessment centres and were evaluated by different staff. Overall ratings from the two ACs correlated well. Ratings on parallel dimensions were also highly correlated. A complex procedure like an AC can't be replicated as precisely as an ability test or even an interview. Cohen and Sands (1978) list some of the factors that are hard to control: assessor/candidate acquaintance, assessors' consensus discussions, the way instructions for exercises are given. The 'group dynamic' aspect of the AC makes an exactly parallel replication impossible.

Inter-rater reliability

Ratings of Leaderless Group Discussions achieve fair to good reliability; reliability of OSS ratings of was similarly fair to good. Hinrichs and Haanpera (1976) review twelve studies of inter-rater reliability, and find generally good agreement in the short term, although agreement after 8 years was understandably very much lower. Jones (1981) reports fair inter-rater reliabilities for ratings of naval officer candidates by trained naval officers. Overall judgements made *after* discussing the candidates achieved higher inter-rater reliabilities. Schmitt (1977) also found inter-rater reliabilities higher after raters had discussed ratings.

It never pays to be complacent about any personnel selection procedure, but reliability doesn't seem a major problem with AC ratings.

VALIDITY

ACs achieve impressively good predictive validity, which accounts for their popularity, and justifies their cost. AT&T's Management Progress Study assessed 123 'new college hires' and 114 non-graduate first-level managers. On follow-up, 8 years later, Table 9.1 shows the Management Progress Study had identified 82 per cent of the college group and 75 per cent of the non-graduates who had reached middle management. The AC achieved a predictive validity of 0.44 for college educated Ss, and 0.71 for non-college educated. The AC also identified 88 per cent of the college group and 95 per cent of the others who didn't reach middle manager level. The AC identified successful and unsuccessful managers equally accurately (Bray and Grant, 1966). Toplis (1976) thinks validity of the Management Progress Study varied markedly from year to year, but may be falling into the Fallacy of Small Numbers. Some AT&T research has used very large samples. A published study by Moses (cited in Byham, 1971) followed up 5943 assessees, and found AC rating correlated well with promotion—but promotions *weren't* made in ignorance of AC results, in contrast to the original Management Progress Study.

Byham (1971) reviewed 22 AC validity studies, and found fifteen positive, with only one negative result (the rest were inconclusive). Campbell and Bray's (1967) study, across four Bell telephone companies, divided candidates into 'acceptable', 'questionable' and 'unacceptable'—but all were promoted to first-level management anyway. While the AC had some predictive validity it also proved

Table 9.1. Results of the AT&T Management Progress Study

Assessment centre ratings	n	Achieved Rank		
		1st line	2nd line	Middle
College Hires				
'Potential middle manager'	62	1	30	31
'Not potential middle manager'	63	7	49	7
Non-college hires				
'Potential middle manager'	41	3	23	15
'Not potential middle manager'	103	61	37	5
All combined				
'Potential middle manager'	103	4	53	46
'Not potential middle manager'	166	68	86	12

to have a very high false negative rate; 46 per cent of 'unacceptable' candidates nevertheless succeeded as first-level managers. False negatives matter more in promotion than in selection. A rejected applicant can apply elsewhere, whereas an employee turned down for promotion he/she really merits stays in the organization, and may start getting resentful.

A later review by Cohen *et al.* (1974) reported median correlations for three criteria:

performance ratings	$r = 0.33$
promotion achieved	$r = 0.40$
rating of potential for further promotion	$r = 0.63$

Hunter and Hunter (1984) correct the median for performance ratings for attenuation, increasing it to $r = 0.43$, which is the value they quote in their 'final league table' for promotion decisions. ACs come last in the 'league table', for promotion decisions. ACs come last in that 'league table', below work sample tests, ability composites, peer ratings, behavioural consistency experience ratings, and job knowledge tests. However the range from best to worst was very small: 0.54 to 0.43; all methods of deciding who to promote are fairly successful. Too few researches using ACs for initial selection have been reported to calculate their place in that 'league table'. British data, especially from CSSB, suggests ACs have good predictive validity in selection also.

Schmitt *et al.* (1984) calculate average validities for assessment centres against four criteria:

performance ratings	$r = 0.43$
achievement/grades	$r = 0.31$

status change $r = 0.41$
wages $r = 0.24$

pooled $r = 0.41$

Schmitt *et al.* corrected for sampling error, but not for criterion reliability. Their estimate for 'true' validity of ACs predicting performance ratings is exactly the same as Hunter and Hunter's—$r = 0.43$. The two analyses overlap to some extent, but Schmitt *et al.* include only studies published in *Journal of Applied Psychology* and *Personnel Psychology*, whereas Cohen *et al.*'s review (which Hunter and Hunter re-analysed) included many unpublished researches. (Too much research on AC validity remains unpublished, and only accessible to the general reader through reviews, some of which aren't very detailed.)

Civil Service Selection Board (UK)

The most senior ranks of the UK Civil Service have been selected since 1945 by CSSB: group discussion, written 'appreciation' of a problem, committee exercise, 'individual problem', short talk, interview and second group discussion, as well as an extensive battery of intelligence tests. Vernon (1950) reported predictive validity data for successful applicants, after 2 years, using supervisor ratings as criterion. CSSB was highly selective—only 1 in 15 were accepted—so Vernon corrected for restricted range. Table 9.2 shows CSSB achieved good predictive validity. The correlations listed in Table 9.2 are not independent, but *cumulative*, representing validity after assessors had seen each exercise. CSSB's overall validity coefficient was high. However, CSSB wasn't the final hurdle; those who passed CSSB faced a Final Selection Board; CSSB could *reject* but not accept. Predictive validity of the Final Selection Board was slightly better ($r = 0.56$).

Anstey (1977) continued to follow up Vernon's sample, until the mid-1970s, when many were nearing retirement. Using achieved rank as criterion, Anstey

Table 9.2. Predictive validity of CSSB, and its components, after 2 years (Vernon, 1950) (Reproduced by permission)

	Observer	Psychologist	Chairman
First discussion	26	34	36
Appreciation	—	—	31
Committee	42	34	41
Individual problem	35	36	42
Short talk	40	—	47
Interview	42	42	48
Second discussion	32	—	—
Final mark	44	49	49

reported an eventual predictive validity, after 30 years, that was amazingly good (r = 0.66, corrected for restricted range). Anstey admits achieved rank and CSSB ratings aren't indpendent, so 'criterion contamination' exists, but argues that CSSB rating wouldn't influence opinion for more than 2 or 3 years, after which 'departments would have formed their own opinions'. All but 21 of 301 CSSB 'graduates' in Anstey's analysis achieved 'Assistant Secretary' rank, showing they 'made the grade' as senior Civil Servants; only three left because of 'definite inefficiency'.

Admiralty Interview Board

Royal Navy officers are selected by individual and group 'command' tasks, group discussions, short talks, interview and an extensive battery of intelligence tests. Gardner and Williams (1973) review the Board's first 25 years, and find the Board's mark correlated very poorly with three indices of speed of promotion (Table 9.3). Adding the results of exams in maths, physics and English to the Board's rating increased the correlations slightly. However the correlations in Table 9.3 weren't corrected for restricted range, test reliability or criterion reliability, so underestimate the Board's true validity.

Table 9.3. Results of the Admiralty Interview Board (Gardner and Williams, 1973) (n = 269)

	Criteria		
	TLCDR	SINDA	SINDB
Ability tests (8)	0.26	ns	ns
Examination	0.35	ns	ns
Board mark	0.22	0.15	0.14
Board mark + exam	0.40	0.12	0.16

TLCDR = 'time to promotion to lieutenant-commander'; this is actually a 'training' criterion, because all officers are promoted to lieutenant-commander. Officers who do better in training get more seniority, so are promoted sooner.

SINDA = time to be promoted to commander.

SINDB = time to be promoted to commander + length of service. This criterion allows for officers who leave the service.
ns = Not significant.

AC compared with other tests

Several studies show ACs achieve better validity than psychological tests. Vernon (1950) found CSSB's test battery had poor predictive validity. Similarly the Admiralty Board found tests alone gave poorer predictions than the whole procedure (Gardner and Williams, 1973). American studies confirm British findings; in particular School and College Aptitude Test has been shown several times to have much poorer predictive validity than an AC (Bray and Campbell, 1968; Moses and Boehm, 1975).

But sometimes other methods are *better* than ACs. Campbell *et al.* (1970) compared AC with a combination of ability test, personality and Biodata, as predictors of managerial effectiveness in Standard Oil Company of New Jersey. The test and Biodata package predicted advancement or effectiveness better than an AC, and was of course much cheaper. Hinrichs (1978) found assessments of management potential from personnel records had predictive validity as good as an AC. Rating potential from personnel records is very cheap, and can be done without the canditate knowing he/she is being assessed (but presupposes the employer keeps good records).

Reservations about AC validity

Narrow data base

While ACs have been used very widely in the USA, the published validity studies derive from relatively few organizations: American Telegraph and Telephone, IBM, Union Carbide, SOHIO, Rohem and Haas, a few state governments, and some hospitals. In Britain published validity data derive almost entirely from WOSB, CSSB and Admiralty Boards.

Criterion contamination

Only two American studies are free from *criterion contamination*, because only those two kept AC results secret until calculating the validity coefficient (Sackett, 1982). The two studies are the original AT&T Management Progress Study, and AT&T's salesmen AC (Bray and Campbell, 1968). The latter rated salesmen's performance during actual sales calls, without knowing the earlier AC rating. The AC had divided salesmen into unacceptable, acceptable and 'more than acceptable'; 24, 68 and 100 per cent of each group were rated as making acceptable sales calls. The correlation between predictor and criterion was high.

Criterion contamination can be blantant: candidate returns from the AC with a good rating and so gets promoted. Or it can be subtle: candidates who have 'done well' at the AC are deemed suitable for more challenging tasks, so 'develop' more. *Criterion contamination* occurs more readily when ACs are used to promote or 'develop' staff; it's really a form of 'self-fulfilling prophecy'. In selection ACs only the candidate is likely to know how many times he/she has been rejected. But one he/she is accepted, a good rating can 'stick', and help him/her progress.

'Face fits'

Critics comment on the 'curious homogeneity in the criteria used for this [validity] research', namely 'salary growth or progress (often corrected for starting salary), promotions above first level, management level achieved and supervisor's ratings of potential' (Klimoski and Strickland, 1977). These criteria 'may have less to do with managerial effectiveness than managerial adaptation and survival'. Klimoski and Strickland suggest ACs pick up the personal mannerisms that top management use in promotion, which may not have much to do with actual effectiveness. They even use the word 'conspiracy'. ACs answer the question 'Does his/her face fit?'

Klimoski and Strickland complain that few studies use less suspect criteria. Cohen *et al.*'s (1974) review finds AC ratings predicted *actual job performance* moderately well, but predicted *higher management ratings of management potential* much better. A later study by Klimoski and Strickland (1981, cited in Hunter and Hunter, 1984) used three predictors, including an AC rating, to predict three criteria, 3 years on, in 140 managers. The AC rating predicted who got promoted, and who got rated as having potential, but not who performed well (Table 9.4). Future rating of performance was only predicted by past rating of performance. On the other hand, Schmitt *et al.*'s review (1984) concludes ACs predict performance ratings *as well as* 'status change', and better than wages. Schmitt *et al.*'s review does confirm Klimoski's argument that 'Face fits' criteria are more popular for ACs. Twelve coefficients, based on 14,662 subjects, used 'status change' and 'wages' criteria, whereas only six coefficients, based on a mere 394 subjects, used performance ratings.

Table 9.4. Validity of three predictors, of three criteria, after 3 years, for 140 managers (Klimoski and Strickland, 1981)

	Criteria		
Predictor	Grade achieved	Rated potential	Rated performance
Rated potential for promotion	0.14	0.51	0.08
Rated current performance	0.06	0.10	0.38
AC rating	0.34	0.37	–0.02

Ritchie and Moses (1983) compared women who had been recommended for promotion after an AC, with ones who hadn't. AC rating correlated with achieved promotion in both 'recommended' and 'non-recommended' groups, which implies AC ratings aren't necessarily a 'self-fulfilling prophecy'. Some women who came back from the AC labelled 'low management potential' still managed to get promoted, and within the restricted range of women rejected for promotion, those who succeeded had been given better AC ratings.

Validity of individual exercises

Bray and Grant (1966) report the contribution of exercises in the AT&T Management Progress Study for *subsets* of subjects only, making it very hard to determine their value overall. They also report the contribution of each exercise to overall ratings, showing that Group Discussion, Manufacturing Problem, and 'In-Basket' correlate with Staff Rating better than do psychological tests. Borman (1982) found five exercises for army recruiting staff all achieved equally moderate validities, perhaps because scores on all five intercorrelated moderately well. There is surprisingly little research on this issue, perhaps because most ACs use the same observers throughout, which makes independent assessment of different exercises difficult. Order of component exercises—In-Basket, supervising incompetent 'assistants', preparing and presenting a case, and two discussion groups—in the AC makes no difference (Cohen and Sands, 1978).

Differences between assessors

An unpublished study by Thompson (cited in Sackett, 1982) found no differences between psychologists and managers. Borman *et al.* (1983) report a more sophisticated analysis than simply comparing each assessor's accuracy with every other's—which makes it fairly difficult *not* to find a difference. They compared the distribution of accuracy scores, with 'random rating–criterion pairs . . . disregarding which assessor had rated the subject', and concluded there is no evidence of true differences between assessors.

Cost

ACs are expensive. ACs usually have one assessor for every two candidates, with a ratio of six assessors to twelve candidates being most typical. Cascio and Silbey (1979) estimate the cost of planning exercises and training assessors at $3200, and the cost of running the AC (staff time, subsistence, etc.) at $2166, plus $198 (subsistence, expenses) per candidate. So a single AC for ten candidates could cost, at 1978 prices, $7346, if held on the organization's own premises. Running costs for a British AC, using hotels, have been estimated at £730 per candidate, and development costs of £12,000 (1978 prices). The difference in value between good and bad employees (Chapter 1) makes these high costs well worth while, especially as the AC achieves fairly high validity. Moses (1973) describes a programme called Early Identification Assessment, an abbreviated form of AT&T's AC for supervisors, that works well and is much cheaper.

What ACs can assess

The layman, especially a committee of such, naturally tends to multiply the dimensions to be rated; the psychologist knows this is a mistake, because factor analysis will almost always find most contribute very little new information. The AT&T study found 25 ratings yielded only eight factors. Vernon (1950) reached the same conclusion some years before; one factor accounted for most of the variance in CSSB ratings.

Sackett and Dreher (1982) analyse ratings on a number of scales, across a number of exercises; Table 9.5 shows ratings of *different dimensions* made after the *same exercise* correlated very highly. In two of the three organizations studied, ratings of the *same trait in different exercises* hardly correlated at all. When the ratings were factor-analysed the factors clearly identified *exercises*, not *traits*. The ACs weren't measuring general decisiveness across a range of management tasks; they were measuring *general performance* on each of four or six tasks. But if decisiveness in Task A doesn't generalize to decisiveness in Task B, how can one be sure it will generalize to decisiveness on the job? In the third organization, ratings of the same trait in different exercises *did* correlate reasonably well, but only because there was pervasive 'halo' in all the ratings. Ratings, of any trait, on any exercise, tended to correlate fairly well. Turnage and Muchinsky (1982) analysed ratings of over 2000 people, on eight traits, across five exercises, and found candidates were rated globally, so ratings of individual traits contributed little extra information. They also found that such limited differentiation as was recorded centred on *exercises* rather than *traits*, confirming Sackett and Dreher's results.

Table 9.5. Multi-Trait Multi-Method Analysis of three assessment centres (Sackett & Dreher, 1982)

	Organization		
	A	B	C
Number of *traits* rated	7	15	9
Number of exercises included	6	4	6
Average intercorrelation of ratings of:			
Different traits within *Same exercise*	0.64	0.40	0.65
Same trait across *Different exercises*	0.07	0.11	0.51

Russell (1985) analysed ratings in sixteen dimensions, plus an Overall Assessment Rating. The sixteen dimensions covered four main areas:

personal qualities,
interpersonal skills,
problem-solving skills,
communication skills,

so each assessor's ratings would ideally yield four corresponding factors. In practice they didn't. Five of the ten assessors' ratings yielded only two or three factors. Furthermore, all ten assessors' ratings yielded one very large factor, four times as big as any other, and identifiable as:

'interpersonal skills' for 5/10 assessors,
'problem-solving skills' for 4/10,
'cognitive ability' for the tenth.

Assessors didn't rate the four dimensions defined by the AC's planners, but used their own individual categories.

Bias

American AC practice emphasizes the importance of the assessors achieving consensus after discussing the candidates (Cohen, 1978). Sackett and Wilson (1982) refer to 'Abundant anecdotal evidence of vice-presidents serving as assessors and exerting considerable influence on consensus decisions'; research on conformity, not to mention common sense, suggests such anecdotes reflect reality. Sackett and Wilson found a simple two-stage decision rule predicted 94.5 per cent of all consensus decisions:

(a) if three assessors (of four) agree on a rating, that value is taken as final;
(b) otherwise the mean of assessors' ratings, rounded to the nearest whole number, is taken as final.

This implies the consensus discussion may often be redundant. Sackett and Wilson suggest the 'disassembled assessment center', in which assessors never meet, but separately view and rate videotapes of AC exercises. However Cook's Law—the more important the decision, the more time must be taken, or must *be seen to be taken*, to reach it—implies discussion will never be abandoned or replaced.

American ACs often use the AT&T model, in which assessors 'observe and record' behaviour, but don't make any evaluations until after all exercises are complete, when assessors share observations and rate candidates. This procedure avoids one sort of biasing order effect—'first impressions'—at the expense of risking another—recency effects.

'FAIR' EMPLOYMENT AND THE ASSESSMENT CENTRE

The AC is often regarded as fair or even 'EEOC-proof', but no selection procedure is exempt. However ACs have been recommended, or even ordered, by courts as 'alternative procedures' (Chapter 12).

Sex

Schein (1975) argues most employers see successful managers as having characteristics, attitudes and temperaments more typical of males than females,
which implies ACs may be biased against women. However ACs don't seem to
create *adverse impact*—as many women as men 'pass'. A large-scale follow up to
1600 female entry-level managers in Bell Telephone found ratings of middle-
management potential predicted achieved rank 7 years later as well as AT&T's
study of male managers (Ritchie and Moses, 1983). Moses and Boehm (1975)
report AC data from AT&T for 4846 women and 8885 men which showed no
adverse impact at all. Table 9.6 shows predictive validity was equally good for
women and men.

Table 9.6. Men and women passing through
AT&T assessment centres (Moses and
Boehm, 1975)

	Women	Men
Total number	4846	8885
More than acceptable	6.1	7.2
Acceptable	28.1	25.6
Questionable	29.0	32.7
Not acceptable	36.8	34.5

Race

An assessment centre for white and non-white female supervisors created some
adverse impact—fewer non-whites 'passed' (Huck and Bray, 1976). Non-whites
got poorer ratings for Administrative Skills, Sensitivity and Effective
Intelligence, but not for Interpersonal Effectiveness. However AC results
predicted job performance equally well for both non-white and white, and
predicted rated potential for advancement for both non-white and white equally
well; the method was proved valid despite adverse impact. In 'mixed' ACs—
male, female, white, non-white—Schmitt and Hill (1977) found a very small
tendency for non-white women to get poorer ratings on forcefulness, communications skills, and for group exercises, if there are more white males
present. Schmitt and Hill note the results are not really significant, either
statistically or practically, but suggest that the *possibility* of bias arising from
group composition is sufficiently serious to merit further investigation.

Age

AC ratings sometimes show small negative correlations with age, which may
create problems in the USA, where it's legally 'unfair' to discriminate against
candidates over 40.

The AC has high 'face' or 'content' validity (Chapters 11 and 12), which probably accounts for much of its popularity, and also probably does give it a measure of protection against EEO claims. Presenting a speech, fighting one's case in a committee, chairing a meeting, answering an 'in-tray', or leading a squad, all have obvious, easily defended 'job-relevance'; they're almost work samples.

CONCLUSIONS

The assessment centre is often referred to as the 'Rolls-Royce' of selection methods. It's certainly expensive, but is it worth the money?

Its advocates, of course, say it's very good value. Some argue assessment centres work precisely because they are expensive. They're expensive because they last a long time, because they typically employ six trained assessors and because they include a wide range of different assessment methods. A range of assessors and assessment methods reduces bias, and gives candidates more chance to expose their strengths and weaknesses. Length gets behind candidates' fronts, to find out what they're really like, or else—if you're a role theorist—they pick those who can play the role of manager indefinitely.

Assessment centres also have the great virtue, these days, of being fairly 'safe'. They look 'fair'; they look plausible; they include samples of the job. They give people a chance to prove themselves. A selection method that's 'fair' *and* accurate can be forgiven for being expensive.

Critics have argued that assessment centres perpetuate the *status quo*, picking managers whose 'faces fit', filling the organization with carbon-copies of top management, if not with yes-men and sycophants. This may be a problem, if top managers are out of date or incompetent. On the other hand this 'criticism' could be interpreted as praise; selecting carbon-copies of present management is better than selecting at random, which is all some methods can achieve.

Other critics might complain the assessment centres are an elaborate charade. WOSB started life as a 'cover plan' to get the Army to use intelligence tests, but military perversity, and Cook's Law, ensured all the elaborate, item-wasting elements survived, or even prospered. Perhaps ability tests contribute most of the AC's predictive validity (although several studies prove otherwise). Or perhaps cheaper, less elaborate elements of the assessment centre are what makes it work.

The fact is—we don't know why ACs work so well. It's an increasingly derided tradition for psychologists to conclude every research paper by saying 'More research is needed'. But sometimes more research really *is* needed: analysis of AC validity is a prime candidate. If we knew which elements of the AC contribute to its success we could improve its predictive accuracy still further, *or* reduce the AC's length and expense, or perhaps achieve both at once.

CHAPTER 10

Miscellaneous Methods

Education, work samples, physique and self-ratings

There are six classes of miscellaneous selection 'test' that don't fit neatly into any other main category.

EDUCATION

Employers in Britain often specify so many 'O' and 'A' level passes; professional training schemes almost always do. American employers used to require high school graduation. Booth *et al.* (1978) suggest people who do well at school are more able, mature and more highly motivated, so they fit into work more easily. It's a lot easier and cheaper to ask how well someone did at school, than to try to assess ability, maturity and motivation. It's important to distinguish *duration* of education from *achievement*; staying at school or college a long time proves less than passing exams or getting good grades.

Amount of education doesn't predict productivity very well. Research in the American petroleum industry concludes mere *duration* of education has zero predictive validity (Dunnette, 1972). However *duration* of education does predict 'survival' in recruits to the US Navy. American college 'Grade Point Averages' (marks from exams and coursework) correlate moderately with training grades, but hardly at all with supervisor ratings (O'Leary, 1980). Education predicts performance ratings in the American armed services very moderately, whereas it predicts 'suitability' ratings rather better (Vineberg and Joyner, 1982); this suggests better-educated individuals make a better impression but don't necessarily perform any better.

Reilly and Chao (1982) summarize research on predictive validity of educational *achievement*, usually Grade Point Average in school or college. Achievement predicted supervisor ratings relatively poorly ($r = 0.14$). Educational achievement predicted 'adjusted compensation' rather better ($r = 0.27$). Harrell *et al.* (1977) found MBA grades predicted earnings after 5 years very well, and earnings after 10 years quite well. However Reilly and Chao caution these correlations may be an artefact; quite often grades set initial salary and so initiate a self-fulfilling prophecy.

Education 'tests' have fallen foul of American 'fair' employment laws in a big way. Some US minorities do poorly at school, so far more of them fail to complete high school. Minimum education requirements may have the effect, perhaps sometimes even the intention, of excluding non-whites. The employer then has to prove the job really needs the educational level or qualifications specified. Meritt-Haston and Wexley's (1983) review of 83 US court cases found educational requirements were generally ruled unlawful for skilled or craft jobs, supervisors and management trainees, but were accepted for the police and for 'professors'. American universities can still, legally, require their teaching staff to have degrees.

Certification/Licensing

You can't practise medicine without being a member of the British or American Medical Association. Medicine, law and a few other professions have established a 'closed shop'. Other professions would like to do the same—personnel management, estate agency (real estate), psychology (in Britain)—but haven't yet succeeded. Anyone can set up in business as a psychologist in Britain. Entrants to some professions in America face a double hurdle; doctors and lawyers must pass degree exams, and also pass state certification exams. The 'validity' of degree exams tends to be taken for granted; common sense says a doctor must have passed medical school. State certification exams, however, have been accused of creating adverse impact, and being 'unfair'. Non-whites tend to fail certification exams for law and teaching more often than whites; they argue the exams are unreliably marked, subject to bias, and have 'no demonstrated validity against criteria of actual law practice' (Ash and Kroeker, 1975).

TRAINING AND EXPERIENCE RATINGS

Also known as: T&E Ratings, E&T Ratings, Traex exam, and Unassembled examination. A rating of applicant's background, by staff member or committee, very commonly used in public sector in USA. T&E ratings are commonly used for jobs requiring specialized backgrounds: engineering, scientific and research. T&E ratings would be useful for selecting academics, but aren't used in Britain. T&E ratings are also useful for trade jobs, where written tests unfairly weight verbal skills. T&E ratings aren't suitable for entry-level jobs where no prior training and skill are required. T&E ratings may create adverse impact on women and non-whites who lack training and experience, but otherwise are rarely the subject of 'fair employment' complaints. Hunter and Hunter's (1984) validity generalization analysis includes 65 validity coefficients for T&E ratings, without giving further detail, and finds a mean 'true' validity of $r = 0.13$. T&E ratings proved fairly ineffective as a selection test, coming seventh of 11 tests analysed.

Hough *et al.* (1983) develop the conventional application form or CV into the 'Accomplishment Record', in which the applicant describes his/her achievements, giving 'a general statement of what was accomplished, a detailed description of exactly what was done, the time period over which the accomplishment was carried out, any formal recognition gained as a result of the achievement (e.g. awards, citations, etc.), and name and address of a person who could verify the information provided'. So far just a typical CV, but with two important differences: (a) the applicant describes accomplishments in eight job areas derived from 'criticial incident analysis' (Chapter 3), and (b) the Accomplishment Record is rated on 'behaviourally anchored' scales (Chapter 5).

Hough *et al.*'s Accomplishment Record was written for lawyers: a high score for *Researching/Investigating* was given to

> I assumed major responsibility for conducting an industry wide investigation of the [deleted] industry and for preparation of a memorandum in support of complaint against the three largest members of the industry ... I obtained statistical data from every large and medium [deleted] industry in the US and from a selection of small [deleted]. ... I deposed [got statements from] *many* employees of [deleted] manufacturers and renters. I received a Meritorious Service award.

A low score on *Researching/Investigating* went to:

> My research involved checking reference books, LEXIS, and telephone interviews with various people—individuals, state officials, etc.

The ratings were highly reliable, and correlated very highly with criterion ratings.

SELF-ASSESSMENTS

Allport once said 'if you want to know about someone, why not ask him? He might tell you.' Self-assessments ask people for a direct estimate of their potential. The CPI Dominance scale infers dominance from the answers people give to 40 questions; a self assessment gets straight to the point: 'How dominant are you?'—on a seven-point scale. A typing test takes half an hour to test your typing skill; a self-assessment simply asks 'How good a typist are you?'

Ash (1980) compared a standard typing test with typists' ratings of their own skill. Ash's best result ($r = 0.59$) suggested Allport was right; people are quite good judges of their own abilities. However Ash's other correlations, for typing letters, tables, figures and revisions, were nowhere near so promising. Levine *et al.* (1977) found self-assessments of spelling, reading speed, comprehension, grammer, etc., correlated rather poorly with supervisor rating. DeNisi and Shaw (1977) measured ten cognitive abilities—mechanical comprehension, spatial orientation, visual pursuit, etc.—and compared test scores with self-assessments;

correlations were very low, suggesting self-assessment couldn't be substituted for tests. Self-assessments have also been used in a battery of tests for bus drivers; Baehr *et al.*'s (unpublished, see Reilly and Chao) self-assesssments were much more elaborate: 72 items, based on a job analysis, and factored down to thirteen scores. Baehr described the self-assessment as one of the two best predictors.

Reilly and Chao's analysis (1982) found the overall validity of self-assessments very low ($r = 0.15$). Mabe and West (1982) analyse 43 studies, and report a much higher mean 'true' validity ($r = 0.42$), partly because they correct for predictor and criterion reliability. They conclude self-assessments had highest validity when given anonymously—not a lot of use to the selector—or when subjects were told self-assessments would be compared with objective tests—which means either giving a test or lying to the subject. Self-assessments also worked better when subjects were used to them, or when subjects were comparing themselves with fellow-workers, which again makes them impractical for selection.

Levine *et al.* (1977) think self-assessments aren't used, because employers suppose people can't or won't give accurate estimates of their abilities. They tested the 'faking' hypothesis by comparing self-assessments of people who knew their typing ability would be tested, with people who had no such expectation. The two sets of self-assessments didn't differ, implying people weren't faking. Other studies however (Ash, 1980) found people overestimated their abilities.

WORK SAMPLE TESTS

Work sample tests used not to be very highly thought of. Guion's (1965a) book on personnel testing devoted just over three pages to work sample tests. McClelland (1973) argues the case for them: 'If you want to test who will be a good policeman, go find out what a policeman does. Follow him around, make a list of his activities, and sample from that list in screening applicants.'

Work sample tests are justified by *behavioural consistency* theory, which argues 'past behaviour is the best predictor of future behaviour' and that 'like predicts like'. Asher and Sciarrino (1974) explain that 'point-to-point correspondence between predictor and criterion' will ensure higher validity, and—perhaps more important these days—less scope for legal challenge. Intelligence tests assess the applicant's *general* suitability and make an intermediate inference—this person is intelligent so he/she will be good at widget-stamping. Testing the employee with a real or simulated widget-stamper makes no such inference (nor is widget-stamping ability quite such an emotive issue as general intellectual ability).

Campion (1972) devised a work sample test for maintenance mechanics. After a thorough job analysis he selected four tasks: installing pulleys and belts, disassembling and repairing a gear box, installing and aligning a motor, pressing a bush into a sprocket and reaming it to fit a shaft. Campion used three supervisor rating criteria: uses of tools, accuracy of work and overall mechanical ability. Campion compared the work sample test with a battery of paper-and-pencil tests: Bennett, Wonderlic, Short Employment Tests (Verbal, Numerical and Clerical Aptitude). The work samples predicted fairly well, whereas the paper-and-pencil tests did very poorly.

Campion describes a classic work sample test, of the type used in Europe and Britain in the 1920s and 1930s, and applied on a large scale in wartime testing programmes. The scope of 'work sample' has widened somewhat in the last 15–20 years. Robertson and Kandola (1982) distinguish four classes of 'work sample':

Psychomotor:	Typing, sewing, using tools.
Individual decision-making:	In-Tray test (see below)
Job-related information tests.	
Group Discussions/Decisions.	

The 'Psychomotor' category covers the classic work sample; In-Tray and group exercises extend the principle to jobs which don't need motor skills. 'Job-related information test' is another name for 'trade test', and hasn't really much in common with a true work sample. Calling a trade test a 'work sample' has the possible advantage of making it more acceptable.

Cascio and Phillips (1979) describe 21 work samples for municipal employees in Miami Beach, covering a wide range of manual, clerical and administrative jobs, from electrician's helper (mate) to parking-meter technician, from library assistant to concession attendant. Applicants for concession attendant were tested on site, out of hours: counting cash, giving change, completing revenue reports, making announcements and dealing with irate customers. Cascio and Phillips argue the tests were very convincing to the applicants. If applicants for electrician had completed the wiring test correctly the lights lit up; if the wiring wasn't correct the bulbs didn't light, and the applicant couldn't deny he/she had made a mistake. Some of the tests had 'realistic job preview' (Chapter 2) built in; quite a few applicants for the post of sewer mechanic withdrew after being tested in an underground sewage chamber. Gordon and Kleiman (1976) claim applicants tested by work sample are better motivated to accept the job than those tested by cognitive ability tests. Cascio and Phillips took the, for psychologists, unusual step of working out how much their tests cost, and arrived at an average figure of $675 to plan each one, and $262 to test a batch of applicants.

Asher and Sciarrino's (1974) review finds work samples better than intelligence and personality tests. Schmitt *et al.* (1984) report a validity generalization analysis for work samples, based on research published in the *Journal of Applied Psychology* and *Personnel Psychology*. They find a 'true' validity (corrected for sampling error only) of $r = 0.38$, one of the higher 'true' validities they report. Dunnette's (1972) analysis of tests in the American petroleum industry found work samples achieved similar validities for Operating and Processing, Maintenance, and Clerical jobs. Hunter and Hunter (1984) find work samples the best test ($r = 0.54$) by a short head, for promotion decisions where, however, all tests give fairly good results. They don't say how many studies contributed to the estimate, nor what type of work sample.

Robertson and Kandola (1982) review validity of work samples from a wider body of research, taking in US wartime researchers, and British research. Median validity for 'Psycho-motor' work samples is quite good ($r = 0.39$) with, however, a very wide range. Robertson and Kandola don't calculate a validity generalization analysis, nor do they appear to have corrected for any source of error, so their median is likely to be an underestimate of 'true' validity. Median validities for job knowledge tests, group exercises and In Baskets are comparable to 'motor' work samples, although job knowledge tests predict training grades much better than job performance.

'Classic' work samples can only be used if the person already has the job's skills; it's clearly pointless giving a typing test to someone who can't type. (Whereas In-Trays and group exercises don't presuppose any special knowledge, skill or experience.) *Trainability tests* are a subtype of work sample, that assess how well the applicant can *learn* a new skill. Trainability tests are widely used in 'Skillcentres' run by the (UK) Manpower Services Commission (Robertson and Downs, 1979). The instructor gives standardized instructions and a demonstration, then rates the trainee's efforts, using a checklist (Table 10.1). Robertson and Downs reports good results for bricklaying, carpentry, welding, machine sewing, forklift truck driving, fitting, machining and even dentistry.

Table 10.1. Part of checklist for trainability test for centre lathe operation (Robertson and Downs, 1979) (Reproduced by permission)

Doesn't tighten chuck sufficiently
Doesn't select correct tool
Doesn't use coolant
Dosen't set calibrations to zero
Doesn't mark lengths on slide

Similar American research on 'miniature training and evaluations', shows subjects how to do something, gives them a chance to practise, then tests them (Siegel, 1978). Siegel's validity data, on small samples, are unimpressive, but he finds the procedure popular with subjects: 'Gave me a chance to prove that I could do some things with my hands, not just my head'. Reilly and Manese (1979) uses trainability tests to select staff for American Telegraph and Telephone's electronic switching system. Performance in seven self-paced lessons

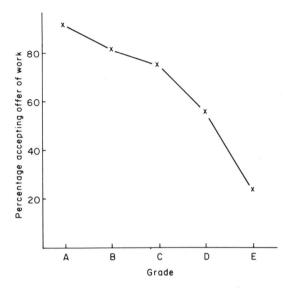

Figure 10.1. Proportion of applicants accepting job offer, after taking trainability test, for each applicant's grade obtained on the test. NB: They were not told the test scores, nor were the test scores used to decide who to make offers to. Data from Downs *et al.* (1978).

predicted time to complete training moderately well. Reilly and Manese present no data on the validity of other tests; 'electronic switching' needs programming skills, so perhaps the Programmer Aptitude Test, which achieves a 'true' validity of 0.91 for training grades (Chapter 7), would do as well, or better, and take less time.

People doing trainability tests can assess their own performance, even though they aren't told the results. Applicants for machine sewing jobs selected themselves for the job (Figure 10.1). Scores on a sewing machine trainability test weren't used to select, but high scorers took up sewing jobs, while low scorers generally did not (Downs *et al.*, 1978).

'Fair employment'

Work samples are currently popular becaue they're 'alternatives' to legally risky ability tests. Are work samples really 'fairer'? Cascio and Phillip's Miami Beach work samples passed as many blacks and Hispanics as whites. Other studies (Gordon and Kleiman, 1976) similarly report work samples create less adverse impact than aptitude or intelligence tests. The 'work samples' in question appear to be paper-and-pencil job knowledge tests. Work samples also create less adverse impact than trade tests; Schmidt *et al.* think trade tests create more adverse impact because they rely more on verbal ability. However, the samples studied are often small: Schmidt *et al.* (1977) compared work sample and trade test for 58 white and 29 non-white metal trades apprentices. Chapter 7 emphasizes how risky it is to draw firm conclusions from small numbers. One study, using a large sample ($n = 450$), did find adverse impact on non-whites (Schoenfeldt *et al.*, 1976).

IN-TRAY TESTS

Applicants deal with a set of letters, memos, notes, reports and phone messages (Figure 10.2). Applicants are instructed to *act on* the items, not *write about* them, but are limited to written replies by the assumption it's Sunday, and they depart shortly for a week's holiday or business trip abroad. The In-Tray is a management work sample—but doesn't need mastery of specific skills, so can be used for graduate recruitment. In-Tray content can be varied to suit the job. The candidate's performance is usually rated (a) overall and (b) item by item. The overall evaluation checks whether the candidate sorts the items into high and low priority, and notices any connections between items. The In-Tray was invented in 1957 by Frederiksen *et al.*, as part of a *training* programme for USAAF officers, was later adopted by American Telegraph and Telephone, and now features in most assessment centres.

In-Tray tests can be scored with acceptable reliability by trained assessors, and achieve reasonable validity. AT&T's Management Progress Study found In-Tray predicted salary level 5 years later, for college-educated subjects and non-college subjects. Wollowick and McNamara (1969) report similar results from the IBM assessment programme. In-Tray performance predicts supervisory effectiveness moderately well ($r = 0.24$ to 0.34) (Brass and Oldham, 1976). Robertson and Kandola (1982) summarize 53 validity coefficients for 'individual, situation decision-making' tests, which include an unspecified number of In-Trays. Median validity, apparently uncorrected for restricted range or limited reliability, was quite high. Several studies (Bray and Grant, 1966; Wollowick and McNamara, 1969) find In-Trays add new information, and don't just cover the same ground as tests of verbal ability or general intelligence. Lopez (1966) compared trainees and experienced AT&T managers; trainees were wordier, grasped fewer implications for the organization, were *less* considerate to others and less alert to important issues. Trainees' decisions were poorer; they *either* reached a final decision too soon without getting all the facts, *or* they delegated decisions entirely to others, without any follow-up.

The In-Tray's main shortcomings arise from the 'Sunday afternoon' asumption; writing replies in a deserted office may be quite unlike dealing with the same issues face-to-face or by telephone on a hectic Monday morning.

IBT/1

From: V Wordy MICE CEMH FIME (Engineering Director)

To: I Prior (Asst Gen Mgr)

I am in receipt of your memorandum of 15th November concerning the necessity for more rapid progress on the revised layout of Number 4 component assembly area and am fully cognisant of the urgency of this matter myself. My strenuous efforts in this respect are not however being assisted by the calibre of some of the personnel allocated to myself for this purpose. A particular obstacle with which I am currently faced lies in the persistent absenteeism of certain members of the workforce who appear to have little interest in contributing an effort commensurate to their present rates of pay. The designated complement of shop floor workers for Assembly Area 4 under the new establishment of 5th October is just adequate for the Area's requisites *on the strict understanding that the full complement are in fact present and available for work* as opposed for example to reading newspapers in the works canteen or absenting themselves for lengthy smoking breaks in the male toilet facilities. Efforts on the part of myself and my foremen to instill a sense of purpose and discipline into a workforce sadly lacking any semblance of either have not so far I am sorry to say received what I would consider adequate backing from the management. I would like to bring to your attention *for your immediate executive action* a particularly blatant case which fully merits in my estimation the immediate dismissal of the employee concerned. Yesterday our revised November schedule calls for us to be securing the transfer of Number III lathe from its former position to its new location some 35 metres nearer the North

Figure 10.2. A sample item from an 'In-Tray' test.

Attempts to add telephones to In-Tray haven't really caught on. Tests that require people to *write* things they normally *say* to others have been criticized by 'fair' employment agencies both sides of the Atlantic.

PHYSICAL TESTS AND APPEARANCE

Some jobs require strength, agility or endurance. Some jobs require, or are felt to require, physical size. Some jobs require dexterity. For some jobs attractive appearance is, explicitly or implicitly, a requirement.

Strength

Tests of physique or strength are used in Britain, usually in an arbitrary, haphazard way. Fire brigades require firemen to climb a ladder carrying a weight. Other employers rely on the company medical checkup, or an 'eyeball' test by personnel manager or foreman.

Some North American employers use physical tests much more systematically. Armco Inc. use a battery of physical work sample tests for labourers, and have extensive data on norms, correlations and sex differences (Arnold *et al.*, 1982). The Du Pont corporation also use physical tests for production workers. American Telephone and Telegraph have developed a battery of three tests for pole-climbing—an assential part of many AT&T jobs (Reilly *et al.*, 1979); employees with good balance, adequate 'static strength' (pulling on a rope) and higher 'body density' (less fat, more muscle) did better in training, and were more likely to 'survive' at least 6 months. The US army loses 9 per cent of recruits during basic training because they aren't up to it physically; more specialized arms, like US Navy underwater bomb disposal, lose over 50 per cent (Hogan, 1985). Hogan finds three tests—1-mile run, sit and reach test and arm ergometer muscle endurance—reduce wastage in bomb disposal training considerably.

Measures of physique and physical performance often intercorrelate very highly; Reilly *et al.* started with fourteen, and found only three necessary. Hogan started with 26, and again found only three necessary. Fleishman (1979) factor-analysed a very wide range of physical tasks and concludes there are nine factors (see Note 1, Chapter 3) underlying 'physical proficiency' (Table 10.2). Fleishman developed *Physical Abilities Analysis*, a profile of the physical abilities needed for a job. Some US organizations employ work physiologists to measure the *oxygen uptake* each job demands, and select people whose 'aerobic' (oxygen uptake) capacity, measured by treadmill, exercise bicycle or step test, is adequate (Campion, 1983).

Schmitt *et al.* (1984) report a validity generalization analysis of tests of physique, and find a 'true' validity of $r = 0.32$. Of 22 validities analysed, fifteen

Table 10.2. The nine factors underlying human physical ability, according to Fleishman (1979)

Dynamic strength   Ability to exert muscular force repeatedly or continuously. Useful for: doing push-ups, climbing a rope.
Trunk strength   Ability to exert muscular force repeatedly or continuously using trunk or abdominal muscles. Useful for: leg-lifts or sit-ups.
Static strength   The force the individual can exert against external objects, for a brief period. Useful for: lifting heavy objects, pulling heavy equipment.
Explosive strength   Ability to expend a maximum of energy in one act or a series of acts. Useful for: long jump, high jump, 50 metre race.
Extent flexibility   Ability to flex or extend trunk and back muscles as far as possible in any direction. Useful for: reaching, stretching, bending.
Dynamic flexibility   Ability to flex or extend trunk and back repeatedly. Useful for: continual bending, reaching, stretching.
Gross body co-ordination   Also known as agility.
Balance   Ability to stand or walk on narrow ledges.
Stamina   Or cardiovascular endurance, the ability to make prolonged, maximum exertion. Useful for: long-distance running.

were for unskilled labourers, six for skilled labour and one for managers. Unfortunately Schmitt *et al.* don't reveal who thinks what aspect of manager's physique important. Chaffin (cited in Campion, 1983) finds the greater the discrepancy between a worker's strength and the physical demands of the job, the more likely the worker is to suffer a back injury—a notorious source of lost output in industry. Furthermore the relation is continuous and linear, and doesn't have a threshold, so an employer who wants to minimize the risk of back injury should choose the strongest applicant, other things being equal.

Physical tests create a very substantial 'adverse impact' on women, who are lighter and less strong on average than men. Nevertheless, physical tests can survive legal scrutiny, if they are carefully validated. AT&T's pole-climbing tests reject 10 per cent of male applicants and 50 per cent of female applicants, without being 'unfair' because AT&T proved conclusively strength is essential in linemen.

Height

'Common sense' says police officers need to be big, to overcome violent offenders and command respect. British police forces still specify minimum heights. American police forces used to set minimum heights, but have been challenged frequently under 'fair' employment legislation. Women are less tall on average than men, and some ethnic minorities have smaller average builds than white Americans, so minimum height 'tests' create 'adverse impact' (Chapter 11) by excluding most women and some minorities. Therefore minimum height tests must be proved 'job-related'. 'Common sense' is surprised to learn American research has found no link between height and any criterion of effectiveness in police officers (Arvey, 1979b). Perhaps American police officers don't need height, bulk or brute force because they are armed. British police forces have always set a separate, lower minimum height for women, so the only group with a possible grievance are shortish men, who might argue that if a 5′ 6″ woman can do the job, so can a 5′ 6″ man.

Dexterity

Manual deterity is needed for assembly work, which is generally semi-skilled or unskilled. It's also needed for some 'professional' jobs, notably dentistry and surgery. Standardized tests of dexterity have been available for many years—e.g. Crawford Small Parts Dexterity Test, Bennett Hand Tool Test—but don't seem to have been used very widely; at any rate the published validation information is rather thin. General Aptitude Test Battery (Chapter 7) includes both Manual and Finger Dexterity tests; GATB is, of course, very widely used in the USA. Many work sample and trainability tests assess dexterity.

Appearance and attractiveness

Wallace and Travers (1938) describe how door-to-door salesmen were selected by a British company in the 1930s. The managing director and his personnel manager 'were both more or less convinced that small dark men are the best', because 'Both of these able gentlemen are small dark men'. Wallace and Travers introduced a more scientific assessment of physique, classifying the salesmen as 'gorillas, orang-utans, chimpanzees, baboons, or mixed anthropoids'. This, and other clues, suggest Wallace and Travers had a fairly low opinion of salesmen.

Is appearance or attractiveness a 'genuine occupational qualification' for any jobs? Acting and modelling certainly. Appearance or attractiveness is often an unstated requirement for receptionists; advertisements often specify 'smart appearance', 'pleasant manner', etc. Appearance, shading into 'charisma', is probably also important for selling, persuading and influencing jobs. Attractiveness used to be dismissed as irrelevant, or because 'beauty is in the eye of the beholder'. Extensive research has proved both assumptions false, and shown people do agree who is and isn't good-looking, and that attractiveness matters a lot, and not just in sexual encounters. Dipboye *et al.* (1977) showed that being physically attractive was worth on average two places in a rank order of twelve when applying for a job.

CONCLUSIONS

Educational qualifications have surprisingly poor validity. Surprising not so much because education is a very widely used test; being in general use certainly doesn't guarantee a test's validity. Surprising rather because education reflects both ability and personality (effort, motivation, co-operativeness), and because Booth *et al.* made a fair case for education's construct validity as a selection test.

Self-assessments appeal to some, because they allow the subject to speak for him/herself. They appeal to others because they're very simple, hence very cheap. Self-assessments have limited validity which, one suspects, might vanish altogether if self-assessments were used for real decisions, not just research.

Work samples have generally very good validity, but are cumbersome, and usually 'local'. 'Transportable' tests are obviously cheaper than ones that have to be developed for every new job. True work samples can only be used for motor tasks, which means they can't select for jobs that are very varied, or involve dealing with people rather than things.

Work samples have two major advantages. They measure how well applicants can do the job, so they measure every attribute needed for the job—strength, dexterity, eyesight—as well as intellectual abilities. Some work samples also measure aspects of interests and even personality (but work samples probably won't be so good at predicting long-term satisfaction, absence, turnover, etc.).

Work sample tests are very 'safe'. 'Fair employment' legislation favours tests that resemble the job as closely as possible. Work samples can be 'content-valid', which means many legal problems are avoided (Chapters 11 and 12).

Physical tests If a job needs strength, it needs strength. Even American courts have admitted that, although a physical test has to be properly validated. On the other hand if a job seems to need height, research suggests it probably doesn't, so height 'tests' aren't useful. Research on attractiveness in other fields suggests it may be very important in selection, but there's not a lot of direct evidence at present.

CHAPTER 11

Validity and Criteria of Productivity

Does it work? How can you tell?

What's the difference between a party game like 'Trivial Pursuits' and a test of verbal ability? What distinguishes Problem Puzzles on a matchbox from a numerical ability test? What's the difference between a magazine's 'Are You a Good Lover' quiz and a personality test?—Validity. Joke tests are fun to do, but tell you nothing. True psychological tests can be used to make decisions, about who will be productive, and who won't be.

A *valid* test is one that works, that measures what it claims to measure, that predicts something useful. Dunnette (1966) defines validity more elaborately as learning more about the meaning of a test. A valid test is backed by research and development. Anyone can string together a few dozen questions about assertiveness; it takes years of patient research, studying large groups of people, collecting follow-up data, to turn the list of questions into a valid psychological test.

The earliest psychological tests were validated, rather roughly. Binet's intelligence test used teacher ratings, and age (the average 10-year-old can solve problems the average 6-year-old can't). Woodworth's Personal Data Sheet selected its questions from psychiatric texts and cases, and checked them against diagnostic status. Since then validating tests has become a major industry, subject to intense legal scrutiny (Chapter 12). The American Psychological Association's Division of Industrial/Organisational Psychology have issued a book on *Principles for the Validation and Use of Personnel Selection Procedures.*

TYPES OF VALIDITY

1. Faith validity

'The man who sold me the test was very plausible.'

The layman is easily impressed by well-presented tests, smooth-talking salesmen, and sub-psychodynamic nonsense. But plausibility doesn't guarantee validity, and money spent on glossy presentation and well-dressed salesmen is all too often money not spent on R&D.

2. Face validity

'The test looks plausible'

Some people are persuaded a test measures dominance, if it's called 'Dominance Test', or if the questions all concern behaving dominantly. Early personality inventories mostly relied on face validity. Allport's A(scendance)–S(ubmission) Reaction Study asks questions about rebuking queue-jumpers, asking the first question at seminars, avoiding bossy people, etc. Early research showed face validity is never sufficient in itself; it does make the test more acceptable to employer and employee.

3. Content validity

'The test looks plausible to experts'.

Experts analyse the job, choose relevant questions and put together the test. The St Louis Fire brigade used 'a' (i.e. one) professional outside consultant, who conducted interviews with 27 fire captains to identify every component of the job and its importance. (The resulting test wasn't a great success—see Chapter 12.)

A content valid test is almost always face valid, but a face valid test isn't necessarily content valid. Content validity depends on job analysis (Chapter 3). Content validation was 'borrowed' from educational testing, where it makes sense to ask if a test covers the curriculum, and to seek answers from 'subject-matter experts'. Content validation regards test items as *samples*, of things workers need to know, not as *signs* which enable the tester to infer what else workers might be able to do.

Content validation was poorly thought of, before the law started taking such a keen interest in selection. Dunnette (1966) said 'this armchair approach to test validation is, at best, only a starting point'. Guion later said (1978) 'there is really no such thing as content validity, ... there is only content-oriented test construction'. Guion describes the APA's own official policy statements on content validation as 'filled with contradiction and confusion', because it was written by a committee (of which Guion was a dissenting member).

Be that as it may, selectors in the USA often have to use content validation or nothing. The APA's *Principles* describe standards for good content validation:

(a) a test developer should define a job content domain, (b) ... the definition should be given in terms of tasks, activities, or responsibilities, or perhaps job knowledge, (c) ... the sample should include all important aspects of the domain, and (d) ...

the qualifications of people who make the various kinds of judgements in the process should be duly recorded.

Distefano *et al.* (1983) describe five stages in content-validating a test for psychiatric aides.

1. Psychiatric aides, nurses and psychologists write an initial pool of basic work behaviour items.
2. Personnel, training staff and nurses review and modify the items to ensure they deal with observable behaviour, and apply to all six hospitals.
3. Items are rated by twenty psychiatric aides and eighteen aide supervisors on two scales:
   (a) essential (for effective performance of the job)/useful but not essential/ not necessary
   (b) task performed every day/several times a week/once a week/less than once a week/never
4. the 78 surviving items are re-written in BARS format (Chapter 5):

   Physically assists patients with bathing, dressing, grooming, and related personal hygiene tasks as needed
   (1) seldom performs correctly according standards expected, and requires constant supervision
   (2) performs below acceptable level, below standards expected, and requires frequent instructions
   . . .
   (5) performs consistently above acceptable level, greatly exceeds standards expected, and almost never requires instructions

5. finally 72 aides are rated.

Lawshe (1975) outlines a formal procedure for establishing content validity. A Content Evaluation Panel, composed of workers and supervisors, rate test items as essential/useful/unnecessary. Their ratings are used to calculate a Content Validity Ratio for each test item:

$$CVR = \frac{N(\text{essential}) - N(\text{total})}{N(\text{total})}$$

Lawshe supplies a table for deciding whether whether CVR is acceptable or not. Finally the Content Validity Index is calculated—the mean Content Validity Ratio of the items retained in the final form of the test.

The (US) Equal Employment Opportunity Commission's (EEOC) Guidelines on selection procedures say

> a selection procedure based upon inferences about mental processes cannot be supported solely or primarily on the basis of content validity. Thus a content

strategy is not appropriate for demonstrating the validity of selection procedures which purport to measure traits or constructs, such as intelligence, aptitude, personality, commonsense, judgement, leadership, and spatial ability.

This ought to limit content validation to work sample tests; employers desperate to find valid, but 'fair', tests (Chapter 12) sometimes try to stretch content validation to 'traits and construct'.

Content valid tests take a long time to write, and are themselves often immensely long. They commonly achieve no greater *predictive* validity than a set of four or five standard, all-purpose aptitude tests (Tenopyr, 1977).

4. Criterion validity

'The test predicts productivity'.

People who score highly on the test are more productive— no matter what the test is called, what the questions are, how plausible the test looks, or how plausible the test's author sounds. What matters is the *criterion*—productivity. Criterion validity has three forms: predictive, concurrent, and retrospective.

(a) Predictive validity

'The test predicts who *will* produce more.'

The most convincing demonstration of a test's validity, because it parallels real-life selection: select *today*, find out *later* if you made the right choice. The same time-lag makes predictive validation slow and expensive. Also referred to as 'follow-up' or longitudinal validity.

(b) Concurrent validity

'The test "predicts" who *has* produced more.'

Concurrent validity is quicker and easier than predictive validity, because subjects can be tested, and the criterion data on productivity collected, at the same time (preferably independently). Also referred to as 'present-employee' or cross-sectional validity.

(c) Retrospective validity

'Past tests "predict" present productivity.'

Also known as 'shelf research', because employers trying to validate or improve selection use data obtained when employees were recruited, but not necessarily collected for selection purposes. Retrospective studies are usually untidy, because the researcher has to make the best of the information available, instead of deciding what data to collect.

Predictive v. concurrent validity

Received wisdom from 1946 held predictive validity superior to concurrent validity. Guion (1965) even said the 'present employee method is clearly a violation of scientific principles'. Why?

1. *Missing persons*. In concurrent, or 'present-employee', studies, people who were rejected, or who left, or who were dismissed aren't available for study. Nor are people who proved so good they have been promoted. In concurrent validation, it is argued, both ends of the distribution of productivity are missing, so *range is restricted.*
2. *Unrepresentative samples*. Present employees ('incumbents') may not be typical of applicants—actual or possible. The applicant sample is often younger than the 'incumbent' sample. The workforce may be all white and/or all male, when applicants include, or ought to include, women and non-whites.
3. *Direction of cause*. Present employees have changed to meet the job's demands. They have often been *trained* to meet the job's demands. So it's really rather trivial to find successful managers are dominant, because managers learn to command influence and respect. (Whereas showing dominant applicants *become* good managers is useful.)
4. *Faking*. Present employees are less likely to fake personality inventories than applicants, because they've already got the job. Guion and Cranny (1982) describe a form of predictive validation that might solve this problem: 'hire, then test'—usually during a training programme. This obviously restricts range, but might get more candid replies.

These four arguments imply concurrent validation research is much less conclusive than predictive validity research. But several reviews of research all conclude the two methods of measuring validity give much the same results (Barrett *et al.*, 1981). Bemis (1968) reviewed 71 predictive validity coefficients and 69 concurrent validity coefficients for General Aptitude Test Battery (GATB), and found virtually no difference. Bemis also found no difference in variance of GATB scores in predictive and concurrent validation samples, showing range hadn't in fact been restricted. Lent *et al.*'s (1971) review also found predictive and concurrent validities the same on average. Why don't predictive and concurrent validities differ?

1. *Restricted range* reduces validity coefficients in predictive validity studies too. In an *ideal* predictive validity study there is no restriction of range,

because every applicant is employed, or applicants are employed at random. In reality this very rarely happens because:

(a) The employer uses test data to select, so there is a *cut-off* point in the distribution of test scores, and *direct* restriction of range (Figure 4.1). If the test has any validity the range of criterion scores is also restricted, because some poor performers will be excluded. If range of test scores and range of criterion scores are restricted, the correlation is necessarily reduced.

(b) Even if the employer doesn't use the test scores to select, the researcher's problems aren't over. The employer will almost certainly use some selection test, and it's quite likely to correlate with the test being validated, which creates *indirect* restriction of range. Suppose the existing selection criterion is educational level (high school diploma/ O levels), and suppose the new test being predictively validated is an ability test. Educational level and ability test scores correlate, so the educational requirement excludes more applicants with low ability scores, which indirectly restricts range on the ability test.

In the Second World War the US Air Force tested 1143 men, then put them *all* through pilot training, regardless of test scores, enabling Flanagan (1946) to calculate an *unrestricted* validity coefficient of $r = 0.66$. Given the unreliability of the criterion, the coefficient probably couldn't have been much higher.

2. *Unrepresentative samples.* Barrett *et al.* says it's perfectly possible to select a sample of present employees who *are* representative of applicants; critics (Guion and Cranny, 1982) agree it's theoretically possible, but doubt if it's often possible in practice, either because the workforce is all white or all male, or because the number of workers available for study is too small to allow researchers to select from within it.

3. *Direction of cause.* The job changes the worker. The force of this argument depends on the test. If taller policemen were more efficient, no-one could sensibly argue efficiency increased height. On the other hand finding that managers express more willingness than the managed to control others is clearly trivial. Most researchers agree concurrent validation is unsatisfactory for personality and attitude measures.

However, reviews that report no difference between predictive and concurrent validity all limit themselves to ability tests. Is direction of cause a problem with ability tests? Reviewers assume not. The layman sees it as self-evident that a year spent working with figures will improve performance on a numerical test. The tester cites high retest reliabilities as proof cognitive abilities are stable, even fixed. (But subjects in retest reliability studies don't have intensive practice between tests.) Barrett *et al.*'s review could find only two studies proving that cognitive ability test scores are 'probably resistant to the effects of work experience'. Anastasi (1981) reviews research on practice and coaching effects with ability tests, and concludes they exist but are small enough to be disregarded. However, the research all deals with coaching and practice for school tests, like the American Scholastic Aptitude Test or the British '11+', and doesn't address the question of the effects of long experience.

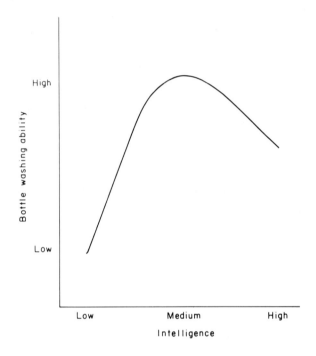

Figure 11.1. A fictional non-linear relationship between a predictor (intelligence) and productivity (bottle-washing).

Ways of calculating predictive validity

Researchers usually report *correlations*, sometimes *differences between group means*. A significant difference between productive and unproductive workers may not be very useful, if the distributions *overlap* too much. A correlation may be misleading if the relation between predictor and criterion isn't *linear*, or isn't *homoscedastic*. Figure 11.1 illustrates a *non-linear* relationship between predictor and criterion: very dull subjects make poor bottle-washers; fairly bright people make good bottle-washers; very bright people are as poor at bottle-washing as the very dull. The example is fictional; reliable examples of non-linear relations between predictor and criterion are scarce. Brown and Ghiselli (1953) found tests of arithmetic and reaction time had a curvilinear relationship with turnover in taxi-drivers.

Figure 6.4 (page 93) illustrates a *non-homoscedastic* relationship. Variability of scores differs in different parts of the distribution. There are 'too many' subjects with high scores on the predictor, but low scores on the criterion. Lack of *homoscedasticity* is also infrequent, although Figure 6.5 does show the results obtained with the American insurance industry's *Aptitude Index Battery* (Chapter 6), on which low scores predict failure, but high scores don't predict success.

A *scatterplot* (Figure 11.2) identifies non-linear or non-homoscedastic data, and also identifies *leverage*, where an apparently large and highly significant correlation turns out to result largely from a single *outlier*, one subject whose scores on predictor and criterion deviate from everyone else's. Researchers should always draw a scatterplot, just in case there's something odd in their data.

Suppressor variables

Sorenson (1966) reports data on selecting motor mechanics, using Bennett Mechanical Comprehension Test (MCT), Survey of Mechanical Insight (SMI),

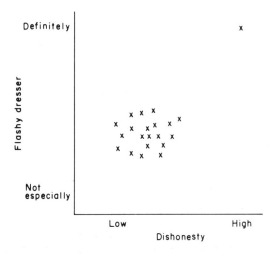

Figure 11.2. A fictional scatterplot of relationship between two variables (being a flashy dresser, and being dishonest) in occupational psychologists, illustrating an 'outlier' (top right) which could create a spuriously high correlation, and cause people to think *all* smartly dressed psychologists are dishonest.

Table 11.1. Illustration of a suppressor variable (Sorenson, 1966) (Copyright 1966 by the American Psychological Association).

	SMI	MCT	BSQ
Supervisor rating	22	–04	30
Survey of Mechanical Insight		71	09
Bennett Mechanical Comprehension Test			–02
Background survey questionnaire			

and a Background Survey Questionnaire. Table 11.1 shows none of these tests predicted supervisor ratings very well; the Bennett MCT didn't predict at all. Nevertheless Sorenson thought MCT could help select motor mechanics, and included it in his regression equation:

$$\text{Rating} = 866 + (10 \times \text{SMI}) - (6 \times \text{TMC}) + (17 \times \text{BSQ})$$

The Bennett MCT test correlates fairly well with general intelligence, whereas the SMI is more of a 'nuts-and-bolts' test which, however, also measures an irrelevant element of general intellectual ability. Some mechanics do well on SMI because they're generally bright, not because they're good mechanics. So 'suppressing' the general intelligence element, by subtracting MCT score, improves selection of mechanics. In practice, according to Wiggins (1973), 'suppressor variables' very rarely prove useful.

5. Construct validity

'The test measures something meaningful.'

Construct validity can focus on a *test*, or on a *trait or ability*.

(a) Test-centred construct validity

Cronbach (1984) discusses the construct validity of the Bennett Mechanical Comprehension Test (MCT).

Experience.   MCT assumes subjects have seen, used or even repaired machinery, so it's unsuitable for people in 'developing' countries. Women tend to get lower scores on MCT, perhaps because they too have less experience with machinery.

Education.   People who have studied physics get slightly higher MCT scores.

General ability.   MCT scores correlate quite highly with general intelligence.

Specific knowledge. Cronbach once hypothesized MCT simply measured knowledge of a few specific mechanical principles—gears, levers, etc. When he tested his hypothesis he found it incorrect; MCT does measure *general* acquaintance with mechanical principles.

Dexterity. MCT scores correlate less well with dexterity in handling tools.

Productivity. MCT's manual lists correlations with performance ratings, and training grades for a variety of occupations: naval aviation cadets, aircraft engine factory foremen, motor mechanics, coal miners, chemical plant operators, millwrights, power utility (power station) technicians. Correlations vary widely; neither job nor criterion seemed to account for any systematic trends.

The Bennett test seems to reflect general intelligence more than being good *with one's hands* with machinery. On the other hand the test also reflects experience and education, perhaps more than a pure test of general intelligence would.

(b) Trait/ability-centred construct validity.

'Need for achievement' is what made America and the West get where they are today, according to McClelland (1971). 'Need for achievement', abbreviated to 'nAch', is *ambition*, to make money, and build a business empire (Cook, 1984). Research on the construct validation of nAch follows seven main lines (Fineman, 1977):

1. *Different measures.* Need for achievement can be measured by the TAT, by other projective tests, including doodles, preference for different tartans, or even designs on pottery, and by personality inventory. Different measures intercorrelate very poorly, if at all, which throws doubt on the existence of a construct.
2. *Reliability.* Retest reliability of measures of nAch is often poor; projective measures, very widely used, are especially unreliable. This again casts doubt on the value of the construct of 'need for achievement'.
3. *Peformance.* Measures of nAch predict who will perform better on a task, because ambitious people are more efficient.
4. *Level of aspiration.* Achievement motivation predicts who chooses more difficult tasks, suggesting ambitious people welcome a challenge. Research on both level of aspiration and performance is disappointingly inconsistent, and effects, when found, are often very small. (Fineman's is a narrative review, with no meta-analysis, so he may have underestimated true effect size).

5. *Upbringing.* McClelland reports research on children building castles out of toy bricks, while parents watched their efforts. Parents of 'high achievers' were warm and encouraging, and physically affectionate; parents of low achievers kept finding fault and telling the child what to do next.
6. *Psycho-history.* McClelland presents some very challenging data, showing for example that literature full of achievement themes preceded, and therefore possibly *caused*, expansion of ancient Greek trade, as measured by the dispersion throughout the Mediterranean of Greek wine jars.
7. *Creating an achieving society.* McClelland thinks both upbringing and culture shape achievement motivation, so changing both should make a whole society achieve more and produce more. McClelland went to India, and tried to do just that, with mixed results.

Construct validation relies on many lines of evidence:

(a) showing a test is internally consistent,
(b) showing the test's questions are relevant (face/content validity),
(c) showing the test correlates with an established measure,
(d) factor analysis,
(e) showing natural or experimental groups differ,
(f) showing the test can predict behaviour,
(g) showing the test *doesn't* correlate with measures it shouldn't correlate with.

Opinions differ widely about construct validation.

Guion (1978) argues all test validation necessarily is construct validation, because the test writer always has a theory about what he/she is trying to measure. Consider 'scrap rate'—a very concrete measure. If high scrap rate is a sign of *carelessness*, workers whose scrap rate is high may be too irresponsible to make good foremen. To test this hypothesis the tester needs other measures of carelessness. On the other hand if scrap rate reflects *clumsiness*, it may not be a bar to promotion, and one seeks tests of physical co-ordination. Taking this broad view of construct validation it becomes virtually synonymous with validation as a whole.

Ebel (1977) takes a much narrower view; constructs are 'a few internal forces of personality', which he thinks don't exist anyway. So 'why do we continue to talk about construct validation as if it were something we all understand and have found useful?'. Certainly examples of constructs, in Ebel's narrow sense, are hard to find. There is some evidence that aggressiveness operates as an 'internal force', present in the aggressive person but not always directly affecting his/her behaviour (Cook, 1984). Otherwise evidence of 'internal forces' in personality remains sketchy and inconsistent.

6. Factorial validity

'The test measures two things but gives them sixteen different labels.'

Factor analysis is a useful component of validation, but insufficient in itself. Knowing *how many* factors a test measures doesn't tell you *what* they are, nor what they can predict.

7. Synthetic validity

'The test measures component traits and abilities that predict productivity.'

The employer tells the psychologist 'I need people who are good with figures, who are sociable and outgoing, and who can type.' The psychologist uses tests of numerical ability, extraversion and typing skills, whose validity had been *separately* proved elsewhere. The separate validities of the three tests are synthesized to yield a compound validity. Lawshe (1952) defined synthetic validation as 'the inferring of validity from a logical analysis of jobs into their elements, a definition of test validity for these elements, and combination of elemental validities into a whole'. Also known as *job component validity*.

Guion (1965b) reports a case study of synthetic validity in a small electrical wholesalers, employing 48 employees, where the largest number of persons doing the same job was three. Clearly a local validation study on conventional lines was quite impossible. Guion identified seven elements in the company's work; each job in the wholesalers required a particular combination of these elements. The company's president and vice-president rank-ordered staff on each criterion successively (omitting those for whom it wasn't relevant). Guion made sure these criterion ratings were as independent as possible; if the criterion consisted largely of 'halo', the whole point of the procedure was lost. All 48 workers then completed GZTS, Graves Design Judgement Test, and some ability tests. Guion compared scores with criterion, and found a different set of scores predicted each criterion (Table 11.2).

So in future the company could identify which of the seven attributes a vacancy requires, and choose someone with acceptable scores on those attributes. Or could they? Guion describes a variation on the theme of the local validation study, in which his *largest* sample size is 48 (Guion doesn't say how many workers each criterion was relevant for). Perhaps the variations in which test predicts which criterion, in Table 11.2, reflect only sampling error. Without cross-validation one doesn't know, and it would be very unwise to make future selections using Guion's data. The basic principle is sound, but proof that a test measures a component of a job needs as large a sample as a predictive validity study.

Table 11.2. Test-Criterion Validity Matrix (Guion, 1965) (Reproduced by permission.)

	Sales-manship	Creative Judgment	Customer Relations	Routine Judgment	Leadership	Detail Work	Work Organization
EAS—Verbal					2.09†		
EAS—Numerical							
EAS—Visual							
Adaptability Test		1.62†					
Design Judgment Test		3.23**	1.82†		2.81†		
GZTS—G	1.73†			1.77†			
GZTS—R						1.76†	
GZTS—A							
GZTS—S	2.21*						
GZTS—E			1.92†				
GZTS—O			2.84*	1.69†		3.01**	
GZTS—F			3.19**			2.35*	
GZTS—T							
GZTS—P					2.09†	3.01**	1.86†
GZTS—M	2.16*						
MAI—Int. Job Perf.					1.77†	2.27*	Note[a]
MAI—Leadership			2.27*				
MAI—Job Att.							
MAI—Relns Others							
R for best 2 tests	.53	.82	.80	(.31)	.65	.47	(—)

*Signif. at 5% level
**Signif. at 1% level
†Signif. at 10% level
[a]Note that 90% of those rated on this element had scores above the company median.

Tests:
EAS	Employee Aptitude Survey			
GZTS	Guilford Zimmerman Temperament Survey			
MAI	Management Aptitude Inventory			
G	General	T		Thoughtfulness
R	Restraint	P		Personal Relations
A	Ascendance	M		Masculinity
S	Sociability	Int. Job Perf		Interest in Job Performance
E	Emotionality	Job Att		Job Attitude
O	Objectivity	Relns Others		Relations Others
F	Friendliness			

Synthetic validation isn't a new idea. In 1923 Viteles described a Job Psychograph, in which a job's requirements were described by the test scores needed. Modern synthetic validation goes beyond just asking the employer what he/she thinks is needed; experts identify the component parts of a job, so synthetic validation is closely linked to job analysis (Chapter 4).

PAQ and GATB

Synthetic validation has used Position Analysis Question (PAQ) (Chapter 3), and General Aptitude Test Battery (GATB) (Chapter 7). McCormick *et al.* (1972)

found PAQ scores predicted GATB *scores* and GATB *validity* (Table 11.3). These results imply PAQ data can be used to predict what profile of GATB scores will be found in people doing a job, and to predict—not so quite accurately—what profile of GATB scores will be found in people doing a job *successfully*. Therefore selectors could use PAQ to choose subtests of GATB that will best select for a particular job.

Table 11.3. Correlations between PAQ dimensions, and PAQ attribute ratings with GATB scores and validity, across 90 jobs

	GATB scores	GATB validity
PAQ dimensions	0.71	0.47
PAQ attributes ratings	0.70	0.44

J coefficients

Experts first rate the importance of various attributes for a job, then use ratings to weight scores on various tests. The J coefficient combines the judgements for the various attributes. J coefficients have mostly been used by the US Civil Service Commission (Primoff, 1959).

Mossholder and Arvey (1984) review these, and several other approaches to synthetic validation, and reach the rather melancholy conclusion that 35 years of research have only shown that synthetic validation is 'feasible', but 'has not done so in a completely convincing manner'. The public expect personnel psychologists to deliver selection systems that work now, not blueprints for what someone (else) might one day achieve.

ASPECTS OF VALIDATION

Cross-validation

This means checking the validity of a test a second time, on a second sample. Cross-validation is always desirable, and absolutely essential when keys are empirically constructed, regression equations are calculated or multiple cut-offs are used, because these methods are particularly likely to capitalise on chance. Locke (1961) gives a very striking demonstration of the hazards of not cross-validating; he found students with long surnames (seven or more letters) were less charming, stimulating, gay, happy-go-lucky and impulsive, liked vodka, but didn't smoke, and had more fillings in their teeth. Locke's results sound quite plausible, in places, but needless to say they completely failed to *cross-validate*.

Tests that aren't cross-validated lead to *fold-back error*, calculating scoring weights from a sample, then applying them to the same sample as if it were independent. Cureton (1950) has a ruder name for un-cross-validated empirical keys and regressions—'baloney coefficients'.

Murphy (1984) notes that most researches published in *Personnel Psychology* and *Journal of Applied Psychology* in the late 1970s did cross-validate—usually by splitting a single sample into two, and calculating validity within each. Murphy considers this pointless; researchers can calculate the stability of validity coefficients or regression equations using formulae based on sample size and number of predictors used. In fact cross-validation serves two different purposes: it (a) checks the sample size is large enough, and (b) checks whether observed effects are robust enough to survive the move to a new sample, a new job or a new location.

The 'Advantage' of small samples

If two small (n = 10) samples are compared, the difference between them must be large to achieve significance—nearly one whole SD between the means (Dunnette, 1966). If the samples are large (n = 1000), a very small average difference can achieve significance (one corresponding to 0.09 SD). This follows logically from the way significance of mean differences is calculated. Dunnette (1966) argued a sample should be large enough to detect true relationships, but *small enough* not to detect trivial ones. A difference between means equivalent to only 0.09 SD may interest researchers, but isn't likely to be much use to selectors. Dunnette suggests 50–60 is the ideal range (which just happened to be the sample size of the typical local validation study). Chapter 7 outlined modern arguments why 50–60 is *nowhere near large enough* to give reliable results. It's important to show a difference or a correlation is large enough to be cost-effective, but there are better ways of deciding than using samples that are too small to give reliable results.

Is validation always essential?

Outsiders often think psychologists are obsessed with validity; some even claim excessive concern with statistics is a sign of an anal personality. Other experts don't keep measuring themselves, and announcing to the world that most of their decisions are unreliable or incorrect. Other scientists don't constantly demand proof of the validity of measures. Ebel (1977) cites the example of the Babcock test of butterfat in cream (in which the fat is dissolved by sulphuric acid, then centrifuged into the neck of the bottle, and measured). No-one demands proof that the Babcock test is valid, that it 'really' measures butterfat in cream. As Ebel says, the Babcock test has 'self-evident' validity. Why can't psychological tests be accepted in the same way?

Ebel's argument is, of course, deliberately ingenuous. Butterfat is real; you can eat it. Intelligence is a 'construct', something inferred from behaviour. The inferential leap from psychological test to productivity is far greater than from centrifuge to fat content. And if ability tests measured something as uncontroversial as butterfat, they might easily achieve the same unthinking acceptance.

THE CRITERION

Over sixty years ago Bingham and Freyd (1926) said: 'the successful employee ... does more work, does it better, with less supervision, with less interruption through absence. ... He makes fewer mistakes and has fewer accidents. ... He ordinarily learns more quickly, is promoted more rapidly, and stays with the company.' Employers hire employees to produce goods and services. Therefore productivity is the criterion of good selection, so any discussion of criteria becomes a discussion of definitions and measures of productivity.

A good criterion should be:

1. *Relevant*, i.e. valid. In one sense this is a tautology; the criterion *defines* success. But criteria have often been attacked as irrelevant, especially in 'fair' employment cases.
2. *Reliable*. Reliability may mean *stability* (over time) or *consistency* (inter-observer, split-half, etc.). Ratings, the favourite criterion, have limited consistency. Efforts to improve rating reliability, such as BARS, are discussed in Chapter 5.
3. *Free of bias*. The criterion doesn't omit important aspects of the job, nor include or over-emphasize unimportant aspects.
4. *Practical*. Information can be obtained at reasonable cost, by procedures management and workers accept.

The quickest way to discredit a validation study is to discredit the criterion. Validation evidence can't be better than the criterion. Guion (1961) sees the 'ultimate criterion' as 'the total worth of a man to the company—in the final analysis', but this can't be measured until the employee's career is complete, which is usually too long to wait—although Anstey's analysis of CSSB (Chapter 9) followed staff from selection almost to retirement.

Objective criteria divide into seven general categories:

1. *Job sample*, or standardized tests.
2. *Training*: training grades; how long it takes to train the worker.
3. *Production*: units produced, sales, research productivity and scientific creativity. Quality can be measured positively by ratings, negatively by scrap, wastage, errors or complaints.

4. *Personnel*: advancement/promotion, length of service, turnover, punctuality, absence, disciplinary action, accidents, sickness.
5. *Financial*: salary/wages, bonus/commission.
6. *Miscellaneous*: trade status, membership of professional bodies, e.g. American Society for Personnel Administration/Institute of Personnel Management.
7. *Survival and gravitation*. People gravitate to jobs that suit them, and which they are good at, and they 'survive' in them. The survival/gravitation criterion is used in research on job analysis (Chapter 3), and in the validation of SVIB (Chapter 8). Much depends on the employer's appraisal system; 'survival' in organizations that don't react to idleness or inefficiency isn't a good criterion. By contrast 'survival' is a very discriminating criterion for life insurance salesmen; only one in five last the first year.

Computerised systems—word processors, supermarket checkouts, etc.—allow both quantity and quality to be measured, precisely, continuously and cheaply. Number of 'key-strokes' measures quantity, while use of the 'delete' key measures quality. The computer criterion is an exciting prospect for the personnel researcher, but a frightening intrusion to the workers and their representatives.

Landy (1987) describes an ultimate 'hands-on', work sample criterion, designed to prove conclusively Armed Services Vocational Aptitude Battery's validity in the face of Congressional criticism. Tank crewmen are observed minutely, in real life, in a real tank, repairing the radio, unjamming the gun and getting the tank from A to B. The research is staggeringly expensive by any but US military standards—with a budget of $40 million. Landy suggests the ultimate criterion can be used to validate less exacting and expensive criteria, such as 'walk-throughs', in which the tank man stands in a mock-up tank, and explains how to unjam the gun, or describes how the vehicle is driven (as opposed to actually doing it). 'Walk-through' criteria could in turn 'lay hands' on rating criteria, and confer validity on them.

Subjective criteria include: supervisor nominations, supervisor ratings, efficiency ratings, self-ratings. Nearly all—95 per cent of US performance appraisal systems use supervisor ratings. However ratings suffer from many systematic defects—leniency, halo, etc.—described in Chapter 5. Many variations in format have been tried, with limited success.

'Nominations' are temptingly simple; employers answer questions such as:

Which of the present workforce are the sort of person you would like more of?

If you had to reduce the workforce by a half, who would you 'let go'?

Nominations make experimental designs difficult if the employer nominates too few or too many individuals, and can be difficult to interpret. The employer may really be happy with most of the present employees, or may really think 90 per cent are a waste of space. Or else a 10–90 per cent split may reflect the employer's biases, so a jaundiced supervisor would like to sack everyone, while one with a sunnier disposition thinks everyone worth retaining.

Survey of selection criteria

Crites (1969) analyses criteria used by 500+ validation studies reported by Dorcus and Jones, for the period 1914–50:

global ratings by supervisor	213	(60%)
output criteria	58	(16%)
sales	16	(5%)
earnings	16	(5%)
accidents	13	(4%)
job level	13	(4%)
survival	10	(3%)
work sample	10	(3%)
promotion	4	(1%)

Twenty years later, Lent *et al.*'s review found 879 of 1506 criteria (58 per cent) were 'supervisor's evaluation'. Promotion has been widely used as the criterion in assessment centre research, which wasn't included in either survey.

The global supervisor rating is clearly the favourite criterion in validation research. Most American employers have appraisal systems, which provide researchers with a ready-made source of criterion data. Many psychologists are sceptical of ratings; Guion (1980) says there's nothing wrong with ratings as a criterion, so long as they are good ratings, and so long as they aren't used as criterion because nothing else is available. Too often psychologists 'accept any [criterion] measure that happens to be lying around'.

Guion (1980) prefers specially designed behavioural criteria to 'ready-made' organizational criteria such as appraisal ratings or turnover. The APA's Task Force on Employment Testing for Minority Groups favours a direct measure of job proficiency, after 6 months to a year on the job. A 'direct measure of job proficiency' means a *work sample*, or can be a good *performance appraisal* system. Few studies use work samples *as criterion*. They are so expensive to develop that employers prefer to use them for selection. But a work sample used for selection can't be used again as criterion; a high correlation would be trivial.

Specially developed criteria attract critical comment; everyone thinks they can devise surefire ways of assessing good workers, and everyone likes telling the psychologist how to do his/here job; whereas output, or supervisor's opinion, for all their flaws, are *final*. How do you know X is better than Y—because he/she makes more widgets per hours, or because the foreman says so?

Critics like to pick some occupation where the notion of a criterion seems particularly silly or inappropriate. Some choose university teachers (college professors); some choose social workers; but the favourite nomination is minister of religion. How can one possibly find a sensible criterion (this side of the Day of Judgement)? Umeda and Frey (1974) used five objective criteria: number of baptisms a year, congregation size, status of job title, number of paid supervisees, and time devoted to professional reading, and five subjective criteria: ratings *by the minister himself* of job satisfaction, job success, human relations skills, public speaking ability, and counselling skill. (It's unusual to use self-ratings as a criterion, for fear of less than total frankness, but ministers of religion are probably a special case.) Either the criteria really were unsatisfactory, or the sample ($n = 92$) wasn't large enough; the attempt to devise a Biodata inventory for ministers failed.

MULTIPLE CRITERIA

Dunnette (1966) cites a hypothetical pair of salesmen, both successful, one diligent and persistent, the other persuasive and charismatic. He argues global criteria are over-simplified and misleading. Psychologists must understand the structure of success to predict it accurately. Therefore validation studies need multiple criteria. Multiple criteria may be subjective or objective. Kingsbury (1923) said the same thing about managers over 50 years ago: 'some executives are successful because they are good planners ... others are splendid at co-ordination and direction, but their plans and programs are defective. Few executives are equally competent in both directions.' Kingsbury is saying management is really two jobs, not one, so selection should be tested against two criteria.

Multiple subjective criteria

It's easy to multiply criterion ratings. It's usually a mistake. Petrie and Powell (1951) used eighteen criterion ratings by matron, ward sister and nurse tutor in their study of nurse selection, but found the average intercorrelation between ratings was 0.75, higher than average inter-rater reliability. Petrie and Powell accordingly summed the ratings to give a single 'Total Rating' criterion.

Crites (1969) reviews factor-analytic studies of ratings of 'vocational success', and finds they yield between three and fifteen factors, of the 'drive and efficiency' and 'sales ability' type. Many studies found large 'halo' effects, which might be an artefact in the ratings, or might mean that success is genuinely unitary. Factor analyses of ratings usually give similar results regardless of what is being rated, or why (Chapter 5). More recent research has used BARS, or variations on the BARS theme, to reduce halo. Dunnette (1976) isolated four main criterion factors in sales and technical jobs: Initiative and Persistence, Personal

Commitment, Knowledge Utilization and Planning, Organizing and Handling Detail. These four factors had low intercorrelations, indicting absence of 'halo'.

Multiple objective criteria

A series of elaborate studies by Taylor and Richard (Richard *et al.*, 1965) factor-analysed 80 criteria of success in doctors, and found up to 30 factors. Both individual criteria and the resulting factors were highly specific; for example age, rank, experience, committee membership and journal editorships defined the Academic Seniority factor. Some factors were decidedly odd: Rejection of Actual Practice, Ease of Scheduling Research Interview. Taylor and Richard's research doesn't throw a lot of light on success in the medical profession.

An earlier British study makes rather more sense of criteria for bus conductors. Six criteria yield two factors (Table 11.4). The first factor is clearly Value to Employer; the second factor has loadings on Disciplinary Action, Shortages (in takings), and Absence, and seems to be a Responsibility factor (Heron, 1954).

Table 11.4. Intercorrelation and factor analysis of six measures of productivity in bus conductors (Heron, 1954) (Reproduced by permission)

		GE	CS	AB	DA	LA	Factor I	Factor II
(Poor) supervisor rating	(SR)	31	51	38	13	49	70	03
(Low) gross earnings	(GE)		10	41	06	24	44	-42
Cash shortages	(CS)			27	23	45	61	32
Absence	(AB)				02	37	28	27
Disciplinary action	(DA)					27	28	27
Lateness	(LA)						70	14

Similar research (Ronan, 1963) factor-analysed objective criteria for skilled trades apprentices and journeymen (Table 11.5). Factor I is clearly a Safe Worker factor, with loadings on Injury Index and Time Lost through Accidents. Factor II has loadings on School Rating and Maths Grade, which makes it the Successful School Work factor. Ronan calls Factor III, with loadings on Promotions and Supervisory Rating, Supervisory Evaluation; cynics might call it the 'face-fits' criterion. Factor IV is an Adjustment factor, with large loadings on Absence Index and Personality Disorder, and smaller loadings on Shop Rating and Grievance. Ronan suggests men with a lot of grievances 'can't get along with anybody'—a suggestion that won't appeal to unions.

Another study factor-analysed a mixture of objective and subjective criteria (sales figures and supervisor ratings), and got three factors, one contributed

Table 11.5. Factors After Orthogonal Rotation (Ronan, 1963) (Reproduced by permission.)

Variables	I	II	III	IV	h^2
Shop Rating	084	-030	008	459	219
School Rating	161	794	0	201	696
Mathematics Grade	006	651	222	281	552
Absence Index	-068	044	339	700	612
Injury Index	844	110	185	-069	763
Lost Time Accidents	808	-151	298	-113	777
Grievances	-020	099	055	342	131
Disciplinary Actions	010	251	389	134	232
Promotions	-308	-029	460	0	307
Supervisory Rating	-006	-131	655	311	543
Personality Disorder	247	-149	-104	830	783

almost entirely by sales figures, the others by the ratings, suggesting the two types of criteria don't mix well (Rush, 1953). Crites (1969) suggests success may have a hierarchical structure, like intellectual ability (Figure 11.3). At the highest level is the *general factor*—'Overall Vocational Success'. At the intermediate level are *group factors*: 'Administrative Skills' and 'Drive and Initiative'. At the level of *specific factors* are individual ratings such as 'company loyalty', and single objective criteria, such as scrap. It's tempting to argue global supervisory ratings measure accurately 'Overall Vocational Success', but the concept as elaborated by Crites is much broader.

Composite or separate criteria?

Objective criteria don't intercorrelate very well, and even subjective criteria sometimes contain separable factors, which gives the selection researcher a choice of strategies: use separate criteria, or combine them in a single composite. American personnel researchers classically favoured separate criteria, each reflecting a different aspect of behaviour at work. Multiple separate criteria have more promise of increasing scientific understanding of success at work, but cost more, and can make validation very confusing. If 20 selection tests are used to predict five criteria, 100 validity coefficients result (several hundred if the researcher corrects for restricted range, unreliability, etc.) Experience suggests the resulting 100 coefficients won't present a very tidy picture. There's more at stake here than neat, publishable results for the researcher; the employer may have to fight a 'fair employment' case on the results (Chapter 12). Combining multiple criteria into a single composite makes the results easier to follow, and easier to defend in court.

Figure 11.3. A hierarchical model of criteria of productivity, adapted from Crites (1960).

As long ago as 1931 Bird proposed an 'efficiency index', based on salary, tenure, salary increase, promotion and supervisor rating. Toops (1944) describes the 'Kelly Bid' system for developing weighted multiple criterion; Umeda and Frey (1974) used three raters—Catholic priest, 7th Day Adventist, Baptist—to assign 100 points or *bids* among ten criterion elements, to determine the relative importance of each in the composite. Some composite criteria are not very successful; Merrihue and Katzell (1955) devised the *Employee Relations Index* (ERI), a composite criterion for managers, based on eight 'personnel' indices: absence rate, 'separation' (resignation), dispensary visits, dismissal, suggestions submitted, disciplinary suspensions, grievances, etc. ERI proved a poor criterion, because most of its components were largely outside the manager's control. No doubt a very bad manager could drive more workers to the dispensary, but most visits reflect a real need.

A simpler, and more logical, system is the Laurent Success Index, based on salary in relation to age (Laurent, 1970). Laurent claims his Success Index is an absolute criterion 'independent of any particular group of individuals or company or currency'—so long as the employer's appraisal system is efficient, and closely linked to employees' salary. The Index obviously wouldn't work in organizations such as British universities, where salary is based on age not merit.

Opponents of composite criteria say they're bound to be unsatisfactory because you can't equate *units produced* with *days off*, or *employee satisfaction* with *scrap rate*. Brogden and Taylor (1950) disagree, and say all criteria can be measured on a common scale—the dollar. A good worker is quite simply one who is *worth more* to the employer; all criteria reduce to dollar or pound value of output. The composite 'accountant's criterion' is used widely in recent American research, especially since Rational Estimate techniques have made it easier to calculate. Schmidt and Hunter use a single criterion in all their meta-analyses (Chapter 7); if the original research used multiple criteria, Schmidt and Hunter combine them into a single composite.

CRITERION PROBLEMS

Criterion contamination

A criterion subject to bias is 'contaminated' (Brogden and Taylor, 1950). Ratings are particularly prone to all sorts of bias: halo, leniency, central tendency, intergroup hostility, desire to keep dangerous rivals at bay and plain spite. More specifically *criterion contamination* means criterion ratings aren't made independently; the rater knows who did well and who did poorly in the selection tests. Most assessment centre research suffers 'contamination', which is very difficult for the researchers to control. Employers are naturally reluctant to spend large sums running assessment centres, and then not be told the results for 8 whole years. Critics argue 'objective' criteria, such as promotion, can be 'contaminated' as easily as ratings.

Dynamic criteria

Ghiselli and Haire (1960) used a battery of tests to predict dollar volume of fares in 56 taxi-drivers, over 18 weeks. Tests that predicted the criterion in the first 3 weeks didn't necessarily predict it in the last 3 weeks. Ghiselli called his paper 'The validation of selection tests in the light of the dynamic nature of criteria'. A *dynamic criterion* is one that changes over time; Ghiselli assumes that taxi-driving after 18 week is somehow different from taxi driving after 3 weeks, so a test that predicts one will not necessarily predict the other. The would-be selector of taxi-drivers must decide whether he/she wants to predict productivity in the short time or in the long term, because the same set of tests won't predict both. A more parsimonious interpretation of Ghiselli's results is that his sample was far too small. Bass (1962) presented similar data for 99 wholesale food salesmen, showing correlations between peer assessments and criterion ratings declined from r = 0.30–0.40 at 6 months interval to $r = 0$–0.20 where the time span was 4 years. Correlations between ability tests and successive criterion ratings fluctuated around a very low mean.

On this rather modest empirical founcation the theory of dynamic criteria rested unchallenged for some 25 years, until Barrett *et al.* (1985) argued there's no evidence that criteria are 'dynamic':

(a) *Changes in performance.* A 'dynamic' criterion implies work performance changes over time. Besides presenting the data taxi-fares, Ghiselli and Haire cited unpublished data that showed that investment salesmen increased their sales by 650 per cent over 10 years, and that their sales were still increasing at the end of the period. The investment sales data are very sketchy; Ghiselli and Haire don't even say if they allowed for inflation. Barrett *et al.* review more substantial research, and conclude there's no evidence performance genuinely changes over time, which imples criteria aren't dynamic.

(b) *Changes in validity.* Ghiselli and Haire's sample was very small, and their results were inconclusive and largely insignificant. Bass's results too were largely insignificant. Barrett *et al.* searched literature published between 1914 and 1984, and found twelve studies where the same criterion was used on two more occasions; 5.8 per cent of the 480 pairs of validity coefficients were different—as many as would be expected by chance.

(c) *Stability of criteria.* Ghiselli and Haire found the first week's taxi fares correlated very poorly ($r = 0.19$) with the 18th week's fares. Most researchers would call this an unreliable criterion, rather than a 'dynamic' one, and would increase their sample size, or average the criterion over enough weeks to achieve acceptable reliability. Barrett *et al.*'s literature search found 55 studies that reported retest reliabilities of criteria; only 24 of the 276 correlations failed to achieve significance. Most criteria, fortunately, are *static*.

Criterion-referenced scales, and 'minimum competency'

The norms supplied with most tests relate the individual to a population: Smith is more dominant than 95 per cent of sale managers, Jones is more intelligent than 15 per cent of lumberjacks. The personnel manager often has to choose the best of the available applicants. But suppose being more intelligent than 15 per cent of lumberjacks isn't intelligent enough? A *criterion-referenced* scale compares applicants with the job's needs, not with each other. The criterion is being able to do the job acceptably well. Early research described minimum intelligence levels needed for various types of work:

Mental Age 5:   dishwashing, simple sewing, peeling vegetables.
Mental Age 6:   mix cement, load freight, use mangle.
Mental Age 10:   sign painter, house painter, laundry worker.

Criterion-referenced testing currently takes two forms. For simpler jobs, job analysis and content validation produce a work sample test that defines the things a person doing that job must know or be able to do. For many professions, certification or training provides a form of criterion-referencing; doctors must have adequate knowledge of anatomy, physiology, biochemistry, etc. In practice both forms of criterion-referencing can't require perfect mastery of everything, and have to set a more or less arbitrary passmark. 'Minimum competency testing' is a form of criterion-referenced testing used in the American school system: an attempt to define what everyone who leaves school ought to be able to do: read, write, perform simple arithmetic, etc.

CRITERIA, 'FAIRNESS' AND THE LAW

Criterion ratings face two problems. They may be accused of bias, or they may simply be ruled unsatisfactory.

Bias in ratings may take several forms: raters may be biased against non-whites; raters may be biased in favour of non-whites ('bending over backwards'); raters may fail to discriminate *amongst* non-whites, so all non-whites get the same rating.

Are criterion ratings racially biased? Early studies found raters, white and non-white, rated their own race more favourably (Cox and Krumboltz, 1958). Later research (Schmidt and Johnson, 1973) found no race effects. Meta-analysis of 74 studies of performance ratings (Kraiger and Ford, 1985) finds they are racially biased—whites favour whites, and non-whites favour non-whites—but confirms that the size of the effect is 'somewhat small'.

US 'fair employment' agencies may also find fault with ratings that are unreliable, subjective or too general. In the very important *Albermarle* case (Chapter 12) criterion ratings were ruled unsatisfactory because they were vague, and their basis unclear. In *Rowe* v. *General Motors* supervisor ratings were again ruled unsatisfactory, because foremen had no written instructions about the requirements for promotion, and because standards were vague and subjective. In the case of *Wade* v. *Mississippi Cooperative Extension Service* the court ruled that supervisor ratings of attitude, personality, temperament and habits had to be 'job-related':

> a substantial portion of the evaluation ratings relates to such general characteristics as leadership, public acceptance, attitudes toward people, appearance and grooming, personal contact, outlook on life, ethical habits, resourcefulness, capacity for growth, mental alertness and loyalty to organisation. As may be readily observed, these are traits which are susceptible to partiality and to the personal taste, whim or fancy of the evaluator.

Criterion ratings may not include generalized assessments of the worker's worth as a citizen or member of the human race; they must limit themselves to whether he/she does his/her work properly.

Nor are objective criteria free from challenge. An employer cannot simply say 'high turnover' and leave it at that; it may be necessary to prove that high turnover creates problems, costs money, or results from employees' restlessness and not from employer's behaviour. 'Fair employment' legislation imposes a duty on the employer to make efforts to 'accommodate' employees: provide a crèche, allow time off for religious festivals, etc. An employer who hadn't 'accommodated' might not be able to defend (no) absence or (good) time-keeping as criteria.

CONCLUSIONS

Face validity isn't really validity at all, although plausibility is always worth having. Factorial validation has its uses, but is only a small part of validation. Construct validation certainly has its place—in developing theories of individual differences, not in proving that selection tests work. Synthetic validation is a promising idea, whose promise has yet to be fulfilled. Content validation has really one thing in its favour—it's legally acceptable in the USA.

This leaves *criterion* validation as the best test of selection. Personnel managers select today, and find out later if they've made the right choice.

In theory true *predictive* validation is best, but *concurrent* validation seems to give the same results in practice, and is easier to do. Concurrent validation isn't acceptable where experience can change scores, so isn't suitable for personality and attitude measures.

Validating selection procedures doesn't look as complicated in the 1980s as it did in the 1960s. Over-interpretation of small samples caused psychologists then to suppose that curvilinearity, non-homoscedasticity or 'suppressor' variables were frequent occurrences; they now turn out to be so infrequent they're hardly worth bothering about. Chapter 7 shows that what validation research really needs is *numbers*. If the researcher hasn't a big enough sample of his/her own to analyse, *validity generalization* allows samples to be pooled, to get big enough numbers. When criterion validation uses large numbers, or pools studies, clear results emerge.

Criterion validation requires a criterion. Again the problem looks different in the 1980s than it did in the 1960s. The simple, universally used, supervisor rating criterion *works*; it can be predicted successfully by selection tests. Elaborate factor-analytic studies of multiple criteria may be of value for understanding work, but they aren't necessary for validating selection. Research on productivity (Chapter 1) and utility (Chapter 13) suggests the best criterion is *worth*—what the employee contributes to the employing organisation.

CHAPTER 12

Minorities, 'Fairness' and the Law

'Getting the numbers right'

The House of Commons of the British Parliament numbers 650 Members of Parliament. Before the 1987 election 28 MPs were women, and all 650 were white.

Once upon a time employers could 'hire at will, fire at will'. They could employ only fair-haired men, or red-haired women, or Baptists, or sycophants, or Freemasons or football players. They could sack men who wore brown suits, or women who wore trousers. They might be forced out of business by more efficient competitors, who chose their staff more carefully and treated them better, but they were in no danger from the law. Employers could also indulge any racial stereotypes they happened to have: don't employ Fantasians because they're all thick; don't employ Ruritanians because they're bone idle; Northerners are thieves; Southerners are sly; Easterners are smartasses, etc. Those bad old days are long past.

Equal Employment Opportunities legislation has 'come of age'; just over 21 years ago Title VII of the (US) Civil Rights Act of 1964 (CRA) prohibited discrimination in employment on grounds of race, colour, religion or national origin (Table 12.1). The Civil Rights Act also prohibited discrimination on grounds of sex; Ash and Kroeker (1975) say the US government didn't originally intend women to be included as a 'protected minority', and that the scope of CRA was extended to include them by hostile senators who thought it would reduce the bill to an absurdity, and lead to its defeat. CRA was joined in 1967 by the Age Discrimination in Employment Act, which prohibited discrimination on grounds of age, between ages 40 and 70, and the Vocational Rehabilitation Act in 1973, which prohibited discrimination on grounds of handicap.

US government agencies were created to enforce the new laws: Equal Employment Opportunities Commission (EEOC), Office of Personnel Management (formerly the US Civil Service Commission) and the Office of Federal Contract Compliance Program. Many individual states have their own laws and enforcement agencies (which this chapter won't attempt to go into). The various agencies issued differing sets of guidelines, until eventually, in 1978, EEOC issued the *Uniform Guidelines on Employment Selection Procedures.*

210

Table 12.1. Key events in the development of 'fair employment' legislation
in USA and UK

USA	UK
1964 Civil Rights Act	
1967 Age Discrimination Act	
1970 First *Guidelines* published	
1971 *Griggs* v. *Duke Power Co*	
1973 Vocational Rehabilitation Act	
1975 *Albemarle Paper Co* v. *Moody*	Sex Discrimination Act
1976	Race Relations Act
1978 *Uniform Guidelines* published	
1981 PACE abandoned by US Government	
1984	CRE Code published
1985	EOC Code published

In Britain the Race Relations Act (1976) set up the Commission for Racial
Equality, which issued its Code of Practice for the Elimination of Racial
Discrimination and the Promotion of Equality of Opportunity in Employment
in 1984. The Sex Discrimination Act (1975) set up the Equal Opportunities
Commission, which issued its Code of Practice in 1985. Both British codes of
conduct are short documents, compared with the *Uniform Guidelines*, and don't
give any very detailed instructions about selection. Note that race and sex

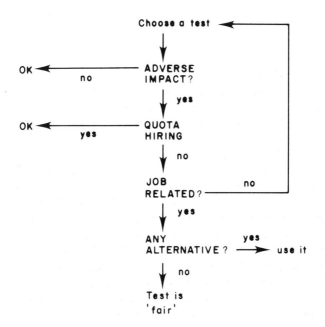

Figure 12.1. Stages in deciding if a test is 'fair'.

discrimination are dealt with by separate laws and separate agencies in the UK. Discrimination on grounds of age isn't illegal in the UK, as staff in the contracting university sector are finding to their cost. Nor is it illegal to discriminate against the handicapped, but there has been a 3 per cent quota system since 1944.

Figure 12.1 shows how 'fair employment' laws work in the USA; British agencies have followed the same general model, and adopted many of the key concepts. If selection (or promotion) excludes too many non-whites or women, it is said to create *adverse impact*. *Adverse impact* shifts the burden of proof (of no discrimination) onto the employer. The employer can remove *adverse impact* by *quota hiring* to 'get the numbers right'. Or else the employer can argue the selection tests are *job-related*. The employer who succeeds in proving tests 'job-related' faces one last hurdle—proving there's no *alternative test* that's equally valid but doesn't create adverse impact.

ADVERSE IMPACT

In Britain 4 per cent of the population are non-white; half are female; so 2 per cent are both female and non-white. If Members of Parliament were selected without regard to sex or race, Table 12.2 shows there would be approximately 325 women MPs, 26 non-white MPs and 13 non-white women MPs.

Table 12.2. Actual composition of the House of Commons before the 1987 election, and 'expected' composition, assuming MPs are selected regardless of sex and race

	Actual	'Expected'	'Expected' (four-fifths)
Male, white	622	312	
Male, non-white	0	13	10
All males	622	325	
Female, white	28	312	250
Female, non-white	0	13	10
All females	28	325	260

Are there fewer women or non-whites in the House of Commons than one would expect? Psychologists immediately think of calculating the chi-squared statistic, which yields highly significant values for all three comparisons, confirming there aren't 'enough' female, non-white or non-white female MPs. The problem with the chi-squared statistic is that it's almost impossible *not* to find a significant discrepancy when analysing large numbers. No employer is likely to have a perfect balance of race and sex throughout a large workforce. In the USA,

Uniform Guidelines introduced the *four-fifths* rule. If the selection ratio (selected/applied) for a protected minority is less than four-fifths of the highest ratio for *any* group, a 'presumption of discrimination' is established.

The proportion of women in the Commons is obviously far less than four-fifths the number of men; the number of non-whites is significantly fewer than four-fifths of 4 per cent of 650; and the number of non-white women significantly fewer than four-fifths of 4 per cent of half of 650. 'Recruitment and selection' for the Commons creates 'adverse impact' on women and on non-whites.

Four-fifths is only a guideline, which doesn't apply to small numbers, where it mightn't achieve statistical significance, nor to very large numbers, such as national statistics on arrest records for hispanic Americans.

Summarizing American experience up to 1979, Miner and Miner (1979) conclude that:

(a) both non-whites *and* women are under-represented as: managers and officials, professionals, technicians and skilled craftsmen;
(b) non-whites *but not* women are under-represented as: sales workers, and office and clerical workers;
(c) women and non-whites are *over*-represented as unskilled workers and service workers.

This leaves only semi-skilled workers not in need of EEOC's services.

Which population?

Is the absence of non-white faces in the Commons justified by saying there aren't any suitable candidates, or that most constituencies have no non-white voters? In America two Supreme Court cases—*Teamsters v. United States* and *Hazelwood School District v. United States*—ruled general population comparisons aren't always relevant; the populations should be those with 'necessary qualifications'. Comparing a district's teachers with its pupils, and finding non-whites *weren't* under-represented, was irrelevant, whereas finding non-whites under-represented as truck drivers was 'probative', because almost anyone can learn to drive a truck. (But not quite everyone; the Czech army in 1935 found recruits with IQs lower than 85 couldn't be trusted with army trucks (Mls, 1935).) The easier the job, the greater the presumption of discrimination if a protected group is under-represented. So perhaps calculations of adverse impact in the House of Commons ought to be based on the non-white middle classes, or non-whites who earn the same salary as MPs.

Sharf—a vocal critic of the EEOC—claims (1982) EEOC use a 'ratchet' tactic when calculating adverse impact; they compare the proportion of non-whites employed by the targeted employer with the *highest* proportion employed by *any* employer, including ones who give preferential treatment to eliminate adverse impact. 'One employer's program of preferential treatment becomes another employer's potential liability'; once the expected proportion has gone up, it can't go back down.

Shifting burden of proof

If there's no *adverse impact*, the case is dropped (or ought to be—Kleiman and Durham (1981) report some courts still go on to investigate promotion decisions even when they *don't* create adverse impact). But if *adverse impact* is demonstrated, the burden of proof shifts to the employer to prove *good business reasons*, which essentially means proving the selection procedure is valid. (Good business reasons don't include saying your customers won't like female/non-white staff, so the absence of non-white and female MPs couldn't be justified by claiming people wouldn't vote for them.) Employers whose 'numbers aren't right' are presumed guilty of discrimination until they succeed in proving their innocence.

QUOTA HIRING

Employers who can't prove 'good business reasons', or don't want to go to the trouble and expense of trying, must 'get their numbers right', by changing their selection criteria. They can adopt 'Affirmative Action' programmes, which set targets for the proportion of non-whites or women in each grade of every job. The Office of Federal Contract Compliance requires any company that supplies the US Government to have an 'Affirmative Action' programme. Other companies adopt an 'Affirmative Action' programme to settle cases brought by EEOC, or to forestall them. Sharf (1982) describes quota hiring as the EEOC's 'hidden agenda'. Miner and Miner (1979) agree that many observers see hiring 'on a random or quota basis' as 'EEOC's ultimate goal' (p. 56). Quotas can be 'hard' or 'soft'. A 'hard' quota requires every other new employee to be non-white; a 'soft' quota tells the personnel manager in effect 'try to find more minorities'. London's Borough of Lambeth, noted for its very progressive policies, announced in 1986 a 'soft' quota for disabled black women in its road-mending teams.

Reverse discrimination

'Affirmative Action' doesn't always end the employer's problems. Employing non-whites implies not employing whites; employing women implies not employing men. White males have been known to resent being passed over in favour of apparently less well qualified or experienced members of protected groups. American Telegraph and Telephone were sued by a male employee who saw a less suitable female promoted instead of him; even though AT&T were following 'Affirmative Action' policies agreed by a 'consent decree', they had to pay the man damages, but didn't have to promote him. The Kaiser Corporation found employers couldn't introduce quotas for minorities *until* they had been sued for discrimination; voluntary introduction of a quota for non-whites discriminated against white employees. (This decision was later reversed by the Supreme Court.)

'JOB-RELATED'

The Tower Amendment to CRA specifically:

> allows employers to give and to act upon the results of any professionally developed ability test provided that such test, its administration or action upon the results is not designed, intended or used to discriminate because of race, color, religion, sex or national origin.

For a while employers thought this allowed them to continue using psychological tests without hindrance.

However American agencies were very suspicious of tests that created adverse impact. David Copus, former Director of National Programmes at EEOC, said:

> when an employer or union attempts to explain the absence of women or minorities from certain jobs by claiming that few if any women or minorities possess the skills, abilities, or other qualifications which are required for the job.... Title VII assumes that Anglo males, females, and minorities are equally qualified for all jobs.

Two events made the 1970s a very bad decade for selection in general, and psychological tests in particular: EEOC's 1970 *Guidelines on Employee Selection Procedures*, and the 1971 Supreme Court ruling *Griggs v. Duke Power Co.*

EEOC's 1970 Guidelines

These set very high standards for validation studies—impossibly high according to critics. The result was most employers would find it very difficult to prove their selection procedures were 'job-related'.

Griggs v. Duke Power Company

Before CRA, the Duke Power Co., in North Carolina, refused to employ non-whites except as labourers. The very day CRA came into effect the company changed its rules: non-labouring jobs needed a high school diploma or satisfactory scores on Wonderlic Personnel Test (a short general intelligence test) and Bennett Mechanical Comprehension Test. The cut-off point was set at national high school graduate average, which 58 per cent of white employees passed, but only 6 per cent of non-whites.

The Supreme Court ruled the company's new rules discriminated—not necessarily intentionally. The Court's ruling attributed non-whites' low scores on Wonderlic and Bennett tests to inferior education in segregated schools. The Court said 'The touchstone is business necessity. If an employment practice which operates to exclude Negroes cannot be shown to be related to job performance, the practice is prohibited.' High School education and high test scores weren't necessary, because existing white employees with neither continued to perform quite satisfactorily. The Court concluded by saying 'any tests used must measure the person for the job and not the person in the abstract'. The Court considered EEOC's 1970 *Guidelines* 'entitled to great deference'—giving the legal seal of approval to a set of very demanding standards.

It's difficult to over-emphasize the importance of the *Griggs* case.

(a) It established the principle of *indirect discrimination*. An employer could be proved guilty of discriminating, by setting standards that made no reference to race or sex, and that were often well-established, 'common-sense' practice. *Griggs* objected to high school diplomas and ability tests. Another case, *Green v. Missouri Pacific Railroad*, ruled exclusion of applicants with criminal records discriminatory, because more non-whites had criminal records. Height, weight and strength tests for police and fire brigade were also excluded. Indirect discrimination can occur in quite unforeseen ways. Arvey *et al.* (1975) compared employers who took a long time to fill vacancies (average of 76 days from closing date to interview) with ones who worked fast (average of 14 days), and found the long wait halved the number of non-white applicants who appeared for interview. The long wait creates adverse impact, and isn't job-related, so it's almost certainly illegal discrimination.

(b) *Griggs* objected to assessing people 'in the abstract', and insisted they be assessed relative to the job. This implicitly extended the scope of the act; employers can't demand employees be literate, or honest, or veterans (ex-servicemen), or good-looking, just because that's the sort of person they want working for them.

(c) General intelligence tests clearly assess people 'in the abstract', so many employers stopped using them, the Tower Amendment notwithstanding.

Critics, such as Sharf (1982), allege 'fair employment' agencies 'have construed the law to their own egalitarian agenda of redistributing jobs', to which end they ignore Supreme Court decisions, or make it impossible for employers to act on them. Miner and Miner (1979) say EEOC commonly use an individual complaint of discrimination as an 'opportunity to look into the whole range of an employer's personnel practices for evidence of barriers to equal opportunity'. It's even been claimed 'EEOC staff includes many bright young people who are out to change the world and [who] have little knowledge of or interest in how the business world operates' (Miner and Miner, 1979). But then the 1960s were a decade of great idealism, and full employment.

The 1970 *Guidelines* and *Griggs* both insisted a test must be *job-related*, if it has created *adverse impact*. 'Job-related' means *valid*—something every occupational psychologist wants, and knows how to measure. In practice 'job-relatedness' meant selection procedures had to include elaborate job analyses, and that content-valid tests had the best chance of being accepted by the courts. General intelligence tests were right out of favour, because they didn't look job-related, and because they created a large adverse impact on some minorities.

Four years after *Griggs*, another case, *Albemarle Paper Co. v. Moody*, examined a 'hastily assembled validation study that did not meet professional standards' (Cronbach, 1980), and didn't like it. The company used Wonderlic Personnel Test and a modern version of Army Beta, and validated them concurrently against supervisor ratings. The court made a number of criticisms of the study's methodology:

(a) The supervisor ratings were unsatisfactory: 'there is no way of knowing precisely what criterion of job performance the supervisors were considering, whether each of the supervisors was considering the same criterion, or whether, indeed, any of the supervisors actually applied a focused and stable body of criteria of any kind'.

(b) Only senior staff were rated, whereas the tests were being used to select for junior posts. 'The fact that the best of those employees working near the top of a line of progression score well on a test does not necessarily mean that that test, or some particular cut-off on the test, is a permissible measure of the minimal qualifications of new workers, entering lower level jobs.'

(c) Only white staff were rated, whereas applicants included non-whites.

(d) Finally, the results were an 'odd patchwork', in which sometimes one test predicted, sometimes another, sometimes both, and sometimes neither. Sometimes Form A of the Wonderlic test predicted, where the supposedly equivalent Form B did not.

Local validation studies with smallish samples sizes usually get 'patchy' results. Occupational psychologists accept this; *Albemarle* showed outsiders expected tests to do better. *Albemarle* created a 'headwind' against aptitude testing in selection (Holt, 1977). Post-*Albemarle*. 'Many people [thought testing] just a gimmick to preserve discrimination. Many more people—maybe even most judges—suspect that it is some kind of mumbo-jumbo on a par with reading tea leaves and examining the entrails of birds.'

An influential paper in the *Harvard Law Review* in 1969 quoted extensively from Ghiselli's *Validity of Occupational Aptitude Tests*, and concluded that 'the likelihood that scores on any particular aptitude test will correlate significantly with performance on any particular job is very slim indeed'. Cooper and Sobol (1969) said the Wonderlic test sometimes didn't predict performance at all, and that it sometimes even correlated negatively with performance. No-one in 1969 had heard of *validity generalization* (Chapter 7), so no-one knew any better. Given that American lawyers are more likely to read *Harvard Law Review* than *Journal of Applied Psychology*, many probably still know no better.

The three forms of validity

The American Psychological Association's (APA) *Standards for Educational and Psychological Tests* distinguished three ways of proving selection procedures worked: content, criterion and construct validation. When EEOC drew up the 1970 *Guidelines*, APA persuaded them to recognize its *Standards*. It seemed a good idea at the time, but went badly wrong. APA's *ideal standards* for validation became EEOC's *minimum acceptable*. EEOC and the courts misunderstood the idea of the three forms of validation, and regarded them as mutually exclusive, whereas most validation procedures contain elements of all three. And the 1970 *Guidelines* didn't accept content or construct validation, except 'where criterion related studies are not feasible'.

The 1978 *Uniform Guidelines* by contrast:

(a) allow content, construct *or* criterion validity;
(b) but require the employer (not the employee) to search for alternative tests;
(c) allow employers to use validity data collected elsewhere;
(d) introduce the 'bottom line' concept of adverse impact.

Adverse impact is calculated from the ratio appointed/applied, not from particular parts of the selection. So could an employer use the Wonderlic test, which creates a very large adverse impact, so long as enough non-whites got through the selection process as a whole? No—the agencies reserve the right to question particular tests that create adverse impact.

Criterion validation

The 1970 *Guidelines* expressed a preference for criterion validation. Miner and Miner (1979) describe an ideal criterion validation study: test a large number of candidates, but don't use the test scores in deciding who to employ, then wait for as long as necessary and collect criterion data. Make sure you have a wide range of scores on the test. If you are using a battery of tests it's advisable to cross-validate the results. Don't use the test scores to make your selection decisions before you have finished the validation study, or you will restrict range. Don't test existing employees and compare test data with criterion data collected at the same time, because existing employees may not be representative of applicants. It sounds quite easy—but there are five reasons why it's difficult, time-consuming, and expensive, in practice.

1. *The criterion.* 'Must represent major or critical work behavior as revealed by careful job analysis' (1970 *Guidelines*). Rating criteria may be accused of bias, especially if non-whites or women get lower ratings. BARS formats (see Chapter 5) are more acceptable than vague graphic scales or highly generalized personality traits. Objective criteria must be justifiable; the employer may have to prove high turnover costs money and isn't the organization's fault. Training criteria are least likely to prove acceptable, and may themselves be ruled to need validation against job performance. Criteria in selection studies are always a compromise, and are never ideal, which makes it very easy to find fault with them.
2. *Sample size.* The correlation between predictor and criterion must be significant at the 5 per cent level—yet the typical local validation study rarely has enough subjects to be sure of achieving this (Chapter 7). EEOC help ensure the sample size is too small by insisting that differential validities for minorities be calculated, and by insisting every job be treated separately.
3. *Concurrent/predictive validity.* The *Uniform Guidelines* favour predictive validity, which takes longer, and costs more. An employer facing EEOC investigation may not have time to conduct a predictive validation study. (The wise employer doesn't wait to hear from the agencies before thinking about validation.)
4. *Representative sampling and differential validity.* The 'Catch-22' of the *Guidelines*. A 'representative' sample contains the right proportion of non-whites and women. The hypothesis of *differential validity* postulates that tests can be valid for whites or males but not for non-whites or females. An employer with an all-white and/or all-male workforce can't prove there's no differential validity without employing women and/or non-whites. Miner and Miner say the Catch was included on purpose: 'the concept was devised by the governmental enforcement agencies in order to pressure companies into hiring more minority group members and women'. Research during the 1970s proved fairly conclusively that differential validity does not exist; tests that are valid for white males are equally valid for women and non-whites.
5. *Adverse impact.* Cognitive ability tests create so much adverse impact on some minorities that the agencies, the courts and the minorities are unlikely ever to accept them, no matter what proof of their predictive validity is produced. Ledvinka (1982) agrees: 'Many employers suspect that, even if

they were to select their employees with unassailably valid tests, the government would find a way to harrass them if their hiring practices had an adverse impact'. The higher the score required on an ability test, the greater the adverse impact. On PACE (vi) 41 per cent of whites, 5 per cent of blacks and 12.9 per cent of hispanics scored over 70, and 8.5 per cent of whites, while 0.3 per cent of blacks and 1.5 per cent of hispanics scored over 90 per cent. The higher the pass mark, the smaller the proportion of non-whites that pass and are eligible for professional careers. Ability tests create most adverse impact on blacks, considerable adverse impact on hispanics, but none on women. Americans of Chinese or Japanese ancestry score better on ability tests than white Americans (Vernon, 1982). No data on adverse impact of ability tests on non-whites are available in Britain.

Kleiman and Faley (1985) review twelve court cases on criterion validity, since publication of the *Uniform Guidelines* in 1978. Their review isn't very encouraging for any employers thinking of relying on proving that their selection procedures actually predict efficiency.

1. Courts often seem to suppose some tests had been completely discredited, and can't ever be valid (notably the Wonderlic Personnel Test). Dunnette (1972) found the Wonderlic test has quite high average predictive validity.
2. Courts often examine item content or format, even though this is irrelevant when assessing predictive validity.
3. Courts often object to coefficients being corrected for restricted range as 'misleading'.
4. Courts' decisions are inconsistent and unpredictable.
5. Courts often ignore or avoid technical issues, and take a 'common sense' approach—to issues like sample size where 'common sense' is generally wrong.
6. Only five of the twelve employers won their cases.

Critics may say psychologists have just been hoist with their own petard. They always claimed their tests were the best way to select staff. They were always ready to dismiss other people's methods as completely invalid. They always insisted validating tests was a highly technical business best left to the experts. But when 'fair employment' agencies took them at their word, the psychologists couldn't deliver an acceptable validity study. Their 50-year-old bluff had been called.

In fact 'fair employment' legislation has done occupational psychologists a service, forcing them to prove more thoroughly that tests are valid and worth using, by validity generalization analysis (Chapter 6), utility analysis (Chapters 1 and 14), and differential validity research (see below). But it takes a long time to get new ideas accepted, especially when the old ones 'have been virtually set in concrete in the ... *Uniform Guidelines*' (Schmidt *et al.*, 1981).

Content validity

In 1964, when the Civil Rights Act was passed, 'content' validity was virtually unheard-of, and not very highly regarded. Guion (1965b) said:

> Content validity is of extremely limited utility as a concept for employment tests. ... [It] comes uncomfortably close to the idea of face validity unless judges are especially precise in their judgements ... evidence has accumulated to show that face validity, like content validity, is not an adequate substitute for empirical determination of predictive power.

'Content' validation improves on 'face' validation to the extent of using experts to analyse the job, analyse the test and conclude the latter relevant to the former. But content validation is clearly inferior to criterion validation; proving that a measure that *does* predict performance is a lot better than finding experts who say it *ought to*.

Guion (1977) later said content validation was added to the 1970 *Guidelines* as an afterthought, for occasions when criterion validation wasn't feasible. A whole generation of psychologists and lawyers have earned a very comfortable living from that afterthought. Content validation became the favourite validation strategy after the *Guidelines* and the *Griggs* case. Criterion validation was impossibly difficult (vs), and the courts couldn't understand construct validation (vi). (Quite a few psychologists admit to finding it a rather nebulous idea.) Content validation has four big advantages:

1. No criterion is required, so it can't be unsatisfactory. The test is its own justification.
2. There's no time interval between testing and validation. The test is 'validated' before it's used.
3. Differential validity can't exist, because there's no criterion.
4. It's easy to defend in court. Every item of the test is clearly relevant to the job. The psychologist doesn't get tied in knots trying to explain the connection between *knowing the opposite of 'big'*, and being able to sell potato crisps. (One of 130 items of the AH4 test which has some predictive validity for retail food salesmen.)

Content validation requires careful job analysis, to prove the test 'is a representative sample of the content of the job' (*Uniform Guidelines*). Test content must reflect *every* aspect of the job, in the *correct proportions*; if 10 per cent of the job consists of writing reports, report writing mustn't account for 50 per cent of the test. It's easy to prove job-relatedness for simple 'concrete' jobs, such as typing tests for typists. Content validation is much more difficult when the job is complex, yet the demands of the *Guidelines* caused many American employers to try content validation, where the problem really needed criterion or construct validation. The public sector in the USA, especially police and fire brigades, have repeatedly developed content-valid selection procedures, and seen them ruled 'unfair'. For example the St Louis Fire Brigade devised a set of promotion tests, misleadingly described as an assessment centre. In one test firemen viewed slides of fires, and *wrote* the commands they would give, which was ruled to over-emphasize verbal ability. Nearly half the fire captain's job is supervision, which the tests didn't cover at all. (The Brigade planned to assess supervisory ability during a subsequent probationary period.) After a series of court hearings and appeals, lasting until 1981, the tests were ruled unfair (Bersoff, 1981).

Construct validation

'A demonstration that (a) a selection procedure measures a construct (something believed to be an underlying human trait or characteristic, such as honesty) and (b) the construct is important for successful job performance' (Questions and Answers on *Uniform Guidelines*). Cronbach gives the example of high school graduation. A narrow approach usually concludes employees don't need to write essays or do sums or even to be able to read, so the "test" isn't job-related. The broader construct validity approach argues it's a reasonable supposition that people who do well at school differ from those who don't, in more than just academic ability, or even intelligence. Cronbach calls the something 'motivation' and 'dependability'. So an employer who doesn't want lazy, undependable employees could exclude them by requiring a high school diploma.

Cronbach's example shows very clearly why construct validation isn't a promising approach. The constructs 'motivation' and 'dependability' are exactly the sort of abstractions that are difficult to define, difficult to measure and impossible to defend in court. The two links—test-to-construct and construct-to-job—are usually both fairly tenuous: 'seminar room abstractions' (Cronbach, 1980). Miner and Miner (1979) say EEO agencies won't accept construct validation unless it includes criterion validation—which makes construct validation superfluous. American experience shows general education requirements are rarely accepted by the courts (Chapter 10).

The fate of PACE

Ironically, 'fair employment' legislation created the biggest problems for state and federal governments, because they must appoint *by merit*. Private employers could, before the Civil Rights Act, select who they liked, how they liked; the public sector had to advertise every post, check every application, use the same tests for every candidate and select the best. The weight of numbers made written tests essential. The US public sector still has to select the best, but has also to 'get its numbers right': so many women, so many non-whites, so many non-white women, etc. After all, if the government doesn't set an example, why should private employers spend time and money to ensure 'fairness'.

PACE (Professional and Administrative Career Examination) was used to select college-level entrants to fill 118 varied US Federal Government occupations: internal revenue officer, customs inspector, personnel manager, international relations analyst, criminal investigator, even archaeologist. PACE consisted primarily of an ability test (Test 500), with bonus points for special experience or achievements. PACE was validated against five criteria, for *four* of the 118 jobs, and achieved a composite validity coefficient of 0.60 (Olian and Wilcox, 1982). PACE had both content and criterion validity, and had every appearance of being an excellent test that most psychologists would be happy to use. Applicants had to achieve a score of 70 on PACE to be eligible for selection. Table 12.3 shows that PACE created a massive adverse impact on blacks and hispanics, but none on women. (*Hirings* based on PACE did create adverse impact on women, because preference was given to veterans (ex-servicemen) who were mostly male.)

Table 12.3. Percentage of PACE Applicants Scoring Unaugmented and Augmented Ratings Above 70 and Above 90, By Race and Sex[a] (Olian and Wilcox, 1982) (Reproduced by permission)

	Unaugmented Score		Augmented Rating	
	70 and above	90 and above	70 and above	90 and above
Whites	41.2	8.5	46.9	13.2
Blacks	5.0	0.3	14.5	0.6
Hispanics	12.9	1.5	19.2	2.6
Males	37.6	7.9	41.2	12.0
Females	36.3	6.6	43.8	10.8
Total	37.0	7.3	42.5	11.4

[a] Source: Compiled from Mento and Northrop, 1980, Table 4.

Pace was challenged in 1979 because:

1. Only 27 occupations of the 118 were included in the job analysis, and only four in the validation study.
2. Validation was concurrent, not predictive.
3. Test fairness wasn't investigated.
4. The Office of Personnel Management (OPM) hadn't tried to find an alternative test that didn't create adverse impact.

OPM were prepared to fight the case by:

(a) citing *validity generalization* research (Chapter 6), to answer point 1.
(b) citing reviews showing concurrent validities don't differ from predictive validities, to answer point 2 (Chapter 11).
(c) citing *differential validity* research (see below), to answer point 3.
(d) reviewing every possible alternative test, to answer point 4 (and concluding PACE was the most cost-effective, and had the highest validity).

The case never came to court; in 1981 the government agreed to abandon PACE over a 3-year period, and to develop alternative tests that create no adverse impact. What these alternative tests might be, and whether they can achieve a predictive validity of $r = 0.60$, remains to be seen.

Risk

'Business necessity' allows some employers to use selection methods creating adverse impact without having to prove their validity exhaustively, if 'the risks involved in hiring an unqualified applicant are staggering'. The case of *Spurlock v. United Airlines* showed America's enthusiasm for equality stopped short of being flown by inexperienced pilots; the court even agreed pilots must be graduates 'to cope with the initial training program and the unending series of refresher courses'. (Presumably no-one told them airline pilots in other countries, including Britain, don't have to be college graduates and often aren't).

Bona-fide occupational qualification (BFOQ)

This is known in Britain as *Genuine* OQ. When Congress was debating CRA, Congressmen and women waxed lyrical about a hypothetical elderly woman who wanted a *female* nurse—white, black, oriental—but female, so they added the concept of the BFOQ: that for some jobs being male, or female, is essential. The agencies interpreted BFOQs very narrowly. Early on, airlines found they couldn't insist flight attendants be female, as a BFOQ. Nor would the elderly woman have been allowed to insist on her female nurse. The scope of the BFOQ is limited in practice to actors and lavatory attendants.

Minimum skills testing

The *Uniform Guidelines* distrust rank-orders, because they may select people who are over-qualified (and who happen not to be non-whites). The *Guidelines* prefer employers to screen out applicants who lack essential skills and then select at random from the remaining pool of applicants. Or, as Cronbach (1980) says, 'Employers who dislike the idea of random choice can achieve nearly the same result by introducing unreliable information such as the interview' (if they have time and money to waste). Common sense says most people can do most jobs, so it's only necessary to screen out the small minority who can't—but common sense is wrong, again. The relation between ability test scores and performance is continuous and linear; the higher the score, the better the employee, for a very wide range of jobs (Schmidt and Hunter, 1981).

ALTERNATIVE TESTS

The 1970 *Guidelines* required employers to prove no alternative test existed that *didn't* create adverse impact, before they used valid tests that *did* create adverse impact. *Albemarle Paper Company v. Moody* overruled this in 1975, on the grounds employers couldn't prove a negative and said: 'it remains open to the complaining party to show that other tests or selection devices, without a similar undesirable racial effect, would also serve the employer's legitimate interest in "efficient and trustworthy workmanship"'. In 1978 the *Uniform Guidelines* placed the obligation to prove a negative back on the employer. Sharf quotes a former head of EEOC:

> There is not any way in which black people tomorrow as a group are going to, no matter what kind of test you give them, score the same way that white people score.... I can't live with that. I think employers can. And I think test validation gives them an A-1 out, because if you validate your tests you don't have to worry about exclusion of minorities and women any longer.... Thus I think that by giving alternatives, we relieve especially minorities of the frustration they inevitably find in taking validated tests.

Culture-free tests

Some ability tests are very obviously culture-bound. The *Information* subtest of the Wechsler Adult Intelligence Scale has 29 items, of which nine must be altered before the test can be used in Britain; few people in Britain, bright or dull, know when Thanksgiving Day is or the distance from Denver to Dallas. If an American test has to be altered before it can be used in Britain, perhaps it needs alteration before it can be used for non-white Americans. Many attempts have been made to find 'culture-free' tests that can be used equally validly on white, non-white, middle-class, working-class, American, British, German, Gurkha, Hottentot—any member of the human race. Some use shapes, some use mazes, some seek universals of human experience. Can culture-free tests reduce or even eliminate adverse impact? No—in fact culture-free tests generally *increase* adverse impact (Arvey, 1972).

Reilly and Chao (1982), and Hunter and Hunter (1984), review a range of 'alternative' tests. None achieve the same validity for selection as ability tests, except Biodata and job try-outs. Biodata inventories are fundamentally arbitrary, so are unlikely to impress the public or the courts as acceptable ways of choosing staff. Job try-outs can only be used where applicants have been trained for the job. But for promotion a range of alternative tests are as valid as ability tests: work samples, peer ratings, job knowledge tests and assessment centres.

Adverse impact of 'alternative' tests

'Test' to a psychologist means a psychological test, but EEOC gives it a much wider meaning: 'background requirements, educational or work history requirements, scored interviews, biographical information blanks, interviewer's rating scales, scored application forms'—and in case they'd overlooked anything—'etc.'. *Any* selection procedure is a 'test', so any selection procedure can be judged by the same rules as ability tests. In practice, the main focus has been on ability tests, because they create most adverse impact, and because Jensen (1969) had drawn everyone's attention to the fact. But most other 'tests' have come under legal scrutiny in the USA at some time; Ledvinka (1982) lists those found to create adverse impact and (sometimes) rejected: education, experience, height and weight, physical agility, (no) criminal record, good credit record, (not) being an unmarried mother, honourable discharge from forces or (no) dishonourable discharge.

Sharf (1982) detects another EEOC 'ratchet' at work here; EEOC have licensed themselves to declare a selection procedure discriminatory in employer B, if they've previously decided it's discriminatory in employer A. If height or weight or 'no-arrest record' has been declared 'not job-related' in organization A, the presumption exists, it's not job-related in organization B (whereas, Sharf notes, 'the employer who wants to transport validity evidence ... finds seven paragraphs of restrictive conditions').

Arvey (1979b) summarizes evidence on adverse impact of different methods (Table 12.3). Every method excludes too many of one protected group or another, usually in at least one way no-one can do much about. The law can't make women as tall and strong as men; the EEOC can't prevent intellectual

Table 12.4. Summary of adverse impact of five classes of selection test on minorities (Arvey, 1979b)

	Blacks	Females	Elderly	Handicapped
Intelligence and verbal tests	AI	+	ai	?
Work samples	+	NE	NE	NE
Interview	+	AI	ai	ai
Educational requirements	AI	+	ai	?
Physical tests	+	AI	?	AI

AI Established evidence of adverse impact.
ai Some evidence of adverse impact.
? No proof of adverse impact, but likely to exist, for some tests, or some persons.
+ Evidence the minority does as well or better than majority on this test.

efficiency falling off with age; 20 years of controversy hasn't closed the gap in test scores and educational achievement betwen white and non-white Americans. On the other hand, Table 12.3 does suggest discrimination against women should be fairly easy to avoid for most jobs. Employers should either eliminate bias from the interview, or eliminate the interview, and rely on ability tests and education (so long as there aren't any non-whites in the applicant pool).

'Sex-plus' discrimination

EEOC and the courts looked very critically at employers who said things like 'no women with pre-school children' or 'no wives of students'. Such 'tests' don't exclude women as such, but subsets of women, hence the name 'sex-plus'. Such requirements are clearly discriminatory, because employers don't say 'no men with pre-school children' or 'no students' husbands'. Validity isn't a defence; it's no use the employer proving women with pre-school children take more time off.

UK PRACTICE

The *Commission for Racial Equality's* (CRE) *Code* recommends employers to keep records of whether 'individuals from a particular racial group ... do not apply for employment or promotion ... [or] fewer apply than might be expected' or 'are not recruited or promoted at all, or are appointed in a significantly lower proportion than their rate of application' (Para 1.40). The *Code* doesn't define 'significantly lower'. The *Code* recommends that 'selection criteria and tests are examined to ensure that they are related to job requirements and are not unlawfully discriminatory' (Para 1.13). The *Equal Opportunity Commission's* (EOC) *Code* similarly says 'selection tests ... should specifically relate to job requirements'. CRE's *Code* is particularly concerned that employers don't require better command of English or higher educational qualifications than the job needs.

CRE first dealt with employers sufficiently ignorant or unsubtle to say things like [we don't employ West Indians because they are] 'too slow, too sly, too much mouth and they skive off' (CRE, 1984a), then with employers whose *recruitment* methods seemed to keep out minorities—usually by recruiting through existing staff. CRE's published Enquiries into alleged discrimination have dealt with taxi-drivers, milkmen, bakery shop assistants, factory workers, foremen and apprentices, bus-drivers, conductors, and inspectors, hospital cleaners—jobs for which selection procedures in Britain are minimal and unsystematic. CRE's latest report deals with the British armed forces, some of whose elite units are notoriously devoid of non-white faces. EOC has concerned itself more with 'sex-plus' discrimination, and with *maximum* entry age limits (because raising a family means women often enter a career later than men).

CRE's and EOC's Codes don't distinguish types of validity, nor have EOC and CRE so far concerned themselves much with tests or selection methods that create 'adverse impact'. To promote drivers and conductors to inspectors, Bradford buses used a home-made essay test of interest in the job, knowledge of local geography, etc. CRE (1983) objected to this test, because Asian candidates found it more difficult, and because it wasn't job-related. CRE later objected to a similar home-made essay test used to select factory foremen, because foremen only needed to write short notes about fairly specific matters (CRE, 1984b). This line of argument has effectively prevented American employers assessing the longer-term potential of staff they recruit.

Only one CRE Enquiry (CRE, 1982) mentions psychological tests. Apprentices at a tractor factory were selected by interview and aptitude tests. Asian applicants did worse on the tests, although there were too few Asians tested (25 in a workforce of 500–600) to prove 'adverse impact'. CRE nevertheless recommended the tests be validated in the company, and appeared to favour their validation for Asians separately. The factory appoints about 30 apprentices a year, and 6 per cent of the local population are Asian, so on average two apprentices a year might be expected to be Asian, which means it will take 100 years to collect enough subjects to make an Asians-only validation study worth doing. Current US thought, on CRE seems to model itself, sees local validity studies as a waste of time (Chapter 7), and differential validity as non-existent (see later).

'Fair employment' laws haven't had the impact in Britain they had in the USA, partly because ability tests aren't used that widely, partly perhaps because the British are less litigious. No employment discrimination cases involving tests have gone to trial in Britain yet, so no legal precedents have been set, and no-one has any idea what a British court would make of a complex dispute over adverse impact and test validity. English law does not allow 'class actions', in which one person's test case can be used to enforce the rights of a whole class of others, e.g. female employees; the British government hasn't introduced 'contract compliance', although some local authorities have; British courts enforce the letter of the law, not what they perceive to be its spirit.

DIFFERENTIAL VALIDITY

Critics often claim tests are valid for the white majority, but not for non-whites. There are two linked hypotheses:

1. *single group validity*—tests are valid for one group but not (at all) for others;
2. *differential validity*—tests are valid for both groups, but more valid for one group than the other.

Critics generally assume tests have lower (or no) validity for non-whites, because their culture, education, etc, differs. The issue gets complex statistically.

Insignificant minority correlations

Some people naively suppose it sufficient to show the test's validity coefficient achieves significance for whites, but not for non-whites. The correlations should be compared with each other, not with zero.

Different correlations

Kirkpatrick *et al.*'s (1968) data on the Pre-nursing and Guidance Examination are often cited as proof that tests weren't 'fair' for minorities. Validity coefficients for whites tended to be higher, or more statistically significant, than those for non-whites.

Meta-analysis

Kirkpatrick *et al.* reported a local validation study, which isn't really capable of proving differential validity. Overall Kirkpatrick *et al.*'s white samples averaged 130, while their non-white samples averaged 70, which means the 'white' correlation is much more likely to achieve significance. Many of the samples, white or non-white, were too small to prove anything. In most comparisons the minority sample is smaller than the white sample, so the correlation is more likely to be insignificant, and more likely to be reduced by *differentially restricted range*. Suppose the selectors accept the top 40 per cent of test scores, and suppose the minority has a lower average score. Obviously fewer members of the minority will be selected, and they will be a *smaller* proportion of the minority's distribution, with a *differentially restricted* range of scores, so their validity coefficient will be lower (Figure 12.2). Meta-analysis (Chapter 7) is needed to demonstrate differential validity.

Schmidt *et al.* (1973) reviewed 410 pairs of non-white/white validity coefficients. In 75 pairs the correlation was significant for whites but not for non-whites, while in 34 pairs it was significant for non-whites but not for whites. At first sight this is (rather weak) evidence that tests are more likely to be valid for whites than for non-whites. However the average non-white sample was only half the size (n = 49) of the average white sample (n = 100), so non-white correlations are less likely to achieve significance. Schmidt *et al.* calculated how often the patterns—white significant and non-white insignificant, and white insignificant and non-white significant—would appear by chance, given the sample sizes. The values calculated—76 and 37—were almost identical to those observed. Schmidt *et al.* conclude that single group validity is 'probably illusory', a 'pseudoproblem'.

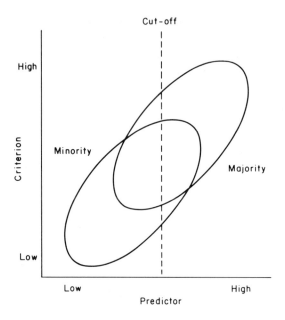

Figure 12.2. Differential restriction of range. A cut-off
on the predictor restricts range more within the
minority group than within the majority group.

If white and non-white sample sizes are the same, the pattern of 'white'
correlation significant but 'non-white' correlation insignificant ought to occur as
often as 'white' insignificant but 'non-white' significant. O'Connor *et al.* (1975)
actually found 25 white significant and non-white insignificant pairs and 17
white insignificant and non-white significant pairs—which doesn't prove a trend.

Differential validity

Single studies of differential validity are similarly inconclusive, because the
sample are too small. Suppose true validities of a test for a job are 0.50 for
whites, and 0.30 for non-whites, and suppose criterion reliability is 0.70 but that
range isn't restricted at all, then each sample needs to number 528, to have a
reasonable chance (90 per cent) of detecting the difference (Schmidt *et al.*, 1980).
Again, only pooling the results of many researches, through meta-analysis, can
give conclusive answers.

Early meta-analyses found no evidence of differential validity. Boehm (1972)
found only seven pairs of correlations from a total of 160 showed differential
validity; most pairs showed the test failed to predict significantly for white *or*

non-white Boehm (1977) later analysed 538 pairs of white and non-white validities, and found differential validity in only 8 per cent. Boehm concluded differential validity was more likely to be 'found' by methodologically inferior studies; neither single group validity nor differential validity was found by any study where both white and non-white samples exceeded 100.

Counting coefficients twice?

But Boehm's (1977) analysis may be misleading. Most validation studies use more than one test and more than one criterion. The tests usually intercorrelate to some degree; so do the criteria. Therefore each correlation between test and criterion is not an independent observation. (Suppose a validation study used Forms A and B of the Watson Glaser CTA, and found both correlated well with ratings of intellectual effectiveness and of originality (Figure 12.3). Does the study report four relationships, or two, or only one?) Hunter and Schmidt (1978), argue that including all 538 pairs of correlations in Boehm's calculation is conceptually the same as including the same correlation ten times—it makes the results look more consistent and more significant than they really are.

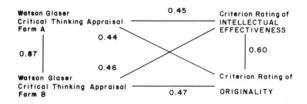

Figure 12.3. (Fictional) 'set' of predictor–criterion relationships, showing fictional correlations between criterion ratings, actual correlation between Forms A and B of the WGCTA and fictional correlations betwween WGCTA and criterion ratings.

Katzell and Dyer (1977) analysed the same 31 studies, but first identified 'sets' of correlated predictors and criteria like the one illustrated in Figure 12.3, then chose *one* pair of correlations at random from each set, so each of the 64 pairs was an independent observation. Ten of the 64 (19 per cent) showed a significant white v. non-white difference. A second random sample of correlation pairs found 31 per cent yielded a significant white v. non-white difference. Katzell and Dyer's re-analysis implies Boehm had allowed true differential validity to be masked by including lots of pairs of correlations that found no difference, which were really the same correlation over and over again under different names.

Exclude insignificant validities?

Hunter and Schmidt (1978) argue *both* analyses, by Boehm, and by Katzell and Dyer, are seriously flawed. Katzell and Dyer excluded pairs in which neither observed validity coefficient was as large as $r = 0.20$. Katzell and Dyer, and Boehm, both excluded pairs where neither correlation was significant—because a test that didn't predict for either race can't demonstrate differential validity. Hunter and Schmidt argue this was a mistake. Validity coefficients often fail to achieve significance because the sample is too small, or range is restricted, or the criterion is unreliable (Chapter 7). So excluding pairs where the correlations were small or insignificant excludes some pairs where there was true validity, and also excludes some pairs where white and non-white validities were identical. Three recent studies that avoid this error find differential validity occurring at chance levels. Bartlett *et al.* (1978) analyse 1190 pairs of black and white validity coefficients and find 6.8 per cent differ, at the 5 per cent level of significance. Hunter *et al.* (1979) analyse 712 pairs, and find 6 per cent significantly different. Schmidt *et al.* (1980b) analyse data for hispanic Americans from 19 studies, and find only 6 per cent of pairs of validity coefficients significantly different.

On balance the hypothesis of differential validity has been disproved. Ability tests can be used equally validly for white and non-white Americans. Humphreys (1973) suggests reversing perspective in a way he thinks many psychologists will find hard to accept: [the hypothesis of differential validity implies] 'Minorities probably do not belong to the same biological species as the majority; but if they do, the environmental differences have been so profound and have produced such huge cultural differences that the same principles of human behaviour do not apply to both groups.'

TEST FAIRNESS

Critics often claim tests aren't 'fair'. Critics often mean non-whites don't score as well as whites, but differences in scores between ethnic groups don't prove a test unfair. In the technical sense of the word, *unfair* means the test doesn't predict the minority's productivity as accurately as it predicts majority productivity. Several models of test fairness have been proposed; the most widely accepted is Cleary's model, based on regression lines. EEOC now accepts Cleary's model of test fairness, which implies American courts ought to.

Figure 12.4 shows the first type of unfair test, where there is true differential validity. When regression lines are fitted to the majority and minority distributions the *slopes* of the lines differ. A *slope* difference means the test predicts productivity more accurately for one group than the other. This chapter has already concluded there's no evidence differential validity exists, which implies there's no evidence *slope* differences do either. Bartlett *et al.*'s (1978)

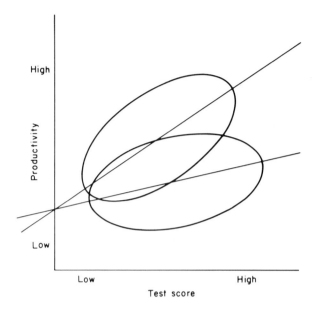

Figure 12.4. An 'unfair' test, showing a *slope* difference. The correlation between test and productivity is higher for majority than for minority applicants.

review finds black v. white difference in slope occur at chance frequency; Schmidt *et al.* (1980) find the same for hispanic Americans.

Figure 12.5 shows the second type of unfair test. Minority and majority differ in test score, but don't differ in productivity. When regression lines are fitted to the majority and minority distributions they *intercept* the vertical axis at different points—so-called *intercept* differences, which indicate bias. Of course the lines rarely have exactly the same intercept in practice, but where intercepts differ they often 'over-predict' minority productivity. In Ruch's unpublished review (see Schmidt *et al.*, 1980) nine out of 20 studies found tests *over*-predicted non-white productivity. Far from being 'unfair' to non-whites, tests may actually favour them.

Figure 12.6 shows a test which is 'fair', even though majority and minority averages differ. A regression line fitted to the two distributions has the same slope, and the same intercept, which means it's one continuous straight line. Test scores predict productivity, regardless of minority or majority group membership. Schmidt *et al.* (1980) review eight studies that show tests don't under-predict non-whites' productivity.

Schmidt *et al.* (1980) think future revisions of the *Uniform Guidelines* should drop the requirement for differential validation by race. Schmidt and Hunter

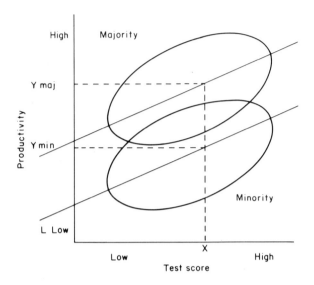

Figure 12.5. An 'unfair' test, showing an *intercept* difference. A given test score (X) predicts lower productivity (Y min) for minority applicants than for majority applicants (Y maj).

(1981) suggest everyone accepts that tests are fair: 'that average ability and cognitive skill differences between groups are directly reflected in test performance and thus are *real*. We do not know what all the causes of these differences are, how long they will persist, or how best to eliminate them.' They conclude 'it is not intellectually honest, in the face of empirical evidence to the contrary, to postulate that the problem [of adverse impact] is biassed and/or unfair employment tests'.

CONCLUSIONS

The *Uniform Guidelines* have been a great burden to American employers. They are rigid and inflexible. They stifle new developments in selection. They force employers to waste time and effort adapting effective methods to meet unrealistic requirements. They give administrators and lawyers power to make decisions about complex technical disputes they often don't understand. The *Guidelines* are misnamed: they don't provide guidance; they create confusion and uncertainty.

The Civil Rights Act has often, only half-jokingly, been called 'the occupational psychologists' charter'. Lawyers too have done quite well from it. But 'fair employment' legislation wasn't meant to benefit psychologists and

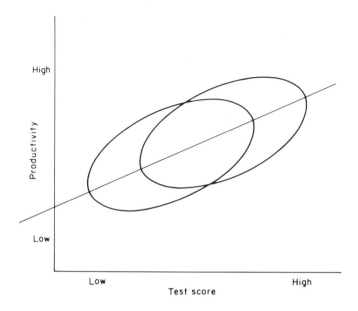

Figure 12.6. A 'fair' test, in which test scores predict productivity
equally accurately for minority and majority applicants.

lawyers; it was intended to help non-whites. According to Ledvinka (1982), it
didn't; the disparity between white and non-white, in wages, prospects, status,
being employed at all, got bigger during the 1970s, not smaller.

If American 'fair employment' agencies' real aim *is* the abolition of selection,
they are doing quite well. In 1963 90 per cent of American employers used
psychological tests in selection; by 1976 only 42 per cent still used them (Miner
and Miner, 1979). Some of the USA's largest employers stopped testing. General
Electric dropped all aptitude tests in the early 1970s to 'get their numbers right',
then realized in the later 1970s that 'a large percentage of the people hired under
the new selection standards were not promotable. GE had merely transferred the
adverse impact from the hiring stage to the promotion stage' (Schmidt and
Hunter, 1981). Similarly US Steel stopped testing apprentices, except to exclude
the very dull, with the result that '(a) scores on mastery tests given during
training declined markedly, (b) the flunk-out [failure] and drop-out rates
increased dramatically, (c) average training time and training cost for those who
did make it through the program increased substantially, and (d) average ratings
of later performance on the job declined'. Schmidt and Hunter wonder aloud if
these trends contributed to America's declining national productivity during the
1970s.

CHAPTER 13

The Value of Good Selection

Calculating the cost of smugness

> We find everywhere a type of organisation (administrative, commercial, or academic) in which the higher officials are plodding and dull, those less senior are active only in intrigue ... and the junior men are frustrated and frivolous. Little is being attempted, nothing is being achieved. (C. Northcote Parkinson).

Sometimes choosing the wrong person has visibly disastrous results: a train crash, a battle lost, the organization disgraced or discredited. Sometimes the results are less striking but still visible: lost customers, minor accidents, frequent absences, damaged equipment, ill feeling, mysterious illnesses—for as long as it takes the employer to realize a mistake has been made. In Britain, employees start acquiring 'employment protection' rights after 6 months' employment, so mistakes become increasingly difficult and expensive to rectify. Another cost of poor selection is more easily overlooked: the good people you reject go and work for your competitors. The scarcer the skill, the bigger the resulting loss.

In some organizations the costs of selecting ineffective staff mount indefinitely, because the organization lacks the mechanism, or the will, to dispense with their services. Some employers tolerate inefficient staff for ever. Naturally morale in such organizations suffers, driving out the remaining efficient workers, until only the incompetent remain, creating the state of terminal sickness so graphically described by Northcote Parkinson. Staff wander aimlessly about 'giggling feebly', losing important documents, coming alive only to block the advancement of anyone more able, 'until the central administration gradually fills up with people stupider than the chairman'. Other diagnostics include surly porters and telephonists, out-of-order lifts, a proliferation of out-of-date notices and *smugness*, especially smugness. The organization is doing a good job, in its own modest way; anyone who disagrees is a troublemaker who would probably be happier somewhere else. Parkinson advises that *smugness* is most easily diagnosed in the organization's refectory. The terminally smug don't just consume an 'uneatable, nameless mess'; they congratulate themselves on having catering staff who can provide it at such reasonable cost—'smugness made absolute'.

236

Just avoid mistakes?

Personnel selectors often see their task as avoiding mistakes, minimizing error. They bring in psychologists as the final check that the candidate is 'safe'. So long as the year's gone by, with no obvious disasters, and no complaints, personnel have done their job.

This negative approach to selection is wrong. Chapter 1 showed productivity is normally distributed. There is a continuous distribution of productivity from the very best to the very worst; selection isn't as simple as avoiding mistakes—not employing a small minority of obvious incompetents or troublemakers. The employer who succeeds in employing *average* staff hasn't succeeded in employing *good* staff; the employer who finds *good* staff hasn't found *excellent* staff. To take the argument to its logical limit, any employer who hasn't got the world's 100 best programmers filling 100 programmer vacancies hasn't maximized productivity. The world's 100 best programmers clearly isn't a realistic target, but programmers in the top 15 per cent perhaps might be, at least for some employers.

HOW TO SELECT

There are five criteria for judging selection tests.

1. *Validity* is the most important criterion. Unless a test can predict productivity there's little point using it.
2. *Cost* tends to be accorded far too much weight by selectors. Cost isn't an important consideration, so long as the test has *validity*. A valid test, even the most elaborate and expensive, is almost always worth using.
3. *Practicality* is a 'negative' criterion, a reason for *not* using a test.
4. *Generality* simply means how many types of employees the test can be used for.
5. *Legality* is another 'negative' criterion—a reason for *not* using something. It's often hard to evaluate, as the legal position on many tests is obscure or confused.

Meta-analysis makes some sense of the confused literature on selection tests, but much remains unclear. Table 13.1 collates the results of five meta-analyses, but should be treated with some caution, as there's insufficient information about some analyses. Hunter and Hunter's analyses are rather sketchily described by *Psychological Bulletin* standards; they do not say where they got their information, nor how they analysed it. It's not at all clear how independent are the analyses in Table 13.1. Dunnette's derives entirely from the American petroleum industry, Vineberg and Joyner's entirely from the American armed services, so these two are independent. Schmitt *et al.*'s analysis derives entirely

Table 13.1. Summary of meta-analyses of selection test validity

	Dunnette (1972)	Reilly and Chao (1982)	Vineberg and Joyner (1982)	Hunter and Hunter (1984)	Schmitt *et al.* (1984)
Chapter 2					
Graphology		'None'			
Chapter 4					
Interview	0.16	0.23		0.14	
Chapter 5					
Reference check		0.17		0.26	
Peer ratings				0.49	0.43
Chapter 6					
Biodata	0.34	0.38	0.24	0.37	0.24
Chapter 7					
Cognitive ability	0.45			0.53	0.25
Perceptual ability	0.34				
Psychomotor ability	0.35				
Aptitude			0.28		0.27
Chapter 8					
Personality					
Interest inventory	0.03		0.13	0.10	0.15
Personality inventory	0.08				
Projective test		'Little'			
Chapter 9					
Assessment centre				0.43	0.41
Chapter 10					
Education	0.00		0.25	0.10	
Academic achievement		0.17		0.11	
T&E ratings				0.13	
Work sample				0.54	0.38
Job knowledge	0.51			0.48	
Job Tryout	0.44				
Self-assessment		'some'			
Physical test					0.32

from studies published in *Personnel Psychology* and *Journal of Applied Psychology*, whereas Hunter and Hunter mostly seem to use unpublished US government data. The biggest overlap seems to be between Reilly and Chao's meta-analysis and Hunter and Hunter's.

With these cautions in mind, let us try to draw some preliminary conclusions, aided by Hunter and Hunter's two 'final league tables' of selection tests. The first 'league table' is for *selection* tests; the second table is for *promotion* tests (Figure 13.1). (Hunter and Hunter classify assessment centres as promotion tests, but they can be used for selection too). Figure 13.1 shows *selection* is much more difficult than *promotion*. Promotion tests all have fairly good average validity

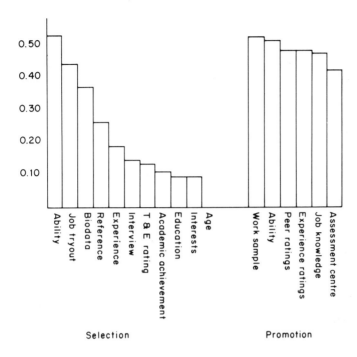

Figure 13.1. Estimates of the validity of various selection and
promotion tests. Data from Hunter and Hunter (1984).

quotients, so personnel managers can choose on the basis of: cost, convenience,
legal problems or the type of staff involved. Promotion should be easier than
selection because the employer is dealing with a *known quantity*; employers have
more, and better, information about existing staff, assuming they have a good
appraisal system and good records. (Although three of the six 'promotion' tests
in Figure 13.1 are not 'historical'.) Selection tests have to be chosen much more
carefully; their validity varies very widely, from a high point of $r = 0.53$ to a low
point of zero. Figure 13.1 also shows the distribution of validity is *skewed*
towards the low end; there are a lot of tests with very limited validity. Table 13.2
summarizes the relative merits of ten selection methods, against the five criteria:
validity, cost, practicality, generality and legality.

Interview costs are given as 'medium/low', because interviews vary so much,
and because they're so much taken for granted that few estimates of their cost
have been made. Biodata costs are given as 'medium', on the assumption the
inventry will have to be specially written for the employer; a 'ready-made'
Biodata inventory would be as cheap as ability or personality tests.

A 'practical' test is one that isn't difficult to introduce, because it fits in easily,
or because no-one objects to it. Ability tests are 'very' practical because they can

Table 13.2. Summary assessment of ten selection tests by five criteria

	Validity	Cost	Practicality	Generality	Legality
Interview	Low	Medium/ high	High	High	Untested
References	Moderate	Very low	High	High	A few doubts
Peer ratings	High	Very low	Very limited	Military only	Untested
Biodata	High	Medium	High	High	Some doubts
Ability	High	Low	High	High	Major doubts
Personality	Low	Low	Fair	?White-collar only	Untested
Assessment centre	High	Very high	Fair	Fairly high	No problems
Work sample	High	High	High	Blue-collar only	No problems
Job knowledge	High	Low	High	Blue-collar only	Some doubts
Education	Low	Low	High	High	Major doubts

be given when candidates come for interview. References are 'very' practical because everyone is used to giving them. Assessment centres are only 'fairly' practical, because they need a lot of organizing, and don't fit into the conventional timetable of selection procedures. Personality tests are only 'fairly' practical, because management and candidates are suspicious of them. Peer assessments are highly impractical because they require applicants to spend a long time with each other, and because people often object strongly to making them.

'Legality' is rated on American experience; no selection test has fallen foul of the law in Britain yet, but Chapter 12 argued that UK 'fair employment' agencies model themselves on American practice, so American experience may be a useful guide to the shape of things to come in Britain.

Most selection tests can be used for any category of worker, but true work samples and job knowledge tests can only be used where there's a specific body of knowledge to test, which means in practice skilled manual jobs. Peer ratings can only be used in the armed services. Personality tests are usually only used for white-collar workers. So too are assessment centres, although they have been used for police officers and enlisted personnel (non-commissioned ranks) in the armed services.

Taking *validity* as the overriding consideration, there are six classes of test with high *validity*: peer ratings, Biodata, ability tests, assessment centres, work sample tests and job knowledge tests. Three of these have very limited *generality*, which leaves Biodata, ability tests and assessment centres.

1. *Biodata* don't achieve quite such good validity as ability tests, and aren't as 'transportable', which makes them more expensive.

2. *Ability tests* have excellent validity, can be used for all sorts of job, are readily transportable, are cheap and easy to use, but fall foul of the law in the USA.
3. *Assessment centres* have excellent validity, can be used for most grades of staff, are legally fairly 'safe', but are difficult to install, and expensive.

Of the three, ability tests are probably best, and certainly the cheapest—so long as the employer doesn't get sued for using them. Chapter 12 showed that ability tests are undoubtedly 'fair', in the technical sense that they predict productivity accurately for male and female, white and non-white. Many American psychologists have argued that the time has come to recognize this fact, and to remove legal constraints on their use.

Ability tests discover what the applicant *can* do; they aren't so good at predicting what he/she *will* do. This implies ability tests needs to be supplemented by something else. Tables 13.1 and 13.2 suggest Biodata as the obvious choice, or perhaps assessment centres (although many assessment centres include ability tests). Personality and interest inventories make a poor showing in Tables 13.1 and 13.2, but possibly not enough studies were included in the analyses. The big gap in our information at present is validity of *combinations* of tests. Would a combination of ability test and Biodata have greater predictive validity than either test alone? Or do they cover essentially the same ground?

4. *Work samples* have excellent *validity*, are easy to use, are generally quite 'safe' legally, but are expensive, because they are necessarily specific to the job. Much the same considerations apply to job knowledge tests, except they're cheaper because they're commercially available, and that they're more likely to cause legal problems because they're usually paper-and-pencil tests.
5. *References* have only 'moderate' validity, but are cheap, easy and fairly 'safe' to use.

Most other tests in Tables 13.1 and 13.2 have low *validity*—but not zero validity. Tests with validities below 0.20 are commonly written off as a waste of time, but in fact can be worth using, if they're cheap, or if they contribute new information. Hence the only test in Table 13.1 that can be definitely dismissed as never worth using is graphology.

CALCULATING THE RETURN ON SELECTION

It's fairly easy to calculate the cost of selection, although most employers only think of doing so when asked to introduce *new* methods; they rarely work out how much *existing* methods, such as day-long panel interviews, cost.

It's more difficult to calculate the *return* on selection. The formula was first stated by Brogden in 1946, but for many years had only academic interest because a crucial term in it couldn't be measured—SD_y, the standard deviation of employee productivity. Until *rational estimate* and *superior equivalents* techniques (Chapter 1) were devised, there was no way of measuring how much more good employees are worth.

Brogden's equation states:

$$\text{Saving per employee per year} = (r \times SD_y \times Z) - (C / P),$$

where: r is the validity of the selection procedure (expressed as a correlation coefficient);

SD_y is the standard deviation of employee productivity in pounds/dollars;

Z is the calibre of recruits (expressed as their standard score on the selection test used);

C is the cost of selection per applicant;

P is the proportion of applicants selected.

Or to put it in plain English, the amount an employer can save, per employee recruited, per year, is:

VALIDITY of the test *times* CALIBRE of recruits *times* SD_y

minus

COST of selection *divided by* PROPORTION of applicants selected.

Here is a worked example:

1. The employer is recruiting in the salary range £20,000 p.a., so SD_y can be estimated—by the 70 per cent 'rule of thumb'—at £14,000. (Or SD_y can be measured by *rational estimate* or *superior equivalents* techniques).
2. The employer is using a test of high level mental ability whose proven validity is 0.45, so r is 0.45.
3. The people recruited score on average 1 SD above the mean for the ability test, so Z is 1. This assumes the employer succeeds in recruiting high-calibre people.
4. The employer uses a consultancy, who charge £480 per candidate.
5. Of ten applicants, four are appointed, so p is 0.40.

The SAVING per employee per year is
  (0.45 × £14,000 × 1) minus (£480/0.40)
  = £6300   minus £1200
  = £5,100

Each employee selected is worth over £5000 a year more to the employer than one recruited at random. The four employees recruited will be worth in all £20,400 more to the employer, *each year*. The larger the organization, the greater the total sum that can be saved by effective selection, hence the estimate given in Chapter 1 of $18 million for the Philadelphia police force, with 5000 employees.

Selection pays off better:

(a) when CALIBRE of recruits is high,
(b) where employees differ a lot in worth to the organization, i.e. when SD_y is high,
(c) where SELECTION procedure has high validity.

Selection pays off less well:

(a) when recruits are uniformly mediocre,
(b) when SD_y is low,
(c) when SELECTION procedure has low validity.

Employers should have no difficulty attracting good recruits in periods of high unemployment (unless the pay or conditions are poor). Chapter 1 showed SD_y is rarely low. But the third condition—zero validity—is all too likely to apply; many selection methods have zero, or near-zero, validity. But if any of the three terms are zero, their product—the value of selection—is necessarily zero too. Only the right-hand side of the equation—the cost of selection—is never zero.

In the worked example, even using a fairly expensive selection procedure, the cost per employee selected is only a fifth of the increased value per employee per year, giving the lie to the oft-heard claim that elaborate selection methods, or psychological assessment, aren't worthwhile. In this example selection pays for itself six times over in the first year. Failure to select the right employee, by contrast, goes on costing the employer money, *year after year*.

Using tests of limited validity

Return on selection is a *linear function of validity*; the higher the validity, the greater the return. The Brogden formula means selection tests can be worth using, even when validity is low—if their cost is also low. Table 13.3 gives three examples. In example 1 the employer uses the Dominance scale of the CPI to select managers. Assume the scale has a validity of $r = 0.25$, and that recruits have an average dominance half a SD above the mean, so $Z = 0.50$. A validity of $r = 0.25$ is often dismissed as useless, sometimes on the grounds that it accounts for only 6 per cent of the variance in selection (0.25 squared $= 0.0625$). Example 1 shows that CPI Dominance would, on the assumptions made, have a worthwhile return for the employer, saving £1275 per employee selected, per year.

Table 13.3. Three examples of utility analyses of selection procedures

	1. CPI-Dominance	2. EPI (pilot training)	3. Panel interview
r	0.25	0.15	0.14
SD_y	£14,000	£14,000	£14,000
Z	0.50	0.50	0.50
Saving	£1400	£1050	£980
C	£25	£1	£200
P	0.20	0.01	0.20
Cost	£125	£100	£1000
Return	£1275	£950	–£20

Example 2 is inspired by Bartram and Dale's (1982) work, using the Eysenck Personality Inventory to select military pilots. EPI's validity was generally low, around $r = 0.15$, a value so low many would automatically dismiss the test. However the EPI is extremely cheap to use—a nominal £1 per candidate is entered in Table 13.3. (On the other hand the Royal Air Force selects very few applicants; Table 13.3 assumes only 1 in 100, so testing costs aren't negligible.) Overall the EPI proves to be worth using. (Especially as Table 13.3 doesn't take account of training costs, which run into six-figure sums per pilot.)

Example 3 shows another selection procedure with low validity—the interview—and illustrates how a selection procedure with low validity can actually waste money. The interview achieves the same potential saving per candidate as the EPI, having the same validity, but costs a lot more. In fact the gain in productivity, for the first year, doesn't cover the cost of selection. Example 3 assumes a panel of ten interviewers, taking an hour per candidate, and values the interviewers' time at £15 per hour, on the accountant's assumption that if they weren't interviewing they could be doing something useful. The other £50 covers cost of secretaries, porters, etc. (If a ten-person interview board sounds preposterously wasteful, reflect that some employers use panels of *25 or more*.)

Utility analysis in practice

Boudreau (1983a) points out that some of Schmidt and Hunter's estimates of savings achieved by good selection are over-optimistic. The value of the increased productivity isn't all 'money in the bank'. Increased production means increased costs: raw materials, overheads, commission, etc. It also means increased taxes. Moreover the *costs* of selection are incurred before the *savings* are made, so interest charges need to be included. Correcting for these omissions reduces estimates of savings by 67 per cent.

On the other hand, Boudreau (1983b) thinks Schmidt and Hunter also *under-estimate* the savings good selection can achieve, because they only analyse one batch of new recruits. In the real world employers are constantly hiring new staff. Boudreau analyses the return on selection over 25 years, by the end of which time *everyone* has been selected by a test with high validity. Boudreau takes the examples of computer programmers, selected with the Programmer Aptitude Test (Chapter 7), which has very high validity ($r = 0.76$). Selection ratio is 0.50. Calibre of recruit is good, representing a Z value of 0.80. Programmers stay with the employer on average for 10 years, so after 10 years the programmer workforce has been completely replaced. Each year the employer recruits 618 new programmers. Figure 13.2 shows the return, in increased productivity, increasing steadily, until year 10, when the whole workforce has been selected by the test. In year 10 the gain is nearly eight million dollars, allowing for increased costs, taxes and interest.

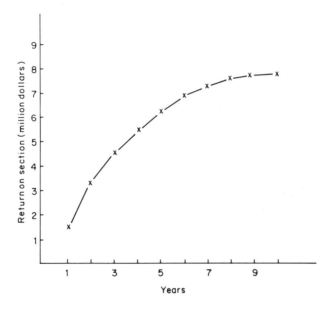

Figure 13.2. Predicted return on a selection programme, over 10 years. Data from Boudreau (1983b).

Coping with 'fair' employment laws

Ability tests select well, and are cheap and easy, but can't be used safely in the USA. Is there any way of using valid tests, notably ability tests, that will satisfy 'fair employment' agencies? Many US employers 'solved' the problem by abandoning tests that created *adverse impact*. Others set a very low cut-off for white and non-white applicants (around IQ 85). Both strategies amount to stopping trying to select at all. Schmidt and Hunter (1981) argue this is a grave mistake, and causes serious loss of productivity. Other employers hire their quota of protected minorities at random, then select within the majority. This is better than 'selecting' the entire workforce randomly, but is otherwise a very bad idea. The randomly 'selected' minority workers will be inefficient in themselves, and will look especially inefficient, working alongside *selected* majority group members.

Hunter *et al.* (1977) propose the *top-down quota* method of 'fair', but reasonably effective, selection. The employer:

chooses a selection ratio, e.g. 20 per cent;
tests applicants;
establishes which applicants belong to which minority,
recruits the best 20 per cent of white applicants;
recruits the best 20 per cent of each minority.

Top-down selection reduces the average test score of the recruits, so it reduces productivity as well. However *top-down* selection reduces productivity far less than *random hiring* or a *common low cut-off*, and somewhat less than a *randomly hired quota* of minorities.

CONCLUSIONS

The illusion of selection

Bad selection isn't just a waste of time; it costs employers a lot of money, year after year. Bad selection methods include the interview, which is a very time-wasting procedure, for candidate and interviewer alike. Yet bad selection methods are still very popular, especially the interview. The interview has survived 60 years of mounting criticism from psychologists, while ability tests, which are very good predictors of productivity, have been practically forced out of business in the USA. Why?

'Summing other people up' is an activity people like to think they are good at, like driving a car, holding their liquor, or making love. Hence people aren't receptive to the suggestion their task could be done quicker and better by ability test, or Biodata inventory. One wonders if the popularity of assessment centres derives as much from the elaborate opportunities to 'sum people up' they give, as from their high validity.

Incompetence + Jealousy = 'Injelitance'?

We are assuming of course that all employers genuinely want the best applicants; Northcote Parkinson thinks this very naive: 'if the head of an organisation is second-rate, he will see to it that his immediate staff are all third-rate: and they will, in turn, see to it that their subordinates are fourth-rate'. Such organizations suffer *injelitance*—'a disease of induced inferiority', compounded equally of *incompetence* and *jealousy*. The 'injelitant' organization doesn't fill up with stupid people accidentally—dull smug people at its core deliberately recruit even duller smugger people, to protect their own positions. And what better way is there to perpetuate incompetence than the interview? Mediocrities can be selected and promoted, using the code words 'soundness', 'teamwork', and 'judgement'. And what greater threat to 'injelitant' individuals can there be than objective tests of ability?, which might introduce unwelcome, disruptive 'clever' people. Parkinson thinks 'injelitance' a terminal illness of organizations, which can only be cured by dismissing all the staff, and burning the buildings to the ground; he does suggest, however, that 'infected personnel' might be 'dispatched with a warm testimonial to such rival institutions as are regarded with particular hostility'.

Cook's Law

An important principle of selection, stated on page 61: the more important the decision, the more time must be spent making it, and *the more time must be seen to be spent making it*. Work samples and simple aptitude tests are good enough for shop-floor workers. Clerical tests are good enough for lowly office workers. But selecting anyone 'important' requires longer, more elaborate selection procedures, taking many man-hours. Panel interviews in the British public sector show Cook's Law to advantage: a panel of ten spends all day interviewing candidates, at vast expense. But usually all the time is spent interviewing—the *visible* part of selection—while far too little time is spent in preparation and analysis.

Cook's Law has a corollary, which is very comforting to occupational psychologists: the more important the selection, the more the employer is willing to pay. It's no more difficult nor time-consuming to assess a potential Managing Director (Company President) than to assess a line manager, but most consultancies charge more, and most employers pay willingly.

Creating an underclass?

An employer who succeeds in recruiting able, productive workers needs fewer of them. If all employers use highly accurate tests to select productive workers the number of jobs will shrink, creating more unemployment. If every employer uses highly accurate tests, people of low ability will find it hard to get work. If employers started exchanging information the ungifted will find themselves never even being shortlisted. The result will be a steadily growing, unemployed, disillusioned and resentful *underclass*. This isn't a new idea; Cattell saw it coming over 50 years ago (Cattell, 1936).

Burning the candle at both ends?

At the other end of the distribution of ability, a shrinking workforce, of more able people, works harder and longer to maximize productivity. In the process they wear themselves out, and have no time left to enjoy life. Many managers already see this happening to themselves. If fewer and fewer people produce more and more, who is going to buy it? How are they going to pay for it?

Is productivity the only end?

This book is a title in a series on *Psychology and Productivity*, so it reviews what psychologists know about selecting people who produce more. This doesn't mean psychologists, including me, think all employers ought to work like that all the time. A world run by cost accountants would be a very dreary place.

Work serves other purposes besides producing goods/services. Work fulfils workers; work absorbs unemployment; work is good for people; work keeps people out of bars; work fills up the day; work brings people together; work prevents urban riots.

References

Algera, J. A., Jansen, P. S. W., Roe, R. A. and Vijn, P. (1984) Validity generalisation: some critical remarks on the Schmidt-Hunter procedure. *Journal of Occupational Psychology*, 57, 197–210.

Allport, G. W. (1937) *Personality: a psychological interpretation.* Holt, New York.

Amir, Y., Kovarsky, Y. and Sharan, S. (1970) Peer nominations as a predictor of multistage promotions in a ramified organisation. *Journal of Applied Psychology*, 54, 462–9.

Anastasi, A. (1981) Coaching, test sophistication, and developed abilities. *American Psychologist*, 36, 1086–93.

Anderson, V. V. (1929) *Psychiatry in industry.* Harpers, New York.

Anderson, C. W. (1960) The relationship between speaking time and decision in the employment interview. *Journal of Applied Psychology*, 44, 267–8.

Andrews, L. G. (1922) A grading system for picking men. *Sales Management*, 4, 143–4.

Anstey, E. (1966) The Civil Service Administrative Class and the Diplomatic Service: a follow up. *Occupational Psychology*, 40, 139–51.

Anstey, E. (1977) A 30-year follow-up of the CSSB procedure, with lessons for the future. *Journal of Occupational Psychology*, 50, 149–59.

Arnold, J. D., Rauschenberger, J. M., Soubel, W. G. and Guion, R. G. (1982) Validation and utility of strength test for selecting steelworkers. *Journal of Applied Psychology*, 67, 588–604.

Arvey, R. D. (1972) Some comments on culture-fair tests. *Personnel Psychology*, 25, 433–48.

Arvey, R. D. (1979a) Unfair discrimination in the employment interview: legal and psychological aspects. *Psychological Bulletin*, 86, 736–65.

Arvey, R. D. (1979b) *Fairness in selecting employees.* Addison Wesley, Reading, Mass.

Arvey, R. D. and Begalla, M. E. (1975) Analysing the homemaker job using the Position Analysis Questionnaire. *Journal of Applied Psychology*, 60, 513–517.

Arvey, R. D., McGowen, S. and Horgan, D. (1981) The use of experience requirements in selecting employees, (unpublished).

Arvey, R. D., Gordon, M., Massengill, O. and Mussio, S. (1975) Differential dropout rates of minority and majority job candidates due to 'time lags' between selection precedures. *Personnel Psychology*, 28, 175–180.

Ash, P. and Kroeker, L. P. (1975) Personnel selection, classification, and placement. *Annual Review of Psychology*, 26, 481–507.

Ash, R. A. (1980) Self-assessments of five types of typing ability. *Personnel Psychology*, 33, 271–82.

Asher, J. J. and Sciarrino, J. A. (1974) Realistic work sample tests: a review. *Personnel Psychology*, 27, 519–533.

249

Banks, M. H., Jackson, P. R., Stafford, E. M. and Warr, P. B. (1983) The Job Components Inventory and the analysis of jobs requiring limited skill. *Personnel Psychology*, **36**, 57–66.

Baron, R. A. (1983) 'Sweet smell of success'? The impact of pleasant artificial scents on evaluations of job applicants. *Journal of Applied Psychology*, **68**, 709–13.

Barrett, G. V., Phillips, J. S. and Alexander, R. A. (1981) Concurrent and predictive validity designs: a critical reanalysis. *Journal of Applied Psychology*, **66**, 1–6.

Barrett, G. V., Caldwell, M. S. and Alexander, R. A. (1985) The concept of dynamic criteria: a critical reanalysis. *Personnel psychology*, **38**, 41–56.

Bartlett, C. J., Bobko, P., Mosier, S. B. and Hannan, R. (1978) Testing for fairness with a modified multiple regression stratgy: an alternative to differential analysis. *Personnel Psychology*, **31**, 233–41.

Bartram, D. and Dale, H. C. A. (1982) The Eysenck Personality Inventory as a selection test for military pilots. *Journal of Occupational Psychology*, **55**, 287–96.

Bass, B. M. (1962) Further evidence on the dynamic character of criteria. *Personnel Psychology*, **15**, 93–8.

Baxter, J. C., Brock, B., Hill, P. C. and Rozelle, R. M. (1981) Letters of recommendation: a question of value. *Journal of Applied Psychology*, **66**, 296–301.

Bayne, R. (1982) Palmistry: a critical review. In Mackenzie Davey, D. and Harris, M. (eds), *Judging people*. McGraw-Hill, London.

Bemis, S. E. (1968) Occupational validity of the General Aptitude Test Battery. *Journal of Applied Psychology*, **52**, 240–9

Bender, W. R. G. and Loveless, H. E. (1958) Validation studies involving successive classes of trainee stenographers. *Personnel Psychology*, **11**, 491–508.

Bernardin, H. J. (1977) The relationship of personality variables to organisational withdrawal. *Personnel Psychology*, **30**, 17–27.

Bersoff, D. N. (1981) Testing and the law. *American Psychologist*, **36**, 1047–56.

Bingham, W. V. and Freyd, M. (1926) *Procedures in employment psychology*. Shaw, Chicago.

Bird, N. (1931) Relationships between experience factors, test scores, and efficiency. *Archives of Psychology, New York*, No. 126.

Bobko, P. and Karren, R. (1982) The estimation of standard deviation in utility analysis. *Proceedings of the Academy of Management*, **42**, 272–6.

Bobko, P., Karren, R. and Parkington, J. J. (1983) Estimation of standard deviations in utility analyses: an empirical test. *Journal of Applied Psychology*, **68**, 170–6.

Boehm, V. R. (1972) Negro–white differences in validity of employment and training selection procedures: summary of research evidence. *Journal of Applied Psychology*, **56**, 33–9.

Boehm, V. R. (1977) Differential prediction: a methodological artifact. *Journal of Applied Psychology*, **62**, 146–54.

Booth, R. F., McNally, M. S. and Berry, N. H. (1978) Predicting performance effectiveness in paramedical occupations. *Personnel Psychology*, **31**, 581–93.

Borman, W. C. (1979) Format and training effects on rating accuracy and rater errors. *Journal of Applied Psychology*, **64**, 410–21.

Borman, W. C. (1982) Validity of behavioral assessment for predicting military recruiter performance. *Journal of Applied Psychology*, **67**, 3–9.

Borman, W. C., Eaton, N. K., Bryan, J. D. and Rosse, R. L. (1983) Validity of army recruiter behavioral assessment: does the assessor make a difference? *Journal of Applied Psychology*, **68**, 415–19.

Boudreau, J. W. (1983a) Economic considerations in estimating the utility of human resource productivity improvement programs. *Personnel Psychology*, **36**, 551–576.

Boudreau, J. W. (1983b) Effects of employee flows on utility analysis of human resource productivity improvement programs. *Journal of Applied Psychology*, **68**, 396–406.

Brass, D. J. and Oldham, G. R. (1976) Validating an In-Basket test using an alternative set of leadership scoring dimensions. *Journal of Applied Psychology*, **61**, 652–7.

Bray, D. W. and Campbell, R. J. (1968) Selection of salesmen by means of an assessment center. *Journal of Applied Psychology*, **52**, 36–41.

Bray, D. W. and Grant, D. L. (1966) The assessment center in the measurement of potential for business management. *Psychological Monographs*, 80, No. 17 (Whole No. 625).

Breaugh, J. A. and Mann, R. B. (1984) Recruiting source effects: a test of two alternative explanations. *Journal of Occupational Psychology*, **57**, 261–7.

British Psychological Society (1985) *The use of tests by psychologists: report on a survey of the members of the British Psychological Society*. BPS, Leicester.

Brogden, H. E. (1950) When testing pays off. *Personnel Psychology*, **2**, 171–83.

Brogden, H. E. and Taylor, E. K. (1950) A theory and classification of criterion bias. *Educational and Psychological Measurement*, **10**, 159–86.

Brousseau, K. R. and Prince, J. B. (1981) Job–person dynamics: an extension of longitudinal research. *Journal of Applied Psychology*, **66**, 59–62.

Brown, C. W. and Ghiselli, E. E. (1953) The prediction of proficiency of taxi-drivers. *Journal of Applied Psychology*, **37**, 437–9.

Brown, S. H. (1978) Long-term validity of a personnel history item scoring procedure. *Journal of Applied Psychology*, **63**, 673–6.

Brown, S. H. (1979) Validity distortions associated with a test in use. *Journal of Applied Psychology*, **64**, 460–2.

Brown, S. H. (1981) Validity generalisation and situational moderation in the life insurance industry. *Journal of Applied Psychology*, **66**, 664–70.

Browning, R. C. (1968) Validity of reference ratings from previous employers. *Personnel Psychology*, **21**, 389–93.

Brush, D. H. and Owens, W. A. (1979) Implementation and evaluation of an assessment classification model for manpower utilisation. *Personnel Psychology*, **32**, 369–83.

Buel, W. D. (1964) Voluntary female clerical turnover: the concurrent and predictive validity of a weighted application blank. *Journal of Applied Psychology*, **48**, 180–2.

Bureau of National Affairs (1979) *Recruitment policies and methods*. BNA, Washington, DC.

Burke, M. J. (1984) Validity generalisation: a review and critique of the correlational model. *Personnel Psychology*, **37**, 93–115.

Burke, M. J. and Frederick, J. T. (1984) Two modified procedures for estimating standard deviations in utility analyses. *Journal of Applied Psychology*, **69**, 482–489.

Buros, O. K. (1970) *Personality tests and reviews*. Gryphon Press, Highland Park, NJ.

Burt, C. (1966) The genetic determination of differences in intelligence: a study of monozygotic twins reared apart. *British Journal of Psychology*, **57**, 137–53.

Byham, W. C. (1971) The assessment center as an aid in management development. *Training and Development Journal*, **25**, 10–22.

Callan, J. P. (1972) An attempt to use the MMPI as a predictor of failure in military training. *British Journal of Psychiatry*, **121**, 553–7.

Callender, J. C. and Osburn, H. G. (1980) Development and test of a new model for validity generalisation. *Journal of Applied Psychology*, **65**, 542–58.

Callender, J. C. and Osburn, H. G. (1981) Testing the constancy of validity with computer-generated sampling distributions of the multiplicative model variance estimate: results for petroleum industry validation research. *Journal of Applied Psychology*, **66**, 274–81.

Campbell, R. J. and Bray, D. W. (1967) Assessment centres: and aid in management selection. *Personnel Administration*, **30**, 6–13.

Campbell, J. P., Dunnette, M. D., Lawler, E. E. and Weick K. E. (1970) *Managerial behavior, performance, and effectiveness.* McGraw-Hill, New York.

Campion, J. E. (1972) Work sampling for personnel selection. *Journal of Applied Psychology*, **56**, 40–4.

Campion, M. A. (1983) Personnel selection for physically demanding jobs: review and recommendations. *Personnel Psychology*, **36**, 527–50.

Carlson, R. E. (1967) Selection interview decisions: the effect of interviewer experience, relative quota situation, and applicant sample on interviewer decisions. *Personnel Psychology*, **20**, 259–80.

Carroll, S. J. and Nash, A. N. (1972) Effectiveness of a forced-choice reference check. *Personnel Administration*, **35**, 42–146.

Cascio, W. F. (1976) Turnover, biographical data, and fair employment practice. *Journal of Applied Psychology*, **61**, 576–80.

Cascio, W. F. (1982) *Costing human resources: the financial impact of behavior in organisations.* Kent, Boston, MA.

Cascio, W. F. and Phillips, N. F. (1979) Performance testing: a rose among thorns? *Personnel Psychology*, **32**, 751–66.

Cascio, W. F. and Silbey, V. (1979) Utility of the assessment centre as a selection device. *Journal of Applied Psychology*, **64**, 107–18.

Cattell, R. B. (1936) *The fight for our national intelligence.* P. S. King, London.

Cattell, R. B. (1965) *The scientific analysis of personality.* Penguin, Harmondsworth, Middlesex.

Cattell, R. B. (1986) The 16PF in personnel work. Seminar at Independent Assessment and Research Centre, London, June 1986.

Cattell, R. B., Eber, H. W. and Tatsuoka, M. M. (1970) *Handbook for the 16PF questionnaire.* IPAT, Champaign, IL.

Cecil, E. A., Paul, R. J. and Olins, R. A. (1973) Perceived importance of selected variables used to evaluate male and female job applicants. *Personnel Psychology*, **26**, 397–404.

Clark, J. G. and Owens, W. A. (1954) A validation study of the Worthington Personal History Blank. *Journal of Applied Psychology*, **38**, 85–8.

Cline, V. B. (1964) Interpersonal perception. In Maher, B. A. (ed.), *Progress in experimental personality research*, vol. 1. Academic Press, New York.

Cohen, B. M., Moses, J. L. and Byham, W. C. (1974) *The validity of assessment centers: a literature review.* Development Dimensions Press, Pittsburgh, PA.

Cohen, S. L. (1978) Standardisation of assessment center technology: some critical concerns. *Journal of Assessment Center Technology*, **1**, 1–10.

Cohen, S. L. and Sands, L. (1978) The effects of order of exercise presentation on assessment center performance: one standardisation concern. *Personnel Psychology*, **31**, 35–46.

Cook, M. (1979) *Perceiving others: the psychology of interpersonal perception.* Methuen, London.

Cook, M. (1984) *Levels of personality.* Holt Rinehart & Winston, Eastbourne, Sussex.

Cooper, G. and Sobol, R. B. (1969) Seniority and testing under fair employment laws. *Harvard Law Review*, **82**, 1598–1679.

Cooper, R. and Payne, R. (1967) Extraversion and some aspects of work behavior. *Personnel Psychology*, **20**, 45–57.

Cooper, W. H. (1981) Ubiquitous halo. *Psychological Bulletin*, **90**, 218–44.

Cornelius, E. T., Denisi, A. S. and Blencoe, A. G. (1984) Expert and naive raters using the PAQ: does it matter? *Personnel Psychology*, **37**, 453–64.

Cox, J. A. and Krumboltz, J. D. (1958) Racial bias in peer ratings of basic airmen. *Sociometry*, **21**, 292–9.

Crites, J. O. (1969) *Vocational psychology*. McGraw-Hill, New York.

Cronbach, L. J. (1980) Selection theory for a political world. *Public Personnel Management Journal*, **9**, 37–50.

Cronbach, L. J. (1984) *Essentials of psychological testing*. 4th edn. Harper & Row, New York.

Cronbach, L. J. and Gleser, G. C. (1965) *Psychological tests and personnel decisions*. University of Illinois Press, Urbana, IL.

Culpin, M. and Smith, M. (1930) *The nervous temperament*. Industrial Health Research Board Report No. 61. HMSO, London.

Cunningham, J. W., Boese, R. R., Neeb, R. W. and Pass, J. J. (1983) Systematically derived work dimensions: factor analyses of the Occupation Analysis Inventory. *Journal of Applied Psychology*, **68**, 232–52.

Cureton, E. E. (1950) Validity, reliability, and baloney. *Educational and Psychological Measurement*, **10**, 94–96.

CRE (Commission for Racial Equality) (1982) *Massey Ferguson Perkins Ltd: report of a formal investigation*. CRE, London.

CRE (1983) *The West Yorkshire Passenger Transport Executive (Bradford Metro): report of a formal investigation*. CRE, London.

CRE (1984a) *St Chad's Hospital: report of a formal investigation*. CRE, London.

CRE (1984b) *Dunlop Ltd, Leicester: report of a formal investigation*. CRE London.

Dawes, R. M. (1971) A case study of graduate admissions: application of three principles of human decision making. *American Psychologist*, **26**, 180–8.

DeNisi, A. S. and Shaw, J. B. (1977) Investigation of the uses of self-reports of abilities. *Journal of Applied Psychology*, **62**, 641–4.

Dipboye, R. L., Arvey, R. D. and Terpstra, D. E. (1977) Sex and physical attractiveness of raters and applicants as determinants of resume evaluation. *Journal of Applied Psychology*, **62**, 288–94.

Distefano, M. K., Pryer, M. W. and Erffmeyer, R. C. (1983) Application of content validity methods to the development of a job-related performance rating criterion. *Personnel Psychology*, **36**, 621–31.

Dorcus, R. M. and Jones, M. H. (1950) *Handbook of employee selection*. McGraw-Hill, New York.

Downs, S., Farr. R. M. and Colbeck, L. (1978) Self-appraisal: a convergence of selection and guidance. *Journal of Occupational Psychology*, **51**, 271–8.

Dulewicz, S. V. and Keenay, G. A. (1979) A practically oriented and objective method for classifying and assigning senior jobs. *Journal of Occupational Psychology*, **52**, 155–66.

Dunnette, M. D. (1966) *Personnel selection and placement*. Tavistock, London.

Dunnette, M. D. (1972) *Validity study results for jobs relevant to the petroleum refining industry*. American Petroleum Institute.

Dunnette, M. D. (1976) Aptitudes, abilities, and skills. In Dunnette, M. D. (ed.), *Handbook of industrial and organisational psychology*. Rand McNally, Chicago, IL.

Dunnette, M. D. (1982) *Development and validation of an industry-wide electricity power plant operator selection system*. Personnel Decisions Research Institute, Minneapolis, MN.

Dunnette, M. D. and Kirchner, W. K. (1959) A check list for differentiating different kinds of sales jobs. *Personnel Psychology*, **12**, 421–9.

Dunnette, M. D. and Maetzold, J. (1955) Use of a weighted application blank in hiring seasonal employees. *Journal of Applied Psychology*, **39**, 308–10.

Dunnette, M. D. McCartney, J., Carlson, H. C. and Kirchner, W. K. (1962) A study of faking behavior on a forced-choice self-description checklist. *Personnel Psychology*, **15**, 13–24.

Eaton, N. K., Wing, H. and Mitchell, K. J. (1985) Alternate methods of estimating the dollar value of performance. *Personnel Psychology*, **38**, 27–40.

Ebel, R. L. (1977) Comments on some problems of employment testing. *Personnel Psychology*, **30**, 55–63.

Elliott, A. G. P. (1981) Some implications of lie scale scores in real-life selection. *Journal of Occupational Psychology*, **54**, 9–16.

Ellis, A. and Conrad, H. S. (1948) The validity of personality inventories in military practice. *Psychological Bulletin*, **45**, 385–426.

England, G. W. and Paterson, D. G. (1960) Selection and employment – the past ten years. In Henneman, H. G. (ed), *Employment relations research: a summary and appraisal.* Harpers, New York.

Epstein, S. (1979) The stability of behavior: I. On predicting most of the people much of the time. *Journal of Personality and Social Psychology*, **37**, 1097–1126.

Farr, J. L. (1973) Response requirement and primacy–recency effects in a simulated selection interview. *Journal of Applied Psychology*, **57**, 228–33.

Fineman, S. (1977) The achievement motive construct and its measurement: where are we now? *British Journal of Psychology*, **68**, 1–22.

Flanagan, J. C. (1946) The experimental validation of a selection procedure. *Educational and Psychological Measurement*, **6**, 445–66.

Flanagan, J. C. (1954) The critical incident technique. *Psychological Bulletin*, **51**, 327–58.

Fleishman, E. A. (1979) Evaluating physical abilities required by jobs. *Personnel Administrator*, **24**, 82–92.

Forsythe, S., Drake, M. F. and Cox, C. E. (1985) Influence of applicant's dress on interviewer's selection decisions. *Journal of Applied Psychology*, **70**, 374–8.

Fowler, R. D. (1985) Landmarks in computer-assisted psychological assessment. *Journal of Consulting and Clinical Psychology*, **53**, 748–59.

Frederiksen, N., Saunders, D. R. and Wand, B. (1975) The In-Basket test. *Psychological Monographs*, **71**, No. 9 (Whole No. 438).

Gardner, K. E. and Williams, A. P. O. (1973) A twenty-five-year follow-up of an extended interview selection procedure in the Royal Navy. *Occupational Psychology*, **47**, 1–13.

Ghiselli, E. E. (1959) The development of processes for indirect or synthetic validity (a symposium). 2. The generalisation of validity. *Personnel Psychology*, **12**, 397–402.

Ghiselli, E. E. (1966) *The validity of occupational aptitude tests.* Wiley, New York.

Ghiselli, E. E. (1971) *Explorations in managerial talent.* Goodyear, Pacific Palisades, CA.

Ghiselli, E. E. (1973) The validity of aptitude tests in personnel selection. *Personnel Psychology*, **26**, 461–77.

Ghiselli, E. E. and Haire, M. (1960) The validation of selection tests in the light of the dynamic character of criteria. *Personnel Psychology*, **13**, 225–31.

Gifford, R., Ng, C. F. and Wilkinson, M. (1985) Non-verbal cues in the employment interview: links between applicant qualities and interviewer judgements. *Journal of Applied Psychology*, **70**, 729–36.

Glass, G. V. (1976) Primary, secondary, and meta-analysis of research. *Educational Researcher*, **5**, 3–8.

Glennon, J. R., Albright, L. E. and Owens, W. A. (1963) *A catalog of life history items.* American Psychological Association, Chicago.

Goldsmith, D. B. (1922) The use of a personal history blank as a salesmanship test. *Journal of Applied Psychology*, **6**, 149–55.

Goldstein, I. L. (1971) The application blank: how honest are the responses? *Journal of Applied Psychology*, **55**, 491–2.

Goodale, J. G. and Burke, R. J. (1975) Behaviorally based ratings scales need not be job specific. *Journal of Applied Psychology*, **60**, 389–91.

Gordon, M. E. and Fitzgibbons, W. J. (1982) Empirical test of the validity of seniority as a factor in staffing decisions. *Journal of Applied Psychology*, **67**, 311-19.

Gordon, M. E. and Kleiman, L. S. (1976) The prediction of trainability using a work-sample test and an aptitude test: a direct comparison. *Personnel Psychology*, **29**, 243–53.

Gough, H. G. (1962) Clinical vs statistical prediction in psychology. In Postman, L. (ed.), *Psychology in the making*. Knopf, New York.

Grant, D. L. and Bray, D. W. (1969) Contributions of the interview to assessment of management potential. *Journal of Applied Psychology*, **53**, 24-34.

Grimsley, G. and Jarrett, H. F. (1973) The relationship of past management achievement to test measures obtained in the employment situation: methodology and results. *Personnel Psychology*, **26**, 317-48.

Guilford, J. P. (1967) *The structure of human intellect*. McGraw Hill, New York.

Guion, R. M. (1961) Criterion measurement and personnel judgement. *Personnel Psychology*, **14**, 141-9.

Guion, R. M. (1965a) *Personnel testing*. McGraw-Hill, New York

Guion, R. M. (1965b) Synthetic validity in a small company: a demonstration. *Personnel Psychology*, **18**, 49-63.

Guion, R. M. (1977) Content validity—the source of my discontent. *Applied Psychological Measurement*, **1**, 1-10.

Guion, R. M. (1978) 'Content validity' in moderation. *Personnel Psychology*, **31**, 205-13.

Guion, R. M. (1980) On trinitarian doctrines of validity. *Professional Psychology*, **11**, 385-98.

Guion, R. M. and Cranny, C. J. (1982) A note on concurrent and predictive validity designs: a critical reanalysis. *Journal of Applied Psychology*, **67**, 239-44.

Guion, R. M. and Gottier, R. F. (1965) Validity of personality measures in personnel selection. *Personnel Psychology*, **18**, 135-64.

Gustad, J. W. (1956) Psychological test reviews: Edwards Personal Preference Schedule. *Journal of Consulting and Clinical Psychology*, **20**, 322-4.

Hakel, M. D. (1982) The employment interview. In Rowland, K. M. and Ferris, G. R. (eds), *Personnel management*. Allyn & Bacon, Boston, MA.

Hakel, M. D., Dobmeyer, T. W., and Dunnette, M. D. (1970) Relative importance of three content dimensions in overall suitability ratings of job applicants' resumés. *Journal of Applied Psychology*, **54**, 65-71.

Hall, W. B. and MacKinnon, D. W. (1969) Personality inventory correlates of creativity among architects. *Journal of Applied Psychology*, **53**, 322-6.

Hansen, J. C. (1976) Exploring new directions for Strong-Campbell Interest Inventory occupational scale construction. *Journal of Vocational Behavior*, **9**, 147-60.

Harrell, M. S., Harrell, T. W., McIntyre, S. H. and Weinberg, C. B. (1977) Predicting compensation among MBA graduates five and ten years after graduation. *Journal of Applied Psychology*, **62**, 636-40.

Harrell, T. W. (1972) High earning MBAs. *Personnel Psychology*, **25**, 523-30.

Harris, J. G. (1972) Prediction of success on a distant Pacific island, Peace Corps style. *Journal of Consulting and Clinical Psychology*, **38**, 181-90.

Hartshorne, H. and May, M. (1928) *Studies in the nature of character. Vol 1. Studies in deceit*. Macmillan, New York.

Heron, A. (1954) Satisfaction and satisfactoriness: complementary aspects of occupational adjustment. *Occupational Psychology*, **28**, 140-53.

Herriot, P. and Rothwell, C. (1983) Expectations and impressions in the graduate selection interview. *Journal of Occupational Psychology*, **56**, 303-14.

Herriot, P. and Wingrove, J. (1984) Decision processes in graduate pre-selection. *Journal of Occupational Psychology*, 57, 269–75.

Herrnstein, R. J. (1973) *IQ in the meritocracy*. Allen Lane, London.

Herzberg, F. (1954) Temperament measures in industrial selection. *Journal of Applied Psychology*, 38, 81–4.

Hinrichs, J. R. (1978) An eight year follow-up of a management assessment center. *Journal of Applied Psychology*, 63, 596–601.

Hinrichs, J. R. and Haanpera, S. (1976) Reliability of measurement in situational exercises: an assessment of the assessment center method. *Personnel Psychology*, 29, 31–40.

Hirsch, H. R., Northrop, L. C. and Schmidt, F. L. (1984) *Validity generalisation results for law enforcement occupations*. US Office of Personnel Management, Washington DC.

Hogan, J. (1985) Tests for success in diver training. *Journal of Applied Psychology*, 70, 219–24.

Hoiberg, A. and Pugh, W. M. (1978) Predicting Navy effectiveness: expectations, motivation, personality, aptitude, and background variables. *Personnel Psychology*, 31, 841–52.

Hollander, E. P. (1965) Validity of peer nominations in predicting a distant performance criterion. *Journal of Applied Psychology*, 49, 434–8.

Hollingworth, H. H. (1922) *Vocational psychology*. Appleton Century Crofts, New York.

Hollman, T. D. (1972) Employment interviewers' errors in processing positive and negative information. *Journal of Applied Psychology*, 56, 130–4.

Holt, T. (1977) A view from Albemarle. *Personnel Psychology*, 30, 65–80.

Holzbach, R. L. (1978) Rater bias in performance ratings: superior, self and peer ratings. *Journal of Applied Psychology*, 63, 579–88.

Hough, L. M., Keyes, M. A. and Dunnette, M. D. (1983) An evaluation of three 'alternative' selection procedures. *Personnel Psychology*, 36, 261–76.

Hovland, C. I. and Wonderlic, E. F. (1939) Prediction of success by a standardised interview. *Journal of Applied Psychology*, 23, 537–46.

Huck, J. R. and Bray, D. W. (1976) Management assessment center evaluation and subsequent job performance of white and black females. *Personnel Psychology*, 29, 13–30.

Hughes, J. F., Dunn, J. F. and Baxter, B. (1956) The validity of selection instruments under operating conditions. *Personnel Psychology*, 9 321–323.

Hull, C. L. (1928) *Aptitude testing*. Harrap, London.

Humphreys, L. G. (1973) Statistical definitions of test validity for minority groups. *Journal of Applied Psychology*, 58, 1–4.

Hunter, J. E. (1983) A causal analysis of cognitive ability, job knowledge, and supervisory ratings. In Landy, F., Zedeck, S. and Cleveland, J. (eds), *Performance/measurement and theory*. Erlbaum, Hillsdale, NJ.

Hunter, J. E. and Hunter, R. F. (1984) Validity and utility of alternate predictors of job performance. *Psychological Bulletin*, 96, 72–98.

Hunter, J. E. and Schmidt, F. L. (1978) Differential and single-group validity of employment tests by race: a critical analysis of three recent studies. *Journal of Applied Psychology*, 63, 1–11.

Hunter, J. E., Schmidt, J. E. and Hunter, R. (1979) Differential validity of employment tests by race: a comprehensive review and analysis. *Psychological Bulletin*, 86, 721–35.

Hunter, J. E., Schmidt, F. L. and Rauschenberger, J. M. (1977) Fairness of psychological tests: implications of four definitions for selection utility and minority hiring. *Journal of Applied Psychology*, 62, 245–60.

Hunter, J. E., Schmidt, F. L. and Pearlman, K. (1982) History and accuracy of validity generalisation equations: a response to the Callender and Osburn reply. *Journal of Applied Psychology*, **67**, 853–8.

Imada, A. S. and Hakel, M. D. (1977) Influence of nonverbal communication and rater proximity on impressions and decisions in simulated employment interviews. *Journal of Applied Psychology*, **62**, 295–300.

Income Data Services Ltd (1985) *Psychological assessment.* Report No. 341. IDS Ltd, London.

Inwald, R. E. and Shusman, E. J. (1984) The IPI and MMPI as predictors of academy performance for police recruits. *Journal of Police Science and Administration*, **12**, 1–11.

Janz, T. (1982) Initial comparisons of patterned behavior description interviews versus unstructured interviews. *Journal of Applied Psychology*, **67**, 577–80.

Jensen, A. R. (1969) *Genetics and education.* Methuen, London.

Jensen, A. R. (1969) ... *Harvard Educational Review.*

Johnson, C. D., Messe, L. A. and Crano, W. D. (1984) Predicting job performance of low income workers: the Work Opinion Questionnaire. *Personnel Psychology*, **37**, 291–9.

Johnson, J. H., Gianetti, R. A. and Williams, T. A. (1979) Psychological systems questionnaire: an objective personality test designed for on-line computer presentation, scoring, and interpretation. *Behavior Research Methodology and Instrumentation*, **11**, 257–60.

Jones, A. (1981) Inter-rater reliability in the assessment of group exercises at a UK assessment centre. *Journal of Occupational Psychology*, **54**, 79–86.

Jones, A. and Harrison, E. (1982) Prediction of performance in initial officer training using reference reports. *Journal of Occupational Psychology*, **55**, 35–42.

Jurgensen, C. E. (1944) Report on the Classification Inventory: a personality test for industrial use. *Journal of Applied Psychology*, **28**, 445–60.

Kane, J. S. and Lawler, E. E. (1978) Methods of peer assessment. *Psychological Bulletin*, **85**, 555–86.

Katzell, R. A. and Dyer, F. J. (1977) Differential validity revived. *Journal of Applied Psychology*, **62**, 137–45.

Kaufman, G. G. and Johnson, J. C. (1974) Scaling peer ratings: an examination of the differential validities of positive and negative nominations. *Journal of Applied Psychology*, **59**, 302–6.

Keating, E., Patterson, D. G. and Stone, C. H. (1950) Validity of work histories obtained by interview. *Journal of Applied Psychology*, **34**, 6–11.

Keenan, A. and Wedderburn, A. A. I. (1980) Putting the boot on the other foot: candidates' descriptions of interviews. *Journal of Occupational Psychology*, **53**, 81–9.

Kelly, E. L. and Fiske, D. W. (1951) *The prediction of performance in clinical psychology.* University of Michigan Press, Ann Arbor, MI.

Kelly, G. A. (1955) *The psychology of personal constructs.* Norton, New York.

Kenny, D. A. and Zaccaro, S. J. (1983) An estimate of variance due to traits in leadership. *Journal of Applied Psychology*, **68**, 678–85.

Kingsbury, F. A. (1933) Psychological tests for executives. *Personnel*, **9**, 121–30.

Kinslinger, H. J. (1966) Application of projective techniques in personnel psychology since 1940. *Psychological Bulletin*, **66**, 134–50.

Kirkpatrick, J. J., Ewen, R. B., Barrett, R. S. and Katzell, R. A. (1968) *Testing and fair employment.* New York University Press, New York.

Kleiman, L. S. and Durham, R. L. (1981) Performance appraisal, promotion and the courts: a critical review. *Personnel Psychology*, **34**, 103–21.

Kleiman, L. S. and Faley, R. H. (1985) The implications of professional and legal guidelines for court decisions involving criterion-related validity: a review and analysis. *Personnel Psychology*, **38**, 803–33.

Klein, S. P. and Owens, W. A. (1965) Faking of a scored life history blank as a function of criterion objectivity. *Journal of Applied Psychology*, **49**, 452–4.

Klimoski, R. J. and Rafaeli, A. (1983) Inferring personal qualities through handwriting analysis. *Journal of Occupational Psychology*, **56**, 191–202.

Klimoski, R. J. and Strickland, W. J. (1977) Assessment centers—valid or merely prescient? *Personnel Psychology*, **30**, 353–61.

Kline, P. (1976) *The psychology of vocational guidance*. Batsford, London.

Knatz, H. F. and Inwald, R. E. (1983) A process for screening out law enforcement candidates who might break under stress. *Criminal Justice Journal*, **2**, 1–5.

Kraiger, K. and Ford, J. K. (1985) A meta-analysis of ratee race effects in performance ratings. *Journal of Applied Psychology*, **70**, 56–65.

Kraut, A. I. (1975) Prediction of managerial success by peer and training-staff ratings. *Journal of Applied Psychology*, **60**, 14–19.

Krzystofiak, F., Newman, J. M. and Anderson, G. (1979) A quantified approach to measurement of job content: procedures and payoffs. *Personnel Psychology*, **32**, 341–57.

Landy, F. (1987) Criteria in personnel selection. Paper presented at the International Conference on Advances in Selection and Assessment, Buxton.

Landy, F. J. and Farr, J. L. (1980) Performance rating. *Psychological Bulletin*, **87**, 72–107.

Latham, G. P., Saari, L. M., Pursell, E. D. and Campion, M. A. (1980) The situational interview. *Journal of Applied Psychology*, **65**, 422–7.

Laurent, H. (1962) Early identification of management talent. *Management Record*, **24**, 33–8.

Laurent, H. (1970) Cross-cultural cross-validation of empirically validated tests. *Journal of Applied Psychology*, **54**, 417–23.

Lawshe, C. H. (1952) What can industrial psychology do for small business (a symposium)? 2. Employee selection. *Personnel Psychology*, **5**, 31–4.

Lawshe, C. H. (1975) A quantitative approach to content validity. *Personnel Psychology*, **28**, 563–75.

Ledvinka, J. (1982) *Federal regulation of personnel and human resource management*. Van Nostrand Reinhold, New York.

Ledvinka, J. and Simonet, J. K. (1983) *The dollar value of JEPS at Life of Georgia*. Working Paper 83–134, College of Business Administration, University of Georgia.

Lent, R. H., Aurbach, H. A. and Levin, L. S. (1971) Predictors, criteria, and significant results. *Personnel Psychology*, **24**, 519–33.

Levine, E. L., Flory, A. and Ash, R. A. (1977) Self-assessment in personnel selection. *Journal of Applied Psychology*, **62**, 428–35.

Levine, E. L. and Rudolph, S. M. (1977) *Reference checking for personnel selection: the state of the art*. American Society for Personnel Administration: Washington, DC.

Levine, E. L., Ash, R. A., Hall, H. and Sistrunk, F. (1983) Evaluation of job analysis methods by experienced job analysts. *Academy of Management Journal*, **26**, 339–48.

Lewin, A. Y. and Zwany, A. (1976) Peer nominations: a model, literature critique and a paradigm for research. *Personnel Psychology*, **29**, 423–47.

Lilienthal, R. A. and Pearlman, K. (1983) *The validity of Federal selection tests for aid/technicians in the health, science, and engineering fields*. US Office of Personnel Management, Washington, DC.

Link, H. C. (1918) An experiment in employment psychology. *Psychological Review*, **25**, 116–27.

Linn, R. L., Harnisch, D. L. and Dunbar, S. B. (1981) Validity generalisation and situational specificity: an analysis of the prediction of first-year grades in law school. *Applied Psychological Measurement*, **5**, 281-9.

Locke, E. L. (1961) What's in a name? *American Psychologist*, **16**, 607.

Lopez, F. M. (1966) *Evaluating executive decision making: the in-basket technique.* American Management Association.

Love, K. G. (1981) Comparison of peer assessment methods: reliability, validity, friendship, and user reaction. *Journal of Applied Psychology*, **66**, 451-7.

McBain, W. N. (1970) Arousal, monotony and accidents in line driving. *Journal of Applied Psychology*, **54**, 509-19.

McClelland, D. C. (1971) *The achieving society.* Van Nostrand, Princeton, NJ.

McClelland, D. C. (1973) Testing for competence rather than 'intelligence'. *American Psychologist*, **28**, 1-14.

McCormick, E. J., Jeanneret, P. R. and Mecham, R. C. (1972) Study of job characteristics and job dimensions as based on the position analysis questionnaire (PAQ). *Journal of Applied Psychology*, **56**, 347-68.

McCormick, E. J., DeNisi, A. S. and Shaw, J. B. (1979) Use of the Position Analysis Questionnaire. *Journal of Applied Psychology*, **64**, 51-6.

McDonald, T. and Hakel, M. D. (1985) Effects of applicant race, sex, suitability, and answers on interviewer's questioning strategy and ratings. *Personnel Psychology*, **38**, 321-34.

McMurray, R. N. (1947) Validating the patterned interview. *Personnel*, **23**, 263-72.

Mabe, P. A. and West, S. G. (1982) Validity of self-evaluation of ability: a review and meta-analysis. *Journal of Applied Psychology*, **67**, 280-96.

Mackinnon, D. W. (1977) From selecting spies to selecting managers. In Moses, J. L. and Byham, W. C. (eds), *Applying the assessment center method.* Pergamon Press, New York.

Mahoney, T. A., Jerdee, T. H. and Nash, A. N. (1960) Predicting managerial effectiveness. *Personnel Psychology*, **13**, 147-63.

Matteson, M. T. (1978) An alternative approach to using biographical data for predicting job success. *Journal of Occupational Psychology*, **51**, 155-62.

Mayfield, E. C. (1964) The selection interview—a re-evaluation of published research. *Personnel Psychology*, **17**, 239-60.

Mayfield, E. C. (1970) Management selection: buddy nominations revisited. *Personnel Psychology*, **23**, 377-91.

Mayfield, E. C. and Carlson, R. E. (1966) Selection interview decisions: first results from a long-term research project. *Personnel Psychology*, **19**, 41-53.

Meehl, P. E. (1954) *Clinical vs statistical prediction.* University of Minnesota Press.

Meehl, P. E. (1978) Theoretical risks and tabular asterisks: Sir Karl, Sir Ronald and the slow progress of soft psychology. *Journal of Consulting and Clinical Psychology*, **46**, 806-34.

Megargee, E. I. (1972) *The California Psychological Inventory handbook.* Jossey Bass, San Francisco.

Meier, S. T. (1984) The construct validity of burnout. *Journal of Occupational Psychology*, **57**, 211-19.

Meritt-Haston, R. and Wexley, K. N. (1983) Educational requirements: legality and validity. *Personnel Psychology*, **36**, 743-53.

Merrihue, W. V. and Katzell, R. A. (1955) ERI—yardstick of employee relations. *Harvard Business Review*, **33**, 91-9.

Miller, K. (1976) Personality assessment. In Ungerson, B. (ed.), *Recruitment handbook.* Gower Press, Aldershot, Hants.

Miner, J. B. (1970) Executive and personnel interviews as predictors of consulting success. *Personnel Psychology*, **23**, 521–38.

Miner, J. B. (1971) Personality tests as predictors of consulting success. *Personnel Psychology*, **24**, 191–204.

Miner, J. B. (1978) The Miner Sentence Completion Scale: a reappraisal. *Academy of Management Journal*, **21**, 283–94.

Miner, M. G. and Miner, J. B. (1979) *Employee selection within the law.* Bureau of National Affairs, Washington, DC.

Mischel, W. (1968) *Personality and assessment.* Wiley, New York.

Mitchell, T. W. and Klimoski, R. J. (1982) Is it rational to be empirical? A test of methods for scoring biographical data. *Journal of Applied Psychology*, **67**, 411–18.

Mls, J. (1935) *Intelligenz und fahigkeit zum kraftwagenlenken.* Proceedings of the Eighth International Conference of Psychotechnics, Prague, pp. 278–84.

Moore, H. (1942) *Psychology for business and industry.* McGraw-Hill, New York.

Morris, B. S. (1949) Officer selection in the British Army 1942–1945. *Occupational Psychology*, **23**, 219–34.

Mosel, J. N. (1952) Prediction of department store sales performance from personal data. *Journal of Applied Psychology*, **36**, 8–10.

Mosel, J. N. and Goheen, H. W. (1958) The validity of the Employment Recommendation Questionnaire in personnel selection. I. Skilled traders. *Personnel Psychology*, **11**, 481–90.

Mosel, J. N. and Goheen, H. W. (1959) The validity of the Employment Recommendation Questionnaire. III. Validity of different types of references. *Personnel Psychology* **12**, 469–77.

Moses, J. L. (1973) The development of an assessment center for the early identification of supervisory talent. *Personnel Psychology*, **26**, 569–80.

Moses, J. L. and Boehm, V. R. (1975) Relationships of assessment center performance to management progress of women. *Journal of Applied Psychology*, **60**, 527–9.

Mossholder, K. W. and Arvey, R. D. (1984) Synthetic validity: a conceptual and comparative review. *Journal of Applied Psychology*, **69**, 322–33.

Muchinsky, P. M. (1979) The use of reference reports in personnel selection: a review and evaluation. *Journal of Occupational Psychology*, **52**, 287–97.

Muchinsky, P. M. and Tuttle, M. L. (1979) Employee turnover: an empirical and methodological assessment. *Journal of Vocational Behavior*, **14**, 43–77.

Mumford, M. D. (1983) Social comparison theory and the evaluation of peer evaluations: a review and some applied implications. *Personnel Psychology*, **36**, 867–81.

Murphy, K. R. (1984) Cost–benefit considerations in choosing among cross-validation methods. *Personnel Psychology*, **37**, 15–22.

Nevo, B. (1976) Using biographical information to predict success of men and women in the army. *Journal of Applied Psychology*, **61**, 106–8.

Northrop, L. C. (1985) *Validity generalisation results for apprentice occupations.* US Office of Personnel Management, Washington, DC.

O'Connor, E. J., Wexley, K. N. and Alexander, R. A. (1975) Single-group validity: fact or fallacy? *Journal of Applied Psychology*, **60**, 352–5.

O'Leary, B. S. (1980) *College grade point average as an indicator of occupational success: an update.* US Office of Personnel Management, Washington, DC.

Olian, J. D. and Wilcox, J. C. (1982) The controversy over PACE: an examination of the evidence and implications of the Luevano consent decree for employment testing. *Personnel Psychology*, **35**, 659–76.

Orpen, C. (1985) Patterned behavior description interviews versus unstructured interviews: a comparative validity study. *Journal of Applied Psychology*, **70**, 774–6.

Owens, W. A. (1976) Background data. In Dunnette, M. D. (ed.), *Handbook of industrial and organisational psychology*. Rand McNally, Chicago, IL.

Owens, W. A. and Schoenfeldt, L. F. (1979) Toward a classification of persons. *Journal of Applied Psychology*, **65**, 569–607.

Pace, L. A. and Schoenfeldt, L. F. (1977) Legal concerns in the use of weighted applications. *Personnel Psychology*, **30**, 159–66.

Parkinson, C. N. (1958) *Parkinson's law*. John Murray, London.

Parry, J. (1959) The place of personality appraisal in vocational selection. *Occupational Psychology*, **33**, 147–56.

Pearlman, K. (1984) *Validity generalisation*. Proceedings of the 92nd Annual Convention of the American Psychological Association.

Pearlman, K., Schmidt, F. L. and Hunter, J. E. (1980) Validity generalisation results for test used to predict job proficiency and training success in clerical occupations. *Journal of Applied Psychology*, **65**, 373–406.

Peres, S. H. and Garcia, J. R. (1962) Validity and dimensions of descriptive adjectives used in reference letters for engineering applicants. *Personnel Psychology*, **15**, 279–86.

Petrie, A. and Powell, M. B. (1951) The selection of nurses in England. *Journal of Applied Psychology*, **35**, 281–5.

Power, R. P. and MacRae, K. D. (1971) Detectability of items in the Eysenck Personality Inventory. *British Journal of Psychology*, **62**, 395–401.

Primoff, E. S. (1959) Empirical validation of the J-coefficient. *Personnel Psychology*, **12**, 413–18.

Psychological Corporation (1978) *Summaries of court decisions on employment testing 1968–1977*. Arthur, New York.

Pursell, E. D., Dossett, D. L. and Latham, G. P. (1980) Obtaining valid predictors by minimizing rating errors. *Personnel Psychology*, **33**, 91–6.

Reilly, R. R. and Chao, G. T. (1982) Validity and fairness of some alternative employee selection procedures. *Personnel Psychology*, **35**, 1–62.

Reilly, R. R. and Manese, W. R. (1979) The validation of a minicourse for telephone company personnel. *Personnel Psychology*, **32**, 83–90.

Reilly, R. R., Zedeck, S. and Tenopyr, M. L. (1979) Validity and fairness of physical ability tests for predicting performance in craft jobs. *Journal of Applied Psychology*, **64**, 262–74.

Richard, J. M., Taylor, C. W., Price, P. B. and Jacobsen, T. L. (1965) An investigation of the criterion problem for one group of medical specialists. *Journal of Applied Psychology*, **49**, 79–90.

Ritchie, R. J. and Boehm, V. R. (1977) Biographical data as a predictor of women's and men's management potential. *Journal of Vocational Behavior*, **11**, 363–8.

Ritchie, R. J. and Moses, J. L. (1983) Assessment center correlates of women's advancement into middle management: a 7-year longitudinal analysis. *Journal of Applied Psychology*, **68**, 227–31.

Roach, D. E. (1971) Double cross-validation of a weighted application blank over time. *Journal of Applied Psychology*, **55**, 157–60.

Roadman, H. E. (1964) An industrial use of peer ratings. *Journal of Applied Psychology*, **48**, 211–14.

Robertson, I. and Downs, S. (1979) Learning and the prediction of performance: development of trainability testing in the United Kingdom. *Journal of Applied Psychology*, **64**, 42–50.

Robertson, I. T. and Kandola R. S. (1982) Work sample tests: validity, adverse impact and applicant reaction. *Journal of Occupational Psychology*, **55**, 171–83.

Robertson, I. T. and Makin, P. J. (1986) Management selection in Britain: a survey and critique. *Journal of Occupational Psychology*, **59**, 45–57.

Robertson, I. and Smith, M. (1987) Personnel selection methods. Paper presented at the International Conference on Advances in Selection and Assessment, Buxton.

Robinson, D. D. (1972) Prediction of clerical turnover in banks by means of a weighted application blank. *Journal of Applied Psychology*, **56**, 282.

Roche, W. J. (1965) A dollar criterion in fixed-treatment employee selection. In Cronbach, L. J. and Gleser, G. C. (eds), *Psychological tests and personnel decisions.* University of Illinois Press, Urbana, IL.

Rodger, D. A. (1959) Personality of the route salesman in a basic food industry. *Journal of Applied Psychology*, **43**, 235–9.

Ronan, W. W. (1963) A factor analysis of eleven job performance measures. *Personnel Psychology*, **16**, 255–67.

Roose, J. E. and Dougherty, M. E. (1976) Judgement theory applied to the selection of life insurance salesmen. *Organisational Behavior and Human Performance*, **16**, 231–49.

Rosenbaum, R. W. (1976) Predictability of employee theft using weighted application blanks. *Journal of Applied Psychology*, **61**, 94–8.

Rosenthal, R. (1979) The 'file drawer problem' and tolerance for null results. *Psychological Bulletin*, **86**, 638–41.

Rothe, H. F. (1946) Output rates among butter wrappers: II. frequency distributions and an hypothesis regarding the 'restriction of output'. *Journal of Applied Psychology*, **30**, 320–7.

Rundquist, E. A. (1947) Development of an interview for selection purposes. In Kelly, G. A. (ed.), *New methods in applied psychology.* University of Maryland Press; College Park, MD.

Rush, C. H. (1953) A factorial study of sales criteria. *Personnel Psychology*, **6**, 9–24.

Russell, C. J. (1985) Individual decision processes in an assessment center. *Journal of Applied Psychology*, **70**, 737–46.

Sackett, P. R. (1982) A critical look at some common beliefs about assessment centers. *Public Personnel Management Journal*, **11**, 140–7.

Sackett, P. R. and Dreher, G. F. (1982) Constructs and assessment center dimensions: some troubling empirical findings. *Journal of Applied Psychology*, **67**, 401–10.

Sacket, P. R. and Harris, M. M. (1984) Honesty testing for personnel selection: a review and critique. *Personnel Psychology*, **37**, 221–45.

Sackett, P. R. and Wilson, M. A. (1982) Factors affecting the consensus judgement process in managerial assessment centers. *Journal of Applied Psychology*, **67**, 10–17.

Sands, W. A. (1978) Enlisted personnel selection for the U.S. Navy. *Personnel Psychology*, **31**, 63–70.

Sands, W. A. and Gade, P. A. (1983) An application of computerised adaptive testing in U.S. Army recruiting. *Journal of Computer-Based Instruction*, **10**, 87–9.

Saville & Holdsworth Ltd (1985) *Occupational Personality Questionnaire: manual.* SHL Ltd, Esher, Surrey.

Schein, V. A. (1975) Relationships between sex role stereotypes and requisite management characteristics among female managers. *Journal of Applied Psychology*, **60**, 340–4.

Schmidt, F. L. and Hunter, J. E. (1977) Development of a general solution to the problem of validity generalisation. *Journal of Applied Psychology*, **62**, 529–40.

Schmidt, F. L. and Hunter, J. E. (1978) Moderator research and the law of small numbers. *Personnel Psychology*, **31**, 215–32.

Schmidt, F. L. and Hunter, J. E. (1980) The future of criterion-related validity. *Personnel Psychology*, **33**, 41–60.

Schmidt, F. L. and Hunter, J. E. (1981) Employment testing: old theories and new research findings. *American Psychologist*, **36**, 1128–37.

Schmidt, F. L. and Hunter, J. F. (1983) Individual differences in productivity: an empirical test of estimates derived from studies of selection procedure utility. *Journal of Applied Psychology*, **68**, 407–14.

Schmidt, F. L. and Hunter, J. E. (1984) A within-setting empirical test of the situational specificity hypothesis in personnel selection. *Personnel Psychology*, **37**, 317–26.

Schmidt, F. L. and Johnson, R. H. (1973) Effects of race on peer ratings in an industrial situation. *Journal of Applied Psychology*, **57**, 237–41.

Schmidt, F. L., Berner, J. G. and Hunter, J. E. (1973) Racial differences in validity of employment tests: reality or illusion? *Journal of Applied Psychology*, **53**, 5–9.

Schmidt, F. L., Hunter, J. E. and Urry, V. W. (1976) Statistical power in criterion related validation studies. *Journal of Applied Psychology*, **61**, 473–85.

Schmidt, F. L., Greenthal, A. L., Hunter, J. E., Berner, J. G. and Seaton, F. W. (1977) Job sample vs. paper-and-pencil tests: adverse impact and examinee attitudes. *Personnel Psychology*, **30**, 187–97.

Schmidt, F. L., Hunter, J. E., Pearlman, K. and Shane, G. S. (1979a) Further tests of the Schmidt–Hunter Bayesian validity generalisation procedure. *Personnel Psychology*, **32**, 257–81.

Schmidt, F. L., Hunter, J. E., McKenzie, R. C. and Muldrow, T. W. (1979b) Impact of valid selection procedures on work-force productivity. *Journal of Applied Psychology*, **64**, 609–26.

Schmidt, F. L., Gast-Rosenberg, I. and Hunter, J. E. (1980a) Validity generalisation results for computer programmers. *Journal of Applied Psychology*, **65**, 643–61.

Schmidt, F. L., Pearlman, K. and Hunter, J. E. (1980b) The validity and fairness of employment and educational tests for Hispanic Americans: a review and analysis. *Personnel Psychology*, **33**, 705–23.

Schmidt, F. L., Hunter, J. E. and Pearlman, K. (1981) Task differences as moderators of aptitude test validity in selection: a red herring. *Journal of Applied Psychology*, **66**, 166–85.

Schmidt, F. L., Hunter, J. E. and Pearlman, K. (1982) Assessing the economic impact of personnel programs in workforce productivity. *Personnel Psychology*, **35**, 333–47.

Schmidt, F. L., Hunter, J. E., Croll, P. R. and McKenzie, R. C. (1983) Estimation of employment test validities by expert judgement. *Journal of Applied Psychology*, **68**, 590–601.

Schmidt, F. L., Mack, M. J. and Hunter, J. E. (1984) Selection utility in the occupation of U.S. park ranger for three modes of test use. *Journal of Applied Psychology*, **69**, 490–7.

Schmidt, F. L., Hunter, J. E., Pearlman, K. and Hirsh, H. R. (1985a) Forty questions about validity generalisation and meta-analysis. *Personnel Psychology*, **38**, 697–798.

Schmidt, F. L., Ocasio, B. P., Hillery, J. M. and Hunter, J. E. (1985b) Further within-setting empirical tests of the situational specificity hypothesis in personnel selection. *Personnel Psychology*, **38**, 509–24.

Schmidt, F. L., Hunter, J. E. and Outerbridge, A. N. (1987) The impact of job experience and ability on job knowledge, work sample performance, and supervisory ratings of
· job performance. *Journal of Applied Psychology* (in press).

Schmitt, N. (1976) Social and situational determinants of employment decisions: implications for the employment interview. *Personnel Psychology*, **29**, 79–101.

Schmitt, N. (1977) Interrater agreement in dimensionality and combination of assessment center judgements. *Journal of Applied Psychology*, **62**, 171–6.

Schmitt, N. and Hill, T. E. (1977) Sex and race composition of assessment center groups as a determinant of peer and assessor ratings. *Journal of Applied Psychology*, **62**, 261-4.

Schmitt, N., Gooding, R. Z., Noe, R. A. and Kirsch, M. (1984) Meta-analyses of validity studied published between 1964 and 1982 and the investigation of study characteristics. *Personnel Psychology*, **37**, 407-22.

Schoenfeldt, L. F., Acker, S. R. and Perlson, M. R. (1976) Content validity revisited: the development of a content-oriented test of industrial reading. *Journal of Applied Psychology*, **61**, 581-8.

Schrader, A. D. and Osburn, H. G. (1977) Biodata faking: effects of induced subtlety and position specificity. *Personnel Psychology*, **30**, 395-404.

Scott, W. D. (1915) The scientific selection of salesmen. *Advertising and Selling*, **25**, 5-6, 94-9.

Scott, R. D. and Johnson, R. W. (1967) Use of the weighted application blank in selecting unskilled employees. *Journal of Applied Psychology*, **51**, 393-5.

Shaffer, D. R., Mays, P. V. and Etheridge, K. (1976) Who shall be hired: a biassing effect of the Buckley Amendment on employment practice. *Journal of Applied Psychology*, **61**, 571-5.

Shapira, Z. and Shirom, A. (1980) New issues in the use of behaviorally anchored rating scales: level of analysis, the effects of incident frequency, and external validation. *Journal of Applied Psychology*, **65**, 517-23.

Sharf, J. C. (1982) Personnel testing and the law. In Rowland, K. M. and Ferris, G. R. (eds), *Personnel management*. Allyn and Bacon, Boston, MA.

Shusman, E. J., Inwald, R. E. and Landa, B. (1984) Correction officer job performance as predicted by the IPI and MMPI: a validation and cross-validation study. *Criminal Justice and Behavior*, **11**, 309-29.

Siegel, A. I. (1978) Miniature job training and evaluation as a selection/classification device. *Human Factors*, **20**, 189-200.

Smith, J. E. and Hakel, M. D. (1979) Convergence among data sources, response bias, and reliability and validity of a structured job analysis questionnaire. *Personnel Psychology*, **32**, 677-92.

Smith, W. J., Albright, L. E., Glennon, J. R. and Owens, W. A. (1961) The prediction of research competence and creativity from personal history. *Journal of Applied Psychology*, **45**, 59-62.

Snedden, D. (1930) Measuring general intelligence by interview. *Psychological Clinic*, **19**, 131-4.

Sorenson, W. W. (1966) Test of mechanical principles as a suppressor variable for the prediction of effectiveness on a mechanical repair job. *Journal of Applied Psychology*, **50**, 348-52.

Sparrow, J., Patrick, J., Spurgeon, P. and Barwell, F. (1982) The use of job component analysis and related aptitudes on personnel selection. *Journal of Occupational Psychology*, **55**, 157-64.

Spencer, G. J. and Worthingon, R. (1952) Validity of a projective technique in predicting sales effectiveness. *Personnel Psychology*, **5**, 125-44.

Springbett, B. M. (1958) Factors affecting the final decision in the employment interview. *Canadian Journal of Psychology*, **12**, 13-22.

Stagner, R. (1958) The gullibility of personnel managers. *Personnel Psychology*, **11**, 347-52.

Sterns, L., Alexander, R. A., Barrett, G. V. and Dambrot, F. H. (1983) The relationship of extraversion and neuroticism with job preferences and job satisfaction for clerical employees. *Journal of Occupational Psychology*, **56**, 145-53.

Strong, E. K. (1955) *Vocational interests eighteen years after college*. University of Minnesota Press, Minneapolis, MN.

Super, D. E. and Crites, J. O. (1962) *Appraising vocational fitness by means of psychological tests*. Harper and Row, New York.

Sydiaha, D. (1961) Bales' interaction process analysis of personnel selection interviews. *Journal of Applied Psychology*, **45**, 393–401.

Taylor, M. S. and Sniezek, J. A. (1984) The college recruitment interview: topical content and applicant reactions. *Journal of Occupational Psychology*, **57**, 157–68.

Tenopyr, M. L. (1977) Content–construct confusion. *Personnel Psychology*, **30**, 47–54.

Thayer, P. W. (1977) Somethings old, somethings new. *Personnel Psychology*, **30**, 513–24.

Thorndike, E. (1918) Fundamental theorems in judging men. *Journal of Applied Psychology*, **2**, 67–76.

Tiffin, J. (1943) *Industrial psychology*, Prentice Hall, New York.

Toops, H. A. (1944) The criterion. *Educational and Psychological Measurement*, **4**, 271–93.

Toplis, J. (1975) Group selection methods. In Ungerson, B. (ed.) *Recruitment handbook*. Gower Press, Aldershot.

Trattner, M. H. (1985) *Estimating the validity of aptitude and ability tests for semiprofessional occupations using the Schmidt–Hunter interactive validity generalisation procedure*. US Office of Personnel Management, Washington, DC.

Tucker, D. H. and Rowe, P. M. (1977) Consulting the application form prior to interview: an essential step in the selection process. *Journal of Applied Psychology*, **62**, 283–7.

Tucker, M. F., Cline, V. B. and Schmitt, J. R. (1967) Prediction of creativity and other performance measures from biographical information among pharmaceutical scientists. *Journal of Applied Psychology*, **51**, 131–8.

Tullar, W. L., Mullins, T. W. and Caldwell, S. A. (1979) Effects of interview length and applicant quality on interview decision time. *Journal of Applied Psychology*, **64**, 669–74.

Turnage, J. J. and Muchinsky, P. M. (1982) Transsituational variability in human performance within assessment centers. *Organisational Behavior and Human Performance*, **30**, 174–200.

Tziner, A. and Dolan, S. (1982) Evaluation of a traditional selection system in predicting success of females in officer training. *Journal of Occupational Psychology*, **55**, 269–75.

Ulrich, L. and Trumbo, D. (1965) The selection interview since 1949. *Psychological Bulletin*, **63**, 100–16.

Umeda, J. K. and Frey, D. H. (1974) Life history correlates of ministerial success. *Journal of Vocational Behavior*, **4**, 319–24.

Valezi, E. and Andrews, I. R. (1971) Individual differences in the decision process of employment interviewers. *Journal of Applied Psychology*, **58**, 49–53.

Vernon, P. E. (1950) The validation of Civil Service Selection Board procedures. *Occupational Psychology*, **24**, 75–95.

Vernon, P. E. (1982) *The abilities and achievements of Oriental North Americans*. Academic Press, New York.

Vernon, P. E. and Parry, J. B. (1949) *Personnel selection in the British forces*. University of London Press.

Vineberg, R. and Joyner, J. N. (1982) *Prediction of job performance: review of military studies*. Human Resources Research Organisation, Alexandria, VA.

Viteles, M. S. (1923) *Industrial psychology*. Norton, New York.

Wagner, R. (1949) The employment interview: a critical summary. *Personnel Psychology*, **2**, 17–46.

Wallace, N. and Travers, R. M. (1938) A psychometric sociological study of a group of speciality salesmen. *Annals of Eugenics*, **8**, 266–302.

Wanous, J. P. (1978) Realistic job previews: can a procedure to reduce turnover also influence the relationship between abilities and performance? *Personnel Psychology*, **31**, 249–58.

Warmke, D. L. and Billings, R. S. (1979) Comparison of training methods for improving the psychometric quality of experimental and administrative performance ratings. *Journal of Applied Psychology*, **64**, 124–31.

Waters, L. K. and Waters, C. W. (1970) Peer nominations as predictors of short-term sales performance. *Journal of Applied Psychology*, **54**, 42–4.

Weekley, J. A., Frank, B., O'Connor, E. J. and Peters, I. H. (1985) A comparison of three methods of estimating the standard deviation of performance in dollars. *Journal of Applied Psychology*, **70**, 122–6.

Wexley, K. N., Yukl, G. A., Kovacs, S. Z. and Sanders, R. E. (1972) Importance of contrast effects in employment interviews. *Journal of Applied Psychology*, **56**, 45–8.

Wiggins, J. S. (1973) *Personality and prediction*. Addison Wesley, Reading, MA.

Williams, S. B. and Leavitt, H. J. (1947) Group opinion as a predictor of military leadership. *Journal of Consulting Psychology*, **11**, 283–91.

Wilson, N. A. B. (1948) The work of the Civil Service Selection Board. *Occupational Psychology*, **22**, 204–12.

Wingrove, J., Glendinning, R. and Herriot, P. (1984) Graduate pre-selection: a research note. *Journal of Occupational Psychology*, **57**, 169–71.

Wollowick, H. B. and McNamara, W. J. (1969) Relationship of the components of an assessment center to management success. *Journal of Applied Psychology*, **53**, 348–52.

Wright, G. (1969) Summary of research on the selection interview since 1964. *Personnel Psychology*, **22**, 391–413.

Wright, O. R., Carter, J. L. and Fowler, E. P. (1967) A differential analysis of an oral interview program. *Public Personnel Review*, **28**, 242–6.

Zdep, S. M. and Weaver, H. B. (1967) The graphoanalytic approach to selecting life insurance salesmen. *Journal of Applied Psychology*, **51**, 295–9.

Zedeck, S., Tziner, A. and Middlestadt, S. E. (1983) Interviewer validity and reliability: an individual difference analysis. *Personnel Psychology*, **36**, 355–70.

Author Index

Subject Index